DAVIDSON COUNTY TENNESSEE

DEED BOOK "P"

PERSONAL PROPERTY DEEDS

15 NOVEMBER 1821– 13 FEBRUARY 1829

Mary Sue Smith

HERITAGE BOOKS
2018

HERITAGE BOOKS

AN IMPRINT OF HERITAGE BOOKS, INC.

Books, CDs, and more—Worldwide

For our listing of thousands of titles see our website
at
www.HeritageBooks.com

Published 2018 by
HERITAGE BOOKS, INC.
Publishing Division
5810 Ruatan Street
Berwyn Heights, Md. 20740

International Standard Book Numbers
Paperbound: 978-0-7884-0784-0
Clothbound: 978-0-7884-8487-2

Davidson County, Tennessee
Deed Book 'P'
Personal Property Deeds
15 Nov 1821 - 13 Feb. 1829

The information in these abstracts was taken from microfilm; the original book is missing. I have used the original spelling, capitalization & punctuation in the lists of articles.

Deed Book P is especially important for African-American research, listing slaves by family units, giving age & physical description. The 'Slave Index' gives only one name but this is associated with the owner and geographical location and hopefully will be of value. Free 'persons of color' are indicated by an (*) and included in both indices.

There are many entries that give family relationships between several generations and localities. A grandparent may be named and located in the mother states and counties of Virginia & North Carolina with descendants located both in Tennessee and other states.

The inventories give us a picture of the early days in Middle Tennessee; listing the home furnishings, books in the home library, early business inventories down to the last pair of sheets in the *Nashville Inn.*

Mary Sue Smith
Nashville, TN
16 June 1997

DAVIDSON COUNTY TENNESSEE
DEED BOOK 'P'

QUINN & ELLISTON of E. LANIER & WIFE
Reg. 15 Nov. 1821   Bill of Sale
Sell to M. H. QUINN & JOSEPH T. ELLISTON 12 negroes &
convey to them all title on account of the life estate vested in AMY W.
LANIER to said twelve negroes whose names and ages are: one
woman by the name of Beck about 40 years of age and her child, Ben,
about three years old; one woman by the name of Patts about 40 years
of age; one woman named Polly, about 21 years of age and child, one
month old by the name of Andrew Jackson; one woman by the name
of Nancy, about 17 years of age and her child, one year old, named
James Monroe; one woman named Isabella, about 16 years old; one
woman named Rose, about fifteen years of age; one man named Billey,
about twenty six years of age; one man by the name of Tom, about
twenty four years; another by the name of Sam, about twenty two
years. 10 March 1821 EDMUND LANIER AMY W. LANIER Wit:
MOSES STEVENS, JOHN A. BODWELL, JAS. CONDON [pp1/2]

JOSEPH ERWIN of R. W. HART
Reg. 15 Nov. 1821   Receipt
Have this day received of ANDREW HYNES, agent for JOSEPH
ERWIN of Louisianna, the following personal property: one negro
boy, named Bob, purchased by JOHN ERWIN in Virginia, aged about
twelve or thirteen years; one sorrel horse, one brown mare, one muley
cow, one red cow, two pided cows, forty two head of hogs, of all
sizes, one Dearborn waggon, or carryall, three feather beds, together
with bedsteads, two tables, one sugar stand, two trunks, sets of knives
& forks, dishes & plates, two ploughs & gears, two hoes & two
chopping axes ... bind myself & my heirs to return all property set
forth to Jos. Erwin, on demand.
Sept. 1821   R. W. HART
Witness: Tho. H. CRUTCHER   [pp2/3]

ROBERT WEAKLEY of WILLIAM McLAURAINE
Reg. 15 Nov. 1821   Bill of Sale
I, WILLIAM McLAURAINE, of Davidson County, have this day sold
to ROBERT WEAKLEY a negro man, named Essia, about thirty
years of age. Oct. 16, 1821   WM McLAURINE
Wit: GEO. WATERS   [pp3/4]

2

ANTHONY W. JOHNSTON of JNO. B. HARDING
Reg. 16 Nov. 1821   Bill of Sale
I, JOHN B. HARDING, of the county of Powhattan and State of
Virginia, have this day sold to ANTHONY W. JOHNSTON one negro
girl by the name of Maria. 25 Nov. 1820 JOHN B. HARDING [seal]
Wit: THO. HARDING, ADDISON EAST, JNO. ELLISTON [p4]

DAVID C. SNOW of A. W. JOHNSON
Reg. 16 Nov. 1821   Bill of Sale
I, ANTHONY W. JOHNSON, did by bill of sale dated 25 Nov. 1820,
purchase of JOHN B. HARDING, of Powhattan County, VA,
purchase a negro girl named Maria for DAVID C. SNOW & his heirs,
and the funds used to purchase same were vested in me as his
guardian. 23 Oct. 1821 ANTHONY W. JOHNSON   [p5]

JOHN COLE of JOHN PORTER
Reg. 19 Nov. 1821   Mortgage
I have sold to John Cole the following property: one waggon & gears,
3 head of horses, 12 head of cattle, 100 head of hoggs, 17 head of
sheep, 3 featherbeds & furniture, household & kitchen furniture; one
loom, the crop that is now made, except so much as will pay the rent.
29 Nov. 1820   JOHN PORTER
Test. SAM. L. WHARTON
Agreed if debt be paid, the above to be null & void.   [pp5/6]

GUY McFADDEN of WM H. NANCE
19 Nov. 1821   Bill of Sale
William H. Nance has sold to Guy McFadden a negro boy slave,
named Christopher, aged between ten & eleven years old.
10 Aug. 1820   William H. Nance
Test: J. COUNCELL   [pp6/7]

ELDRIDGE NEWSOM of B. JOSLIN
19 Nov. 1821   Deed of Trust
Whereas at the Oct. Term 1821 of the Court of Pleas & Quarter
Sessions for Davidson County Eldridge Newsom, as administrator of
ROBERT EVANS, Dec'd, recovered a judgement against BENJAMIN
JOSLIN and his son RICHARD JOSLIN; Joslin has conveyed the
following negro slaves as security: Hannah, about 19 years old, & her
children, Nancy & Henry; Jenny, about 45 years old; Peter about 15
years old; Esther, about 16 years old; Milley, about 28 years old, and
her children, Jerry & Wesley; Maria, about 14 years old. If debt &
interest are paid, the sale to be null & void.

29 Oct. 1821   Benj. Joslin
J. C. GUELL, WILL COOPER   [pp7-10]

IRWIN & HOOVER of W. HEWLETT
20 Nov. 1821   Deed of Trust
I, William Hewlett, of Nashville, sell all my household & kitchen
furniture and all my shop tools & stock in trade to Phillip Hoover.
19 Nov. 1821   WILLIAM HEWLETT
[schedule of household & kitchen furniture}
2 featherbeds, bedsteads & furniture, complete, one crib or cradle
complete, one side board, one bureau complete with a large looking
glass, one Jackson Press, 2 end tables, one large table, one tea table,
one small bureau, one dozen red chairs, 1/2 dozen common chairs; one
pair looking glasses, 3 trunks with their contents , shovel, tongs and a
pair brass handirons, one pair common handirons, one set tea china
complete, 4 decanters and all the glasses, plates, dishes, bowls and all
the Queensware in my possession, one cott and one bag feathers; all
my kitchen furniture; my sadlers materials unmanufactured, all my
saddles, bridles, martingals together with every thing in my line that
may be manufactured for twelve months, 3 showcases, 2 stoves &
pipes.   [pp10-12]

JOSEPH WILLIAMS of R. SEARCY'S Extrs.
20 Nov. 1821   Bill of Sale
This Indenture made 6 Oct. 1821 bet. Stephen CANTRELL, James W.
SITLER & Jesse BLACKSPAN of Nashville, Exrs. of Robert Searcy,
dec'd & Joseph WILLIAMS, Sr., of Surrey County, NC, by his
Attorney, Thomas L. WILLIAMS of the other part. The Executors
convey & sell to Joseph Williams all the right, title, claim, etc. that
Robert Searcy, dec'd had to the following property now in the
possession of John P. ERWIN: one negro boy, named Tom; one girl,
Maria; one boy, Squire, and one girl child, Rose; one pianoforte, 1
violin, 1 mantle clock & ornaments; one bookcase, two cardtables, one
work stand, one small secretary, one large chair, one piano stool, 2
dozen Windsor chairs, one new carpet, sundry music books, one old
carpet, one pair looking glasses, six pictures, one pr andirons, shovel
& tongs, two fenders, one hearth rug, four beds, bedsteds & furniture
including clothing for the same, one Bureau, one writing desk &
drawers, one press, sundry glass & chinaware & crockery ware, 3 setts
knives & forks, 2 dozen silver tablespoons, 2 dozen tea & desert silver
spoons, silver ladles, one set dining tables, one map and sundry kitchen
furniture; also the following books: 1 sett Encyclopedia, 20 Vols;
Rollins ancient history, 8 Vols; Shakespeares plays, 8 Vols;

4

Massachusetts reports, 14 Vols; Bacons Abridgment, 7 Vols; Cranchs reports, 9 Vols; American Law Journal, 6 Vols; American Digest, 2 Vols, Chitty Pleading, 3 Vols, Chittys Criminal Law, 4 Vols, 4 Vols.; Comyn on Contracts, 2 Vols.; East Reports, 16 Vols.; Jacobs Law Dictionary, 5 Vols; 1 large Bible; Tennessee Reports, 2 Vols; Douglas Reports, 2 Vols; Roberts on Fraud, 1 Vol.; Blackstones Commentarieis, 4 Vols; Peak;s Evidence, 2 Vols; American State Papers, 12 Vols.; Metford's Pleading, 1 Vol.; Teds Practice, 1 Vol.; Natura Creviurn, 1 Vol.; Williams Law Dictionary, 1 Vol.; Commercial Dicitionary, 3 Vol.; Woodfals Junius, 2 Vol.; Gillies History, 3 Vols.; Campbells rhetoric, 1 Vol.; Robertsons Charles 5th, 5 Vols.; Wrasals France, 2 Vols.; Rollins Belles Lettres, 4 Vols.; DeLePlaines Repository, 2 Vols.; Life of Sir William Jones, 1 Vol.; Court of Berlin, 2 Vols.; being the same property bought at the Marshalls sale on 9 June 1820. Step. CANTRELL J. W. SITLER J. BLACKFAN/BLACKSPAN
Wit: Geo. SHALL   R. SANDERSON [pp12-14]

HENRY CRABB of RICHARD C. CROSS
Reg. 20 Nov. 1821   Bill of Sale
I, Richard C. Cross, do this day sell to Henry Crabb a negro man slave, named Edmund, about thirty years of age, of a black colour.
29 Oct. 1821   R. C. CROSS
Wit: Alexander BARROW, D. B. GREER   [p14]

WHARTON & CANTRELL, Extrs. of E. COOPER
Reg. 22 Nov. 1821   Mortgage
I, Edmund Cooper have sold to Jesse Wharton & Stephen Cantrell, executors of the will of George M. DEADRICK, dec'd, the following negro slaves; one named Sterling, about 28 years old; one named, Mansco, about fifteen; one, named Louisa, about eighteen years; one named Hannah, about 45 years. If notes are paid, this agreement to be void.   EDM'D COOPER
Wit: John McNAIRY, L. P. CANTRELL   [pp15-16]

JOHN MAYFIELD of WM DICKERSON
1 Dec. 1821   Bill of Sale
I, William Dickerson, of Rutherford County, have sold to John Mayfield a mulatto woman slave, named Rebecca, 26 years old in March next, this 19th Feb. 1817.   WILLIAM DICKERSON
Wit: Berryman G. WELLS   [p16]

SAMUEL CHAPMAN of JAMES A. CANNON

5 Dec. 1821   Bill of Sale

I, James A. Cannon, have sold unto Samuel Chapman the following: 7 feather beds, bolsters & pillows, 16 blankets, 21 quilts, 8 pr. of sheets, 7 bedsteads, 1 sideboard, 1 Secretary, 10 Tables, 2 Presses, 1 Sofa, 2 dozen chairs, 2 carpets, 2 pair of andirons, 16 Tablespoons, 2 Ladles, 2 doz teaspoons, 1 pr. sugar tongs, 2 doz. plates, 1 doz. knives & forks, 8 dishes, 2 tureens, 1 set castors, 10 wine glasses & tumblers, 4 glass jars, 3 decanters, 5 tea Boards, 2 doz. cups & saucers, 3 teapots, one coffee urn, 1 sugar dish, 2 cream pots, 1 stand bed curtains, 7 trunks, two foot stools, 2 looking glasses, 1 candlestand, 2 pitchers, 2 cows & 1 calf, 1 tea canister, 5 candle sticks, 14 pots, kettles & ovens, 1 hand bellows, 2 tea kettles, 1 Roaster, 1 potrack, 2 tubs, 10 crocks, 3 pails, 2 tin buckets, 1 colinder, 1 Demijon, 3 stone Jars, 2 sugar canisters, 1 barrel of vinegar, 2 cotts, 10 barrels, shovel tongs & poker, 3 umbrillas, 3 pr. pot hooks, 2 coffee mills, 1 gridiron, 6 Smoothing irons, 5 tin pans, 1 skillet, 1 cooler, 2 Sifter, 1 Side saddle, and all the right, title & claim I have to the estate of Thomas ROYLE, dec'd; land, negroes and all of her property that may fall to my share.
JAS. A. CANNON
Wit; J. W. McCOMBS   S. V. D. STOUT   [pp17/18]

EDWARD SCRUGGS of JOHN BRACKEN

12 Dec. 1821   Bill of Sale

I, John Bracken, of Sumner County, TN, have this day sold to Edward Scruggs one negro woman, named Fanny.
20 Nov. 1820   JOHN BRACKEN
Wit: Robt W. GREENE, J. H. GREEN   [p18]

JOSEPH & ROBERT WOODS of DEVEREUX WYNN

31 Dec. 1821   Bill of Sale

I, Devereux Wynn, of Wilson County, TN, have sold to J. & Robert Woods a negro boy, named Cary, aged about 12 years old; a negro boy, named Henry, aged about six years old; negro boy, named Peter, aged about six years; negro girl, named Moriah, aged about seven.
18 April 1821   DEVEREUX WYNN
Test. James HENDERSON,   Rich'd A. ECHOLS   [p19]

THOMAS PRITCHETT of W. B. ROBERTSON

28 Jan. 1822   Bill of Sale

14 Nov. 1821   Received of Thomas Pritchett payment in full for a negro boy, named Gairy, about thirteen years old, sound, sensible & healthy. WM. B. ROBERTSON

Wit: Duncan ROBERTSON, I[saiah] CURREY   [p19]

JOHN BEARLEY of JOHN REACE
16 Feb. 1822   Bill of Sale
I, John Reace, have sold to John Bearley a certain yellow slave by the
name of Melley, aged nine years old.
30 Jan. 1822   JOHN (X) REACE
Test: S. SHANNON   Mich'l GLEAVES [p20]

MICHAEL GLEAVES of JOHN BEAZLEY
15 Feb. 1822   Bill of Sale
I, John Beazley, have sold to Michael Gleaves a certain yellow girl
slave by the name of Melley, aged nine years old.
2 Feb. 1822   JOHN BEAZLEY
Test: John J. HINTON   A. PATTON [p20]

WILLIAM JAMES of WILLIAM WISENOR
16 Feb. 1822   Bill of Sale
I, William Wisenor, have sold to William James a negro girl, named
Dorcas, about nine years of age. 26 May 1821   W. WISENOR
Thos. P. YEATS, Whid bell WHITE
Henry EWING 2nd Feb.1822 N. EWING   [p21]

WILLIAM H. McLAUGHLIN of JNO CRIDDLE adm'r
Reg. 16 Feb. 1822   Bill of Sale
I, John Criddle, administrator of the goods & chattles of Lemuel
KENNEDY, dec'd, by order of the Court of Pleas & Quarter Sessions
of Davidson, have proceeded to sell a negro, boy named, about
fourteen years of age at public auction to William H. McLaughlin.
2 Feb. 182   JN CRIDDLE, administrator
Test: Wm HOWTELL   John B. MANNIFEE [p22]

CHARLES BALLENTINE of L. BALLENTINE
16 Feb. 1822   Bill of Sale
I, Lemuel Ballentine have sold to Charles Ballentine a negro boy,
named Isaac, between four & five years of age.
22 January 1821   LEMUEL BALLENTINE
Test:ISAAC B.SULLIVANT, POLLY D.BALLENTIN [p23]

JEREMIAH PIERCE of JOHN CRIDDLE
Reg. 16 Feb. 1822   Bill of Sale
Received of Jeremiah Pierce payment in full for a negro girl, named
Jenney, about six years old. 3 Sept. 1818   JOHN CRIDDLE

Test: Jno S. COX, Lem'l KENNEDY   [23]

WILLIAM MARTIN of NATHAN BENNETT
Reg. 16 Feb. 1822   Bill of Sale
I have this day to William Martin one negro boy, named Major, aged
seventeen years old. 2 July 1816   NATHAN BENNETT
Test: William HEATON   [p24]

ELEANOR LOGUE of DAVID LOGUE
Reg. 16 Feb. 1822   Bill of Sale
I, David Logue, have sold to Eleanor Logue a negro man, named
Dennis, about thirty three years of age. 12 Feb. 1821
DAVID LOGUE
Test: David SMILEY, Lemuel TINNEN [p24]

ZACHARIAH STULL of JAMES FULTON
Reg. 16 Feb. 1822   Bill of Sale
I, James HERVEY, agent for James Fulton, both of the County of
Jackson, TN, have this 15th Feb. 1808, sold unto Zachariah Stull one
negro woman, named Esther, about 28 years old and her three
children, Piaty, Prudence & Sally.   JAMES HERVEY
Test: E. D. MOORE I. F. WILLIAM [p25]

ELIZABETH RANDALL with AQUILLA RANDALL
Reg. 16 Feb. 1822   Article   of   agreement
made & entered into this 7th day of Dec. 1816, bet. Elizabeth Randal,
widow of Greenberry RANDAL, dec'd, of the one part, and Aquilla
Randal, brother to Greenberry, dec'd, of the other: Elizabeth Randal
agrees to board her two children & keep them in clothing, lodging and
'dec't' so long as she is allowed to keep all of the property that her
husband died possessed of, both real and personal ... agreeable to the
valuation of Isaac WALTON ... to be put to the use of the children;
Cordeley RANDAL & Amandey Green RANDAL.
ELIZABETH (X) RANDALL   AQUILLA RANDALL
Test: Isaac WALTON, William WALTON   [pp25-26]

JOHN C. McLEMORE of ROBT. SEARCY's Extrs.
Reg. 16 Feb. 1822   Bill of Sale
I have this day sold to John C. McLemore a negro fellow, Lewis,
about twenty five years of age; also his wife, Winney, a negro woman
twenty eight or thirty years of age
.21 Jan 1822   STEPHEN CANTRELL, Exr.

Test: Joel PARRISH   [p26]

JAMES McCUTCHEN of JNO STOBAUGH
Reg. 16 Feb. 1822   Bill of Sale
I hereby sell unto James McCutchen a negro girl slave, named Rose,
aged about 18 years, and her child, aged about two years.
17 July 1820   JOHN STOBAUGH
Wit: Th. HILL   [p27]

McNAIRY & WEAKLEY of WM McLAURINE
Reg. 22 Feb. 1822   Deed of Trust
William McLaurine of the one part and Nathaniel A. McNairy &
Robert Weakley of the other; McLaurine has sold to McNairy &
Weakley one negro woman, named Mary, about twenty one years; one
girl, Nancy, about fourteen; one old negro woman, named Agnes,
about 50; one waggon & gears, two ploughs, five houghs, two head of
hogs, forty head of cattle, one bay mare, one sorrell mare, two axes,
two pots, two ovens, 2 tin kettles, 1 brass kettle, 1 spider, 1 pr flat
irons, four tubs, 2 pales, 8 tin buckets, 1 wire Sifter, 2 trays, 1 pr
andirons, 1 churn, 1 mans Saddle, 1 bridle, one womans saddle &
bridle, one case & bottles, one Bureau, one walnut table, one poplar
table, 6 windsor chairs, 4 rush bottomed chairs, 2 feather beds &
bedsteds, 2 under beds, 4 pr blankets, 8 counterpanes, 8 pr sheets, one
Spinning wheel, 2 pr cars, 5 waiters, 10 china dishes, 2 dz plates, 2
pitchers, 2 leathern trunks, 4 tin trunks, 6 silver tablespoons, 6 silver
tea spoons, 1 set of china, 2 coffee pots, 1/2 dz knives & forks, one
rifle gun, 1 doz old books, 1 looking glass, one set castors, 2 pr
candlesticks, 1 pr fire tongs, 1 pr iron wedges, 1/2 doz. tablecloths.
All of the above is now in possession of William McLaurine at his
residence near the upper ferry adjacent to Nashville; together with the
crop of corn growing on his farm.
William McLaurine being indebted to Thomas CRUTCHER; the estate
of William HOBSON, dec'd; Madison McLAURINE; estate of
DAVIS; estate of YOUNG; & to George McLAURINE. If debts are
paid, this agreement is to be void. 16 Oct 1821
Wm McLAURINE, N.A. McNAIRY, R. WEAKLEY [pp28-30]

JOSEPH WILLIAMS, Sr. of ROBT PURDY, Marshall
Reg. 22 Feb. 1822   Bill of Sale
Robert Purdy, Marshall of the District of West Tennessee of the one
part and Joseph Williams, Sr., of Surry Co., NC, of the other; whereas
Daniel W. GANTLY & John GANTLY, citizens of NY, on 1 July
1819, recovered a judgment in the Circuit Court of the U.S.for the

Dist of West TN against John P. ERWIN ...remains unpaid and a writ was issued 20 July 1821, and exposed to public sale on 28 Nov. 1821, and Stephen CANTRELL, as Attorney in fact of Joseph Williams, Sr. became the purchaser of the following: one gold watch, one pr of pistols, one Bureau, one large map, one Atlas, one small Atlas, two writing desks, 6 waiters, 2 fenders, 4 prs plated & brass candlesticks, one Safe, 2 prs brass andirons, one wheelbarrow, one large chair and sundry books; Hune & Smottels England, 8 Vols; Federalist Parkherst Lexicon; Ainsworth Dictionary; Johnsons Dictionary, 2 vols; Cookes Reports; Tennessee Reports, 2 Vols; Haywoods Reports, 4 Vols; Revised Laws & Acts of Assembly, 3 Vol; Bosanguel & Puller, 5 Vols; Johnsons Reports, 17 Vols; Johnsons Digest; Sugden on Vendors; Easts Crown Law, 2 Vols; Dallas Reports, 4 Vols; Tidds Practice, 2 Vols; Chitty on Wills; Swift Peak; McNally & McNally's Evidence, 4 Vols; Powell on Mortgages; Newland on Contracts; Fonblanques Equity, 2 Vol.; Tollers Law of Exrs; Sergeant on Attachment; Days Reports, 2 vol.; Johnsons Cases; 3 Vols; Saunders Reports, 3 Vols; Roberts on Fraud; Roberts on Conveyances; Harrisons Chancery, 2 Vol.; Maddochs Chancery, 2 Vols; Blakes Chancery; Watson on Partnership, Law of Carriers; Wheaton Reports, 5 Vols; Tidds Practice, 1 Vol; Every Man his own Lawyer; Clarks Assistant, Lawyers Magazine, 3 Vols; Bays Reports; 2 Vols; Sullivans Lectures; Gilbert on Eseccutions; Kyd on Awards; Raymonds Reports; Amblers Reports; Chancery Pleading, Spirit of Laws, 2 Vol; Metfords Pleading; Chittys Law of Nations; Study of Law; Principles of Taxation; 2 Setts Harris & Wm Henry's Reports, 6 Vols; Burke on Sublime; Dictionary of Quotations, Arthors; Blackstone; Brady on Distress; Montague on Set Off; Gilberts Evidence; Young France, 2 Vol; Rains French Wars, 4 Vols; Lanes On Pleading; Moroes Geography, 2 Vols; Sullernans Travels, 2 Vols; Coopers Equity; Rush on the Mind; 50 Vols of misc. books & novels.
8 Nov. 1821 Rob. PURDY, Marshall, W. Tenn.
Test: Silas LOCKE   J. M. SMITH   [pp30-32]

THOMAS YEATMAN of ROBT PURDY, Marshall
22 Feb. 1822   Bill of Sale
Whereas on 1 July 1819, Daniel W. GANTLY & John GANTLY, of NY state recovered a judgment in the Circuit Court of the U.S. for the District of West Tennessee against John P. ERWIN & balance remaining due a writ was issued 20 July 1821 and a levy was made on a negro woman, Claret, & sundry books & paper goods ... exposed for sale on 28 Nov. 1821, & Thomas Yeatman was last & highest bidder.
28 Nov. 1821 ROB. PURDY

Test: J.M . SMITH   [pp32/33]

MINERVA, SOPHIA, JULIA ANN, ANDREW J, ARRAMINTA &
THO. J. DICKINSON
22 Feb. 1822   Deed of Gift
I, Jacob DICKINSON, for natural love & affection, have given to my
children, Minerva, Sophia, Julia Ann, Andrew J., Arraminta & Thomas
J. Dickinson, the following named negro slaves: Abraham, Jerry, Lucy,
Sophia, John, Mary, George & Angelina; for the purpose of raising,
supporting & educating my children and supporting their mother & my
wife, Mrs. Dickinson.21 Sept. 1821   JACOB DICKINSON
ROBERT SMILEY, ARRAMINTA SMILEY [pp33/34]

JAMES CRAWFORD of WILLIE BARROW
22 Feb. 1822   Deed of Trust
24 May 1821, Arch'd McNEILL conveyed to Willie Barrow, as
trustee, articles of property for the use of James Crawford & Andrew
NAPIER, of the City of New York, trading under the firm of *James
Crawford & Co.* & they have purchased   of Arch'd McNeill the
property conveyed to me under the trust for the sum of one dollar.
31 Jan. 1822   W. BARROW
Wit: Th. HILL, Alpha KINGSLEY   [pp34/35]

EPHRAIM H. FOSTER of THOMAS TALBOT
22 Feb. 1822   Bill of Sale
I, Thomas Talbot, convey to Ephraim H. Foster a negro man, named
Charles, aged about twenty two years, and a negro woman, named
Judith, about twenty years old. 24 July 1821   THOMAS TALBOT
Test: J. H. TALBOT, E[lihu] S. HALL [p35]

LEONARD KEELING of JOHN N. & JOHN HAYNIE
6 March 1822   Deed of Trust
John Neal Haynie & John Haynie have placed in the hands of Leonard
Keeling debts due to William SNEED, one new wagon & gears, one
white horse, one white mare, one yearling colt, one bay horse, one
dark sorrel horse, six head of cattle, one bedstead & furniture, one
Breakfast table, six windsor chairs, 3 Barshear ploughts, one shovel
plough, 6 hoes, 2 axes, 2 pots, 1 oven, 1 skillet, 40 head hogs. If
debts are not paid to Sneed before 1 Jan. 1823, as much property as
need be to pay the debt, may be sold by Keeling. 14 Jan. 1822
     JOHN N. HAYNIE   JOHN HAYNIE
Wit: William L. FRANSLEY, John G. CHILES [p36]

It is understood the above named property is to remain in the hands of John N. Haynie & John Haynie. Wit: Felix ROBERTSON [p37]

ELVIRA NUCKOLS of DREWRY SCRUGGS
30 Apr. 1822   Deed of Gift
Drury Scruggs, of Sumner County, TN, to Elvira Nichols, daughter of JANE & STERLING NUCKOLS; for the love and affection for Elvira and in tender consideration I bequeath to Elvira a negro girl, named Fanny, aged about nine years old.Oct. 1821   DRURY SCRUGGS [pp37/38]

ROBERT L. BROWN of REBECCA STEWART
8 May 1822   Deed of Trust
Rebecca Steward has sold & conveyed to Robert L. Brown the following: Daniel, about 20 years old; Barbary, about ten years old; 4 feather beds, two coverlids, six counterpins, five sheets, 4 bedsteds, 4 pots, 2 ovens, 2 skillets, 6 puter plates, 2 puter dishes, half dozen knives & forks, half dozen delf plates, 1 one dish, half dozen delf cups & saucers, one sugar pot, one coffee pot, one pair flat irons, tongs & shovel, one case of Black Bottles, one looking glass, one chest, one table, four old axes, one weeding hoe, one old plough, one pr. old drawing chains & haims, two wheels & check reel, two pair cotton cards; all of the above in the possession of Rebecca Stewart, at her residence on the plantation of Samuel WEAKLEY. Rebecca Steward is indebted to the following: Thomas STEWART, in the state of KY; Mr. COOK, Attorney in Clarksville; William HINTON; Agness STEWART. If notes are not paid in two years, property may be exposed to public auction. 20 Apr. 1822 REBECCA(X)STEWART ROBERT L. BROWN   [pp38/39]

JAMES WRAY of ENEAS WALKER
8 May 1822   Mortgage
I, Eneas Walker, sell to James Wray the following: 1 brown mare, 1 yoke of oxen. If debt is paid, this deed to be void.
1 Sept. 1821   ENEAS WALKER
Test: Alexander WALKER, Landon C. FARROR [p40]

ISABELLA A. & WILLIAM W. KAIGLER of D. KAIGLER
8 May 1822   Deed of Gift
I, David Kaigler, for natural love & affection I bear unto my beloved daughter, Isabella Kaigler, and my beloved son, William W. Kaigler, convey to them a negro girl by the name of Esther, between eleven & twelve years of age. 7 March 1822   DAVID KAIGLER

Test: James GRIFFARD, Wilford H. RAINS [pp41/42]

JOHN McCLELLAN of JOHN CRIDDLE
8 May 1822   Bill of Sale
I John Criddle, sell to John McClellan, of Williamson County, TN, two negro slaves; Sally, aged about twenty one and Isham, aged about twenty five. 19 April 1822 JNO. CRIDDLE   [p42]

RICHARD BOYD of WILLIAM GRUBB
8 May 1822   Bill of Sale
I, William Grubbs, have sold and delivered to Richard Boyd the following negroes: one woman, named Null, 18 years of age, and her child, named Alfred, about two years of age.
14 Nov. 1820   WILLIAM GRUBB
Test: Wm GILSON, R. GILSON   [p43]

BEAL BOSLEY of ROLAND CATO
8 May 1822   Bill of Sale
I, Roland Cato, have sold & delivered unto Beal Bosley a negro girl, by the name of Anjea, of a dark complexion, about eighteen years old.
30 Oct. 1821   Roland (X) Cato
Test: Jno. NICHOL, James BELL [p43]

JOHN NICHOL of BEAL BOSLEY
9 May 1822   Bill of Sale
I, Beal Bosley, have sold and delivered unto John Nichol a negro girl, named Anjea, being the same I purchased of Roland Cato.
7 Nov. 1821   BEAL BOSLEY
Test: James BELL   [p43]

THOMAS CRUTCHER of SAMUEL ELAM
9 May 1822   Bill of Sale
I, Samuel Elam, have sold to Thomas Crutcher two negro men: George, about twenty six years old; the other, named Emberer, about twenty eight years old; one riding carriage & harness, two bay horses, one mule and one sorrel mare. 4 March 1822   JOHN ELAM
Test: Hays BLACKMAN, M. C. ROANEY [p45]

JOSIAH HORTON of MILTON SWIFT
9 May 1822   Bill of Sale
I have sold to Josiah Horton three negro slaves; a negro woman named Dolly, about twenty three years, of yellow complexion, and her two

children; Minerva, a little more than three years, and Katharine, about eighteen months. 20 April 1822   MILTON SWIFT
Test: Th. CLAIBORNE, Nathan EWING [p46]

JOHN SHUTE of JOHN STROTHER
9 May 1822   Bill of Sale
I have this day sold to John Shute a certain negro fellow named Squire, about nineteen years of age. 25 July 1821
                    JNO STROTHER
Test: Jno. M. HILL, John DREWRY [pp46/47]

JOHN SHUTE of P. W. LONG
9 May 1822   Bill of Sale
I have this day sold to John Shute a negro boy, named Nathan, about fifteen years of age. 14 July 1821 P. W. LONG
Test: Tho. LONG   [p47]

JOHN C. McLEMORE of WM. L. MITCHELL
9 May 1822   Bill of Sale
I have this sold to John C. McLemore a mulatto boy, named Mat, about eleven years of age, being the same boy I purchased from John POOR. 25 Feb. 1822   WM L. MITCHELL
Test: John DECKER, R. SANDERSON [p48]

JOHN C. McLEMORE of ROBERT H. ADAMS
9 May 1822   Bill of Sale
I have this day sold to John C. McLemore a mulatto boy slave, named Gabrial, about thirteen years old. 8 April 1820   ROBT H. ADAMS
Test. J. BLACKFAN/BLACKSPAN? [pp48/49]

JOHN C. McLEMORE of THOS. HOPKINS
9 May 1822   Bill of Sale
I have this day sold to John C. McLemore one negro fellow, named Pleasant, about seventeen years of age.
24 March 1822   THOS. HOPKINS
Test: Patrick H. DARBY, Fr. A. ROSS   [p49]

McLEMORE & McNAIRY of S. D. HAYES
21 May 1822   Bill of Sale
I have this day sold to John C. McLemore & Boyd McNairy the following slaves: Ben, about nineteen years old; George, about thirty years old; Ama, about twenty four years old; Maria, about seventeen years old. 16 March 1822   S. D. HAYES

Test: Willo. WILLIAMS, W. BARROW   [p50]

THOMAS CRUTCHER of SAMUEL ELAM
21 May 1822   Deed of Trust
I sell to Thomas Crutcher all interest I have in the following negroes:
Will, Phill, Pleasant, Nero, Little Phill, Charles, Plutarch, Billy,
Claiborne, Jerry, Hanna and her child, Edy and her child, Ellick, Tony,
Giles, Rachel, Sylvia, Lucy, Edward, Phillis, Atkins, Dorcas, Patsey,
Amy, Stephen, Embro and Harriet. Samuel Elem, together with several
other persons, on 4 Sept. 1818, made several notes to Andrew
ERWIN, for the purchase of the *Bell Tavern* in Nashville...this is a
continuation of that debt. 8 March 1822   SAM ELAM
Test: John CATRON, John GUNNING [pp50-52]

JOSEPH W. HORTON of WILLIE BARROW
4 June 1822   Deed of Trust
I convey to Joseph W. Horton a certain negro slave, named Nero, of
dark complexion, about twenty eight years old. If debt is paid, this
conveyance to be void. 26 April 1822   W. BARROW
Test: Andrew HAYS, James GRERRARD   [pp52/53]

IRWIN, HILL & STOUT of THOMAS G. BRADFORD
4 June 1822   Mortgage
To secure debt to James Irwin & S.V.D. Stout and endorsements
made by Thomas Hill, I hereby mortgage the printing office, type,
press, stock on hand; also the household furniture about the office.
29 Aug. 1821   T. G BRADFORD
Wit: Nelson THORNTON   [pp53/54]

MILTON SWIFT & JOSIAH HORTON
4 June 1822   Agreement
A suit was instituted against Milton Swift by David WILMOTH;
Duncan ROBERTSON, George LOUTHER & John WILSON became
appearance bail for Swift; said securities have surrendered Swift in
open court and Swift is unwilling to be confined in the Jail, he has this
day sold to Josiah Horton, sheriff, three negroes; one yellow negro
woman, named Dolly, aged about twenty two or three; two negro girl
children of said woman, Minerva, about three years and Catherine,
aged about eighteen months. 20 April 1822   J. HORTON
Test:Th. CLAIBORNE, Nathan EWING   [pp54/55]

SARAH HANKS of ANN M. HEWLETT, admrx
1 July 1822   Bill of Sale

I, Nancy M. Hewlett, sell to Sarah Hanks, the wife of Richard HANKS, a negro woman named Violet, about 20 years old, and her child, named Harrel, about two years of age. After the decease of the said Sarah Hanks, said negroes, and their increase, shall belong equally and jointly to the heirs of Richard & Sarah Hanks. 19 Apr. 1822 ANN M. HEWLETT, admx ofGeorge HEWLETT, dec'd
Test: N.A . McNAIRY   [p56]

LEWIS EARTHMAN of JOHN REESE
29 July 1822   Bill of Sale
I have sold to Lewis Earthman a negro man, named Tom, aged about thirty years, now absconded.20 Dec. 1821   JOHN (X) REESE
Test: William (X) BINKLEY, John M. (X) PAGE   James MARSHALL, Isaac EARTHMAN, Jr. [p57]

LEWIS EARTHMAN of CHARLES BIDWELL
29 July 1822   Bill of Sale
I have sold to Lewis Earthman one negro man, named Jim, about twenty seven years, a blacksmith by trade, but at this time absconded, at Earthmans risk.   If the said negro come into my hands, I will endeavour to deliver him to Earthman, but Earthman is to pay all expence in advertising. 20 Dec. 1821   CHARLES BIDWELL
Test: Jno. STUMP, John M. (X) PAGE, James MARSHALL [p58]

HARDY S. BRYANT of J. L. YOUNG
3 Aug. 1822   Deed of Trust
Hardy S. Bryant, as adm. of Daniel YOUNG, dec'd against John L. Young on a note due the estate... John L. Young does sell to Hardy S. Bryant the following negroes: Lawrence, about forty five years old; Armistead, about 12 years old, Nelly, about forty five years old and her youngest child. 30 May 1822 J. L. YOUNG
Witness: Wm ALLEN, Duncan G. ROBERTSON, Isaiah CURRY [pp59/60]

ELISHA WILLIAMS of THOS. HUDSON
8 Aug. 1822   Bill of Sale
I, Thomas Hudson have sold the following negro slaves to Elisha Williams: Nancy, a woman; Daniel, a boy; Mary Ann, Elvia, Jefferson, Lydia, Washington & Egbert, together with their future increase.
26 June 1822   THOS. HUDSON
Test: Will. WHITE, Henry EWIN [pp60/61]

DAVID VAUGHT of SAMUEL F. GREEN
8 Aug. 1822   Bill of Sale
I, Samuel F. Green, have sold to David Vaughn one negro boy know by the name of Jack, and one negro girl, known by the name of Lucy. 28 Jan. 1822   SAM'L F. GREEN
Wit: William PHILIPS, Sam'l STULL [p61]

DAVID VAUGHN of WILSON OVERALL
8 Aug. 1822   Bill of Sale
I, Wilson Overall, have sold to David Vaughn a negro fellow, named Kellece, about twenty eight years of age; which negro slave I convenant for myself, my heirs, also for Isaac OVERALL, William OVERALL, Nathaniel OVERALL & Betsey ROBERTSON to warrent the right & title. 19 Oct. 1821   WILSON L. OVERALL
Test: R[euben] A. HIGGANBOTHAM [p62]

RANDAL EWING of JOS. HOOPER
8 Aug. 1822   Bill of Sale
I, Joseph Hooper, have sold to Randal McGavock Ewing, of Williamson County, a negro man slave, named Robin, aged between 41 & 43 years. 1 May 1822 JOSEPH HOOPER
Wit: David PARKER, Matthew PATTERSON   [pp62/63]

JAMES NEWSOM of B. JOSLIN
8 Aug. 1822   Bill of Sale
I have sold to James Newsom a negro girl named Mariah, aged about thirteen. 18 July 1822   BENJAMIN JOSLIN [p63]

WILLIAM PEAY of ELIAS PEAY
8 Aug. 1822   Bill of Sale
I have sold to William Peay three negro slaves; one girl by the name of Elisa, about seven; one girl, named Lucinda, about four; one negro woman, named Milley, about twenty eight years.
25 Jan. 1822   ELIAS PEAY
Wit: John McCAIN, Tho'S THOMPSON [p64]

ROBERT FARQUHARSON of J. P. ERWIN
8 Aug. 1822   Bill of Sale
By an order of the Court of Pleas & Quarter Sessions, April Term 1822, I, John P. Erwin, was ordered to sell the negro slaves belonging to the estate of William VAUGHN, dec'd, who died intestate ... after 20 days advertising in the *Nashville Whig* ... did proceed to sell.

Robert Farquharson, became the purchaser of negro man, Bob. 11 May 1822
J. P. ERWIN, Commissioner   [pp64/65]

JOHN CATRON of F. STUMPS Exrs.
8 Aug. 1822   Bill of Sale
Frederick Stump, in his lifetime, did sell to John Catron a negro boy named Manscur, about sixteen years of age. Now to confirm said sale, we, the executors of Frederick Stump, sell & deliver to John Catron the negro boy, Manscur. 16 July 1822
PHILIP SHUTE   JNO CRIDDLE   [pp65/66]

ARCHIBALD BOYD of JOS. H. McEWIN
9 Aug. 1822   Bill of Sale
I have sold to Arch. Boyd one negro girl slave named Molusina. 18 Aug. 1821   J. H. McEWIN
Alex. RICHARDSON   [pp66/67]

JESSE WHARTON of J. N. MANEFEE
9 Aug. 1822   Bill of Sale
I have sold to Jesse Wharton the following negro slaves; George, aged about 45 years; Esther, about 28 years and her three children, Sam, about 7 years old; Minerva, about 5 years old; Phillis, about three years and Charlotte, about 18 months old. Whartons holds Manifees bond, payable to John NICHOLS, & endorsed by him, Jonas MANIFEE, Jr. & Daniel A. DUNHAM.
26 Feb. 1822   J. N. MENEFEE
Wit: Stephen CANTRELL, R. SANDERSON   [pp67/68]

ROBERT FARQUHARSON of J. HORTON, shff
9 Aug. 1822   Bill of Sale
a judgment obtained in Nov. 1821, Circuit Court by LARGE & WALN vs Joseph PORTER, adm. of James PORTER, dec'd; writ issued May term; levied on four negroes; Eve & her child, Bonaparte, Cynthia, & Allen; belonging to James Porter, dec'd; exposed for sale at the courthouse in Nashville - Robert Farquhason being highest bidder, sell to him said slaves. 29 July 1822   J. HORTON, shff of Davidson County
Test: Henry CRABB, J. W. HORTON   [pp68/69]

LYTLE & WOODS of A. RICHARDSON
9 Aug, 1822   Deed of Trust

I, Alexander Richardson, convey to Robert Woods & William Lytle the following property: 3 large, 1 small, 4-posted bedsteads, 2 large & 1 small feather beds, 1 large mattress, 6 pillows, 3 Bolsters, ---pr blankets,---pr sheets & counterpanes, & bed quilts, 1 pr chinz bed curtains, 1 large bedroom chair, 20 white chairs, 1 wardrobe, 1 Bureau & bookcase, 1 Bureau, 3 toilett tables & furniture, 3 toilett glasses, 2 sett bedsteps, 11 paper window blinds, 2 wash stands, 3 Suirging Bookshelves, 1 Spice can, 1 Japan sugar case, 1 writing Desk, 1 Sett Northumberland Tables, 2 dining tables, 1 Breakfast table, 1 Ladies workstand, 2 candlestands, 2 small Tables with drawers, 1 Safe, 1 pr Gilt look glasses, 1 Mahogany frame looking glass, 4 floor carpets, 2 Rags, Bradd rod for Carpet & Stair & Hall carpeting, 1 lamp for hall, 1 sideboard, 4 Dimitz curtains & Cornice, 3 fenders, 3 setts & irons for shovel & tongs, 1 Sett scarlett waiters, 1 sett Japan waiters, 2 set mantle ornaments, one scarlet settee, one old green settee, 26 Red chairs, 1 Sett fine tea china, 1 Sett common tea china, 1 Dinner set, knives & forks, all kitchen furniture of every description, 13 milch cows, one cart & water cast, one negro man, Davy, one man, Jacob & his wife, Kitty, and a girl, Maria.
Alexander Richardson is indebted to: Branch Bank of TN at Nashville, with Wm LYTLE & Thomas CLAIBORNE endorsees; another with James STEWART & Stephen CANTRELL; another with John NEWNAN & John HARDINGS; another with William LYTLE & John McNAIRY; to N. & J. DICK & Co. of New Orleans; to Nathaniel POYNTZ & Co.; Ephrain H. FOSTER; William LYTLE; H. SOUGHTY. All to remain in the possession of Richardson until expiration of term of note.6 June 1822   Alex RICHARDSON
Test: Addison EAST, David IRWIN   [pp69/72]

THOMAS YEATMAN of J. HORTON, Shff
9 Aug. 1822   Bill of Sale
Whereas a judgment was returned in favor of John W. TILFORD against John P. ERWIN ...goods & chattels were exposed to public sale on 11 July 1822 & Thomas Yeatman was highest bidder: one patent cooking stove & furniture, one Franklin stove, one new floor carpet, 1 small childrens bureau, 1 office Secretary, one small writing secretary, 4 milch cows, 1 mans saddle & bridle, 1 womans saddle & bridle, one pr saddle bags, 1 Rifle gun, one Barrel whiskey, 1 Barrel loaf sugar, 1 Barrel Brown sugar, 1/2 Bag coffee, about 100lbs Bacon; about 500 lbs beef; one negro bed & clothing, 1 chicken coop, 2 portraits, 1/2 Barrel fish, 1/2 Bar Tea, Box Candles, Demijohn of wine, sundry Law Books;Runnington on Ejectment, 1 Vol; Powell on Contracts, 1 Vol., Powell on Devises, 1 Vol., Hargraves Law Traits,

19

1 Vol. Sanders on Uses, 2 Vols., Washingtons Reports, 2 Vols., Henning & Mumfords Reports, 9 Vols., Cains New York Cases, 1 Vol., NY Term Reports, 3 Vols., Benneys Reports, 6 Vols., Dumford & East Reports, 8 Vols., Bunens Reports, 5 Vols, atkyns Report, 3 Vols., cokes Reports, 9 Vols., Coopers Reports, 1, Lord Raymond, 3 Vol., C. Wheaton, 1 Vol., 18th Johnson, 1 Vol., American Presidents, 1 V., Scotts Revisal, 2 Vols., Shepherds Touchstone, 2 Vols., Yeatis Reports, 4 Vol., Sellens Crompton, 2 Vol., Ceropers Reports, 2 Vol., Sterns works, 6 Vols., Parents assistant, 2 Vols. I therefore convey to Thomas Yeatman the aforesaid.   11 July 1822
                    J. HORTON, shff   [pp72-74]

MOSES NORVELL of JOHN H. WILKINS
12 Aug. 1822   Deed of Trust
I, John H. Wilkins, have conveyed to Moses Norvell the *Clarion* Printing Office, cooking & household furniture, type, press, cases, etc. to secure debt of Thomas G. BRADFORD, for which Thomas HILL may be liable. 1 Sept. 1821   J. H. WILKINS
Test: Th. H. McKEEN, Alex. READ [pp74/75]
State of Tennessee   July Sessions 1822   White County
Deed from John H. WILKINS to Moses NORVELL proven by oath of Alexander REED.   Jacob A. LANE, Clk.

THOMAS CHILDRESS of FRANCES CURTIS
19 Aug. 1822   Bill of Sale
I, Frances Curtis, have this day sold to Thomas Childress, of Alabama Territory, Lauderdale County, a mulatto woman slave, named Sharlotte, and her two children, Patt & William, for the love & affection I bear my daughter, Patsey, wife of Thomas CHILTON ... in consideration of one dollar to me paid.
12 Dec. 1818   FRANCES CURTIS
Wit: R. W. GREENE, Alex. EWING [p76]

PETER DOUGLAS of CHAS. SMITH
28 Aug. 1822   Bill of Sale
I, Charles Smith, of Todd County, KY, have this day sold to Peter Douglass a negro slave girl, named Milley, about seventeen years old and a negro boy about the age of thirteen, named Charles.
Chas. SMITH
Test: P. CRADDOCK, Hays BLACKMAN [pp76/77]

LUCINDA R. K. & GEORGE W. WILSON of P. DOUGLAS
I assign all my right & title to within described slaves to Lucinda R. K.
Wilson & George W. Wilson. 10 Oct. 1821 PETER DOUGLAS
Test: H. F. HAZARD
    In the Supreme Court of Errors & Appeals for the 4th Judicial
Circuit of TN at Nashville - July Term 1822
    The assignment of this Bill of Sale from Peter DOUGLAS to
Lucinda R. K. WILSON & George W. Wilson ack. in open court by
Peter Douglas.   [p77]

TIMOTHY DEMONBREUN of T. DEMONBREUN, Jr.
28 Aug. 1822   Bill of Sale
I, Timothy, Jr., convey to Timothy, Sr., the following property; 1
sorrel mare, 1 bay mare, 1 two-yr old sorrel filley, 1 2 yr old bay horse
colt, 1 bay yearling horse colt, 1 brown yearling filley, 5 cows, 2 three
yr old steers, 9 head of cattle, under three years old, 14 head of sheep,
65 head of hogs, 2 beds & furniture, 2 tables, 1 large pot, 1 large oven,
1 large skillet, 2 small skillets, 1 cart & gears together with my
standing crop of corn, about 20 acres. If paid within 15 months to be
void. 27 July 1822 TIMOTHY DEMONBREUN, Jr.
Wit: Andrew FAHY, W. F. GREEN [pp77-79]

JOHN HARMAN of JOHN H. LEWIS
13 Nov. 1822   Bill of Sale
Ernest BENOIT conveyed, in trust, a negro man slave, named Harry,
to John H. LEWIS in March 1820. ... said Harry was sold at auction
on 14 Sept. and John HARMON was highest bidder. I therefore
convey Harry, aged about thirty two years, to John Harmon.
20 Sept. 1822 JOHN H. LEWIS, Trustee
Test: Philip W. LONG, Isaiah CURREY [pp79/80]

STEPHEN CANTRELL of ALFRED M. CARTER
12 Nov. 1822   Bill of Sale
I, Alfred M. Carter, of Carter County, TN, have this day sold to
Stephen Cantrell & Co., a negro girl, named Harriett, aged about
thirteen years. 11 Nov. 1819 A. M. CARTER
Test: Robert SANDERSON [pp80/81]

STEPHEN CANTRELL of C. D. McLEAN
13 Nov. 1822   Bill of Sale
I, Charles D. McLean, sell to Stephen Cantrell, Jr. a negro woman,
named Lucinda, about twenty years old. 6 May 1820 C. D. McLEAN

ALEXANDER PORTER of JNO. HARMON
13 Nov. 1822   Bill of Sale
I, John Harmon, have sold to Alexander Porter a negro man slave, named Henry, about thirty two years of age.
21 Sept. 1822   John Harmon
Test: Robt. W. GREENE, John ELLISTON   [p82]

ALEXANDER PORTER of NORVELLS
13 Nov. 1822   Bill of Sale
We, William NORVELL and Nathaniel NORVELL, of Bedford County, TN, have sold to Alexander Porter a negro girl of light complexion, named Patsey, about eighteen years of age. 14 Sept. 1822 WM NORVELL by William Norvell, Jr., his att'y in fact, N. J. NORVELL
Test: J. THOMPSON, Robt. W. GREENE [pp82/83]

ZACHARIAH NOELL of W. L. SHUMATE
13 Nov. 1822   Bill of Sale
I, Willis L. Shumate, have sold to Z. Noell one negro man named Jacob, about thirty five years of age.
24 Oct. 1822 WILLIS L. SHUMATE [p83]

JOSIAH HORTON of JOHN CRIDDLE
13 Nov. 1822   Bill of Sale
I have this day sold to Josiah Horton the following furniture and stock: one Bureau, and glass furniture, one press and table furniture, six windsor chairs, seven common chairs, one clock, two circular tables, one dining table, one set brass candlesticks, two large looking glasses, one dressing table and glass, three beds & furniture, one chest, two cows & calves, one pair shovel & tongs, three pr. andirons, one mans and one womans saddle, one bay horse & all the kitchen furniture - it being formerly the property of H. H. LEAGUE, of Stewart County, TN, purchased by me at sheriffs sale.
22 Oct. 1822 JNO CRIDDLE   [p84]

JOHN C. McLEMORE of WM. B. McCLELLAN
13 Nov. 1822   Bill of Sale
I, William B. McClellan, of Williamson County, TN, sell to John C. McLemore one negro woman named Sinda (Linda?), about twenty seven years old. 24 July 1822 Wm B. McCLELLAN

Test: Joseph SHAW   [p85]

JNO. C. McLEMORE of N. B. PRYOR
13 Nov. 1822   Deed of Trust
I have this day sold to John C. McLemore one negro fellow named
Ned, about twenty six years old; subject to the following conditions -
on 23 Jan. 1819, I gave my note at the sale of the personal estate of
Thomas WILLIAMS, Dec'd, at the *Farmers & Mechanics Bank of
Nashville* ..McLemore is my endorser ..if I pay said note & interest
this Bill of Sale is void.24 Oct. 1821   N. B. PRYOR
Test: W. COOPER, J. C. GUILD [pp85/86]   Oct. Sessions 1822 -
proven by the oath of <u>Charles</u> Cooper, one of the subscribing
witnesses.

JNO. C. McLEMORE of N. B. PRYOR
13 Nov. 1822   Bill of Sale
Nicholas B. Pryor executed to John C. McLemore a Deed of Trust on
a negro man named Ned, to secure debt to the heirs of Thomas
Williams...McLemore having paid said note, I hereby deliver negro
man, Ned, to McLemore. 17 Oct. 1822   N. B. PRYOR
Test: Joseph SHAW   [pp86/87]

JOHN C. McLEMORE of THOMAS HOPKINS
13 Nov. 1822   Bill of Sale
I, Thomas Hopkins, of Warren County, KY, have this day sold to John
C. McLemore the following negro slaves and their increase: Patsey, a
negro woman about thirty seven years; her son, Alexander, a mulatto
boy about twelve years old; her daughter, Harriett, a mulatto girl about
ten years old. 13 Aug. 1822 Thos. HOPKINS
Test: Joseph SHAW, Hays BLACKMAN   [pp87/88]

JOHN C. McLEMORE of THOS. HOPKINS
13 Nov. 1822   Bill of Sale
I have this day sold to John C. McLemore the following negro slaves:
Patsey, and her two children, Alexander & Harriett - the same I sold to
him on 18 Jan. last - I have also bargained to sell to him two other
negroes, which I have verbally contracted for with Daniel SWADER,
the present owner: a negro girl about sixteen years of age and a negro
boy about fourteen, and to deliver to said McLemore in Nashville, or
to his father, Nathaniel McLEMORE, residing on Mill Creek, about
ten miles from Nashville. 21 June 1822   THOS. HOPKINS
Test: Joseph SHAW   [pp88/89]

JOHN BLAIR of RUSSELL SULLIVENT
13 Nov. 1822   Mortgage
I assign my interest in one bay mare, one sorrel hors, one black mare,
all my cattle & hogs, my crop of corn & tobacco unless I pay John
Blair the sum I own him by 1 April 1823.
25 Sept. 1823   RUSSELL SULLIVENT
Test: Hardy S. TOWNS   [pp89/90]

JOHN LUCAS of ROBERTSON & RICHARDSON
13 Nov. 1822   Bill of Sale
We, Elijah ROBERTSON, Booker F. RICHARDSON, legatees,
relinquish all right and interest of a negro girl named Matilda, property
of the estate of Charles ROBERTSON, dec'd., to John LUCAS,
legatee. 26 Sept. 1822
ELIJAH ROBERTSON, B. F. RICHARDSON
Test; J. NEWLIN   [pp90/91]

ELIJAH ROBERTSON of RICHARDSON & LUCAS
13 Nov. 1822   Agreement
We, Elijah ROBERTSON, Booker F. RICHARDSON & John
LUCAS, legatees of the estate of Charles ROBERTSON, dec'd, have
mutually agreed to & with each other that Elijah Robertson has
received one negro man named Harry, 21 years of age, property of
said estate, as a full portion. 26 Sept. 1822
    B. F. RICHARDSON JOHN LUCAS
Test: J. NEWLIN   [p91]

ALEXANDER C. EWING to JERMAN & POWELL
13 Nov. 1822   Bill of Sale
We, Robert Jerman, of Wilson County, TN, & Thomas Powell, of
Rutherford County, have sold to Alexander C. Ewing, of Williamson
County, TN, a negro man slave named Isom, aged twenty four or
twenty five years. 14 Aug. 1822
 ROBERT JERMAN   THOS POWELL
Wit: O. B. HAYES, Benj. LITTON [pp91/92]

SOMMERVILLE & McGAVOCK of E.B. & S.C. ROBERTSON
15 Nov. 1822   Deed of Trust
Eldridge B. Robertson & Sterling C. Robertson, of Giles County, TN,
on the one part and John Sommerville & Jacob McGavock of the other
part. Eldridge B. is indebted to the Bank of the State of TN, ... note
to Stirling C., endorsed to John CATRON and to secure same, sell to
John Sommerville & Jacob McGavock the following negro slaves:

Jenney, about thirty years of age; Ben, about twenty two years of age; Lovorerea, about six years of age; Charles, about four years of age. If debt is not paid said negroes are to sold to satisfy the debt; said negroes are to be put into the possession and safe keeping of John Catron. 9 Oct. 1822

Eldridge B. ROBERTSON   Sterling C. ROBERTSON
Wit: Jno. BELL, Isaac SITLER   [pp91-95]

GEORGE W. GIBBS of JAMES R. McMEANS
18 Nov. 1822   Deed of Trust
To secure a note to the Bank of the State of TN, James R. McMeans conveys to George W. Gibbs a negro boy named Bryant, a girl named Seller, and another girl named Synthia. If note is not paid, he shall proceed to sell them at public auction. 2 Oct. 1822

JAMES R. McMEANS
Test: Joel PARRISH, C. COOPER [pp95/96]

THE STATE BANK of WILLIAM WHITE
18 Nov. 1822   Mortgage
I, William White, convey to the Bank of the State of TN the following slaves: Betty, Jack, Carter, Washington, Jackson, Randal, Delphi, Betsey, Hannah, Minia, Frankey, Amey, Little Anne, Hancy, Daniel, Nelson, Ned, Jenney, Mary, Hasty, Isbell. If note is paid, this deed to be void. 25 May 1822   WILL. WHITE
Test: G. W. GIBBS, C. COOPER   [pp96/97]

JOS. & ROBT WOODS of J. HORTON, Shff
18 Nov. 1822   Bill of Sale
a writ was directed from the Court of Pleas & Quarter Sessions that the sheriff levy on goods & chattles of Henry TIRRASS and were exposed to sale on 26 Feb. 1822 and Joseph & Robert Woods being the last and highest bidders became the purchasers of the following property: one negro woman named Prudence; one pianoforte & stool; one press containing one set tea china, glassware, knives & forks, castors, Silver spoons, bread tray, one set dining tables, one wash stand, 2 Sugar boxes, 1 pr silver candlesticks, one dozen chairs, one pr andirons, one fender, 4 small waiters, 1 lot crockery, one bedstead, bed & furniture, one bureau, one wash stand, one looking glass, one small table, 6 chairs, one grass carpet, 2 tables, one carpet, one settee, 2 looking glasses, 12 chairs, one Bedstead, one sugar press, one lowposted bedstead, bed & furniture, one bedstead & furniture for children, one pr andirons, one work stand and glass, one bedstead, bed

& furniture, one stove, a lot of kitchen furniture, one <u>Deep</u> Stone & jars, one mans saddle. 26 Feb. 1822   J. HORTON, Shff
Test: J. P. ERWIN   [pp97/98]

ROBERT WOODS of J. HORTON, Shff
18 Nov. 1822   Bill of Sale
at the suit of Robert LANIER, circuit court of Davidson County - May 1822 - to me directed that of the goods & chattles of Eli TALBOT ... I have taken 1 oval table, 1 large dining table, 1 Doz. chairs, 1 Secretary, 1 Bookcase, 1 looking glass, 1/2 doz. pictures, 3 mantle ornaments, 1 doz. knives & forks, 1 doz. large coffee cups & saucers, 1 doz. teacups & saucers, 1 doz. plates, 4 dishes, 4 Goblets, 1 doz. wine Glasses, 3 tumblers, 1 large tumbler, 1/2 doz jelly glasses, 1 doz cordial glasses, 2 glass dishes, 2 decanters, 1 large glass bowl, 2 pickle urns, 1 pr. of castors, 2 Japanned boxes, 1 pr. of Salts, 3 brushes, 1 Clarinet, 1 Violin & case, 1 large teaboard, 4 waiters, 1 lot of silver spoons, 1 soup spoon, 1 cream spoon, 1 pr of sugar tongs, 1 large carpet, 1 stair carpet with rods, 2 small carpets, a lot of books, 1 large bedstead, mattress & bolster, 1 bureau, 1 cradle & bed. 1 pr. fenders, 1 tin roaster, 1 Candlestand, 1 wash stand, 1 Dressing table, 1 little bedstead, 2 tubs, 1 tray, 1 brass kettle, 1 pr. Waffle irons, 2 dutch ovens, 1 skillet, 1 gridiron, 4 pr sheets - purchased by Robert Woods, as last and highest bidder. 11 Oct. 1822   J. HORTON, shff
Test: Th. HILL   [pp99/100]

WILLIAM WRAY of ISAAC ALLEN
19 Nov. 1822   Mortgage
Isaac Allen has sold to William Wray all the Cotton Factory and Wool Carding Machinery now in the possession and use of said Isaac, on the lot of ground and in the houses owned by Hiram WHITE; also 5 head of horses, by which said machinery is worked, four of which are blind; also two beds & steads & furniture, 12 chairs, 1 Bureau, Tables, cups, saucers, dishes, plates and all other household furniture/kitchen furniture, 3 cows, one calf. If debts are paid this Indenture to become void. 4 Sept. 1822   ISAAC (X) ALLEN
Test: Nathan EWING, Henry EWING   [pp100/101]

BERNARD VANLEER of JAS. D. MILLER
19 Nov. 1822   Deed of Trust
I have sold to Bernard Vanleer - in trust - the following: one bureau, three tables, one candlestand, a desk & bookcase, 70 Volumes of books, 4 beds & bedsteads with the necessary clothing, one cot, one cradle, a knifebox, one large teaboard, two small waiters, one bread

tray, all my knives & forks, my Queensware & chinaware, one large silver soup ladle, eight silver tablespoons, one doz. silver teaspoons, one mustard silver spoon, two salt silverspoons, one pr. of silver sugar tongs, one silver watch, one pair of steel sugar nippers, two candlesticks, one Demijohn, all my glassware & all my crockeryware, one small bellows, one pr of brass andirons, two shovels, one poker, all my pots & kettles, one copper washpan, all my tinware & woodenware of every description, one coffee mill, two large trunks, one Claronet, one brace of pistols, all my flatirons, fourteen chairs, a large quantity of timber, which I keep for the purpose of stocking ploughs, eleven hundred clapboards, a quantity of cedar rails, all my iron & steel, all my coals, all my work in my shop which is now finished, all my tar ... to secure my debt to the firm of *A. W. Vanleer & Co*, to enable me to carry on my blacksmith shop.
28 March 1822   J. D. MILLER
Test: David F. MILLER, J. H. LANIER [pp102/103]

THOMAS CRUTCHER of NICHOLAS B. PRYOR
19 Nov. 1822   Deed of Trust
I convey to Thomas Crutcher the following property; one negro woman named Hulda, aged about 26 years, and her two children, Sophia & Amanda; also a negro woman named Betty, about 38. In trust - note to the Bank of the State of Tennessee at Nashville, with Thomas Crutcher, John C. McLEMORE, & Ephraim H. FOSTER, as endorsers. If note is paid, this trust to be void.
10 Jan. 1822   N. B. PRYOR
Test: Sam. M. PRICE, Hays BLACKMAN [pp103/105]

JOSEPH & ROBT. WOODS of ECKOLS & WYNNE
23 Nov. 1822   Bill of Sale
Richard A. ECKOLS & Deverin WYNNE, both of Wilson County, TN, have sold to Joseph & Robert Woods a certain negro man named Willis, of dark complexion, about twenty four years old. We defend the title especially against a bill now pending in the Supreme Court wherein Britian DRAKE is complainant & Richard A. ECKOLS, Joel ECKOLS and Joseph & Robert WOOD are defendants. 30 Oct. 1821
        Rich'd A. ECKOLS   Deverin WYNNE
Test: Soloman CLARK, Benj'n F. LEWI [pp105/106]

FOSTER, CAMPBELL & McGAVOCK of J. WHITESIDE
23 Nov. 1822   Bill of Sale
I, Jenkin Whiteside, have sold to Robert C. Foster, Michael Campbell & Jacob McGavock one male negro, named Dave Hiram, about eight

years old, to hold for the use of William RUTHERFORD's family; Elizabeth, the wife, and Felix, Susan, Thomas, Polly, Elizabeth & Benjamin RUTHERFORD, the children.
15 May 1822 J. WHITESIDE   [pp106/107]

BOOKER F. RICHARDSON of LUCAS & ROBERTSON
23 Nov. 1822   Bill of Sale
We, B. F. Richardson, Elijah Robertson & John Lucas, legatees of the estate of Charles Robertson, dec'd, agree that Booker F. Richardson receive one negro boy, named Hiram, 12 years old. 26 Sept. 1822
    ELIJAH ROBERTSON JOHN LUCAS   [p107]

JOHN A., MARY J. & CORNELIA READ of JONES READ
14 Dec. 1822   Deed of Gift
I, Jones Read, for the natural love & affection I have for my three grandchildren, John A., Mary Jane & Cornelia Read (all of them the children of my son, Thomas J. Read and his present wife, the daughter of Gen'l Thomas WASHINGTON, dec'd), give a negro woman by the name of Charity, and all of her increase, to be equally divided by the children when they become of lawful age. To the above named children and all those that he, the said Tom, may have by his present wife.31 May 1822   JONES READ   [pp107/108]
Signed in the presence of Th. HILL 3rd June 1822 E. TALBOT

JOHN A., MARY J., & CORNELIA READ of JONES READ
14 Dec. 1822   Deed of Gift
I, Jones Read, for love & affection...for my grandchildren [see previous entry] give the following articles: household & kitchen furniture - three feather beds, Bolsters & Pillows, two hair mattresses, four bedsteads, two bureaus, one looking glass, two dressing glasses, three tables, one work stand, one Sugar chest, one set of blue dining wear, one set of tea ware, Six large silver spoons, twelve silver teaspoons, two dozen knives & forks, twelve glass tumblewrs, one set plated castors, five flower pots, two pair of brass andirons, two pair shovel & tongs, two ovens, two kettles, two floor carpets, one hearth rug, one passage carpet, one Secretarys desk, thirteen Windsor chairs, fifteen pair of blankets, twelve pair cotton & linnen sheets, Seven bedcovers, three tubs, six pails, one saddle & bridle ... to be equally divided as they become of age. 31 May 1822 Jones READ
Th. HILL   3 June 1822   E. TALBOT   [pp108/109]

EMELINE, BENJAMIN, THOMAS J. & JAS. RUCKER of JONES READ
14 Dec 1822   Deed of Gift
I, Jones Read, for the natural love & affection I have for my grandchildren, Emeline Rucker, Benjamin Rucker, Thomas J. Rucker, & James Rucker, (the children of Jonathan Rucker who married my daughter Polly) and all the children the said Jonathan Rucker may have by his present wife, Polly Rucker, my daughter; give & grant a certain negro woman, by the name of Jude, and all the increase I bequeath to them & their lawful heirs forever, to be equally divided when any of those children become of lawful age. 16 July 1822
JONES READ   [pp109/110]

MARY JANE READ of JONES READ
14 Dec. 1822   Deed of Gift
I, Jones Read, for natural love ... for my granddaughter, Mary Jane Read, daughter of Thomas Read, give unto her a yellowish girl slave, named Fanny, about ten years old, which I bought of John HOPKINS.
25 May 1822   JONES READ
Test: Th. HILL   E. TALBOT   [p110]

CORNELIA READ of JONES READ
14 Dec. 1822   Deed of Gift
I, Jones Read, for natural love...for my granddaughter, Cornelia Read (daughter of Thomas J. Read) give a negro girl slave, named Mary, about five years old.31 May 1822   JONES READ
Test: Th. HILL   E. TALBOT   [p111]

BOYD McNAIRY of JOHN L. YOUNG
18 Dec. 1822   Conditional Bill of Sale
I, John L. Young, sell a negro woman slave named Nelly, about thirty five years old & blind in one eye, to Boyd McNairy; to secure debt to McNairy & his partner James OVERTON. Upon payment of debt within six months, this mortgage to be void.
31 Oct. 1821   J. L. YOUNG
Wit: R. T. WALKER, JAS. WALKER [pp111/112]

THOMAS WASHINGTON of JOHN SHELLY
26 Dec. 1822   Bill of Sale
I, John Shelly, have this day sold to Thomas Washington a negro woman slave, named Polly, about thirty two years of age, and her child, Nancy, about four years of age. 5 Dec. 1822
JOHN SHELLY   [p112]

NANCY M. CROSS & others of I. PIERSON & wife
6 Feb. 1823   Deed of Gift
for the natural love & affection we bear to my children, Nancy M
Cross, Poettan B. Cross, James B. Cross, William E. R. Cross, give
the following property: one cart & steers and one horse, one cow &
yearling, ten head of hogs, one bed & furniture to Poettan B. Cross; to
James B. Cross - one young yoke of steers, one mare, one cow &
yearling, ten head of hogs, one bed & furniture; to William E. R. Cross
- one cow & calf, one horse, ten head of hogs, one bed & furniture; to
Nancy M. Cross - one colt, one cow & calf, one bed & furniture, ten
head of hogs, one cupboard & furniture, thirty head of geese, one
writing desk, 3 pots, 1 dutch oven & spider, 1 pr. smoothing irons, 1
pr. hand irons, household & kitchen vessils of every kind; all the
balance ... plows, etc. to be divided equally among them; rents to be
divided equally; corn, tobacco & bacon to be divided equally; one
womans saddle to Nancy M. Cross. 20 Jan. 1823
ISAM(X)PIERSON DELILAH(X)PIERSON   [pp112/113]

ABERNATHY of ABERNATHY
14 Feb. 1823   Bill of Sale
I, Charles Abernathy, have this day sold to David Abernathy a negro
woman named Eliza, aged thirty four years.
3 Sept. 1822   Charles Abernathy
Wit: Laban ABERNATHY, Wm CURTIS, Thomas IRWIN [p114]

WILLIAM CALDWELL of EDMOND GAMBLE
14 Feb. 1823   Bill of Sale
I have sold to William Caldwell a negro woman named Easter, about
22 or 23 years old, together with her youngest child, named Joe, about
13 months old. 24 June 1809   E. GAMBLE
Test: Jas. H. GAMBLE   [p114]
...ack. in open court by Edmond Gamble to be his act & deed &
ordered to be registered. Nathan Ewing, Clerk of Court

DAVID VAUGHN of R. & R. C. DREWRY
14 Feb. 1823   Bill of Sale
We have sold to David Vaughan one negro girl named Tanny. 9 March
1822   R. C. DREWRY   Rich'd DREWRY
...ack. in open court by Richardson C. Drewry & Richard Drewry
                                                                [p115]

JOSEPH W. HORTON of J. & R. DREWRY
14 Feb. 1823   Bill of Sale
We, John Drewry & Richard Drewry have sold to Joseph W. Horton
three negroes; a woman named Jenny of black complexion, about
twenty four years old & her two children, Julia, about 30 months old,
& Squire about eleven months old. 22 Jan. 1823
                    JNO. DREWRY   RIC'D DREWRY
Test: L. NOELL   [pp115/116]

WILLIAM H. McLAUGHLIN of THOMAS L. WILLIAMS
14 Feb. 1823   Bill of Sale
I, Thomas L. Williams, of Knox County, TN, trustee, for the use of the
heirs of J. P. & F. L. ERWIN, by deed of Trust, executed by Joseph
WILLIAMS, Sr., of Surrey County, N.C., convey to William H.
McLaughlin one negro boy named Thomas, aged about 15. 30 Dec.
1822 THOMAS L. WILLIAMS, by his attorney in fact   J. P. ERWIN
Test:H. P. LLOYD, S. B. MARSHALL [p116]

MADISON McLAURINE of WEAKLEY & McNAIRY
3 March 1823   Bill of Sale
We, Nathaniel A. McNairy & Robert Weakley, as Trustees of William
McLaurine, Deed of Trust dated Oct. 16, 1821 - do sell to Madison
McLaurine of Madison County, TN, a negro girl named Nancy and a
negro woman named Agness, named in said trust - also all the
household & kitchen furniture. 30 Dec. 1822
N. A. McNAIRY, Trustee   R. WEAKLEY, Trustee
Test:George W. McLAURINE, Jno HOBSON [pp116/117]

BRENT SPENCE of JOS. HOLT
25 March 1823   Bill of Sale
I, Joseph Holt, have sold to Brent Spence a negro woman slave named
Fillis, about thirty years of age. 15 Jan. 1823   JOS. HOLT
Test: V. D. COWEN, SIMON PIGOTT   [pp117/118]

BASS & SPENCE of Wm CHAMBERLANE
25 March 1823   Bill of Sale
William Chamberlane, of Simpson County, KY, has sold to BASS &
SPENCE a certain yellow female slave, named Minde, about twenty
years of age, and her male child, about eighteen months old.
25 Sept. 1822   WM CHAMBERLIN
Test: Benjamin W. BEDFORD, W. H. BEDFORD   [pp118/119]

31

THOMAS CRUTCHER of ROGER B. SAPPINGTON
10 April 1823   Deed of Trust
Roger B. Sappington has conveyed to Thomas Crutcher the following
negroes; Bently, Abraham, Isham, Mingo, Pinny & her four children,
Mary Phillis, Daniel & Robert. Roger B. Sappington is indebted to the
Bank of the State of TN, with William LYTLE, Jr, Edwin SMITH,
Martin SMITH, Jacob C. SMITH, Elliott HICKMAN & Thomas
HICKMAN as securities. Until the expiration date said negroes to
remain in possession of Sappington. 14 May 1822
ROBERT B. SAPPINGTON   [pp119/120]

JOHN A. RAWLINGS of THOMAS SHANNON
19 May 1823   Power of Attorney
I, Thomas Shannon, of Hardin County, TN, appoint John A. Rawlings,
of said County, my true and lawful Attorney in fact.. authorized to
release from imprisonment one negro man, named Squire, now
confined in the common jail in Nashville ... also authorized to made
sale of said negro man to any person as completely as I myself could
do.8 April 1823   THOS. SHANNON
Test: James W. COMBS, John HOLLAND[pp120/121]
...proven in open court by oaths of Combs & Holland, Apr. Sessions
1823   Alexander W. SWEENEY, Clerk - Hardin Co. TN

LEE SHUTE of THOMAS SHANNON
19 May 1823   Bill of Sale
I, Thomas Shannon, have sold to Lee Shute a negro man named
Squire, about twenty three years old. 19 Apr. 1823
THOMAS SHANNON, by JOHN A. RAWLINGS, his Attorney in
fact
Test: Nathan EWING, Joseph L. EWING, Henry EWING [p122]

THOMAS KIRKMAN of CHARLES McKERAHAN
19 May 1823   Bill of Sale
I, Charles McKerahan, acknowledge I have received all the personal
property specified in *Exhibit A - Exhibit B* - said property has been
loaned to myself & my family ...   CHA. McKERAHAN
Test: James ERWIN
Exhibit A
Thomas Kirkman bought at sheriffs sale the following property of
Charles McKerahan - taken by execution of Davidson County Court at
the suit of PETWAY & CUREN?
1 looking glass, 1 Bureau, 1 Desk, 1 Bedstead, 1 Sugar Chest, 3
Blankets, 1 Bedcord & Screws, 3 Sheets, Knives & forks, chinaware,

one book case, one press, 1 candlestand, 1 pot, 1 skillet, 1 oven, 1 oven, 1 pr firedogs, 1 lot of Books, 1 pr of saddlebages, 1 small trunk & books, 1 map of America, 1 pot - Total = $61.31/4 + Hauling to house - $2.00 = $63.31/4

Exhibit B

1 Table, 1 Doz. chairs, 2 Feather Beds, 1 Looking glass, 2 counterpins, 3 sheets, 1 tablecloth, 3 blankets, 1 pr. brass andirons, shovel & tongs, 1 bell metal kettle, 1 copper tea kettle, oven & pot, knives & forks, 1 set castors, 3 Decanters, 1 Doz. cups & saucers, 1 saucepan, Tea Potts, Dishes/plates, 1 pr. smoothing irons, 1 Tin Bucket, 1 Pewter Bason. 6 March 1823   [pp122-124]

MARY JANE READ of JONES READ
23 May 1823   Deed of Gift
I, Jones Read, in consideration of the love & affection I have for my granddaughter, Mary Jane Read, have given her a yellowish girl slave named Angelina, about ten years old, which I bought of John HOPKINS. 25 May 1822   JONES READ
Test: Th. HILL, E. TALBOT   [p124]

JOHN C. McLEMORE of E. B. ROBERTSON
23 May 1823   Bill of Sale
I, Eldridge B. Robertson, of Giles County, TN, have sold to John C. McLemore the following six negro slaves: Daniel, about thirty five years of age; Rachel, his wife, about thirty two years of age; her daughter Maria, about sixteen years of age; Levi, son of Rachel, about ten years of age; Milley, her daughter, about seven years of age; Monroe, son of Maria, born in January last.
11 Apr. 1823   ELDRIDGE B. ROBERTSON
Test: G. M. FOGG, J. ROANE   [p125]

RACHEL STUMP & others of J. F. STUMP
23 May 1823   Deed of Relinquishment
I hereby surrender up to the executors of Frederick Stump the plantation on Whites Creek and the two negroes, Stephen & Lucy, which are in my possession .. to hold for the benefit of the estate. I also surrender and quit claim to my stepmother, Rachel Stump & my Brothers Thos. J. Stump, Philip S. Stump and Tennessee M. A. Stump any interest vested in me to all the property conveyed in a deed of gift from Frederick Stump to them or to Philip SHUTE, in trust for their use, dated 25 Nov. 1819.---April 1823   JOHN F. STUMP
Test: James TRIMBLE   Geo. S. YERGER [p126]

SOLOMON CLARK of WILLIAM HAMILTON
23 May 1823   Bill of Sale
I, William Hamilton, have sold & conveyed unto Solomon Clark one
negro man named William, about thirty five years of age, two beds &
furniture, one bureau, one sugar chest, one candlestand, one dining
table, six Windsor chairs & ten thousand feet of plank, two cows &
calves. 27 July 1822   Wm HAMILTON
Test: J. W. SITLER, B. G. MILLER [p127]

WILLIAM JAMES of JOS. JOHNSON
31 May 1823   Bill of Sale
I, Joseph Johnson, of Robertson County, TN, have sold to William
James three negroes: Elizabeth, about twenty three years of age; Dick,
about three years of age; Bella, about one year old - the two children
being the produce of Elizabeth. 18 Feb. 1823   JOS. JOHNSON
Test: M. GLEAVES, Henry R. CARTMILL   [pp127/128]

THOMAS L. WILLIAMS of JOS. WILLIAMS, Sr
31 May 1823   Bill of Sale
Joseph Williams, Sr., of the County of Surry, N.C. [consideration of
one dollar] convey to Thomas L. Williams, of Knox County, TN, one
negro woman named Claret; one boy named Thomas; one girl, Maria;
one boy, Squire; one girl, Rose; one Piano Forte & all the goods &
chattles now in possession of John P. ERWIN in Nashville, which
were conveyed by the executors of Robert SEARCY, dec'd, to Joseph
by deed dated 6 Oct. 1821, together with all the goods & chattles now
in the possession of John P. Erwin, conveyed to Joseph by Robert
PURDY, Marshall for West Tennessee, deed dated 28 Nov. 1821. ...
for the following purpose & no other ... to the entire use and benefit of
the joint heirs and children of John P. Erwin and his present wife,
Frances L. Erwin.... notes of - Doc't ZACK of Alabama, James
CARTER, William M. BERRYHILL, W. BROFORD.
Thomas L. Williams may appoint an agent to manage the property
hereby conveyed on behalf of the children of John P. & Frances L.
Erwin. 8 Nov. 1822 JO. WILLIAMS
Test: Alex WILLIAMS, H. P. POINDEXTER, Nicholas L.
WILLIAMS
[proven in Court of Pleas & Quarter Sessions - Surry Co., N.C. - Nov.
Sessions 1822 Joseph Williams, Clerk
          By Jo Williams, Jun., D.C.
- [Reg. in Book R, page 127, Surry Co., N.C.]
I, Alvin S. DUVALL, a presiding magistrate in Surry County, NC, do
certify that Joseph Williams is the sworn & acting Clerk of the County

Court of Surry and that Joseph Williams, Jr., is his lawful & acting deputy. 18 Apr. 1822   [pp128/131]

JOHN GRANT of OAKLEY JONES
13 June 1823   Bill of Sale
Received payment in full for a negro boy named Henry. 10 Sept. 1822
OAKLEY JONES
Test: W. GARNER, W. D. DORRIS
United States of America
District of West Tennessee [pp131/132]

JOHN GRANT of OAKLEY JONES
13 June 1823   Bill of Sale
Received payment for a negro girl named Julia Ann. 10 Sept. 1822
OAKLEY JONES
Test: W. GARNER, W. D. DORRIS
Circuit Court of the United States of America, Dist. of West TN
[p132]

SAMUEL C. MARLIN & JOHN ELLISTON
18 Aug. 1823   Article of Agreement
Marlin binds himself to build Elliston a framed house 18 x 30, one story high with 5 windows 10 by 12, 18 lights, 2 front shutters, venetian, 3 back, button, 4 door pannelled, one chimney in the end of the house with two fireplaces, one fireplace large enough for kitchen, 1 fireplace of good quality. Marlin is to furnish all materials except the plastering. Elliston binds himself to give Marlin a deed for 25 ft. of ground on broad street - the property purchased by RICHMOND. 14 Aug. 1822   JNO ELLISTON   SAML C. MARLIN
Test: John MILLER, John MURRELL [pp132/133]

JOHN SOMMERVILLE, cashier & ROBERT W. GREENE
19 Aug. 1823   Assignment
I, Robert W. Greene, assign to John Sommerville, cashier of the Branch Bank of the State of Tennessee, 50 shares of capital stock in the said Bank to cover payment of my notes due. 16 July 1823
ROBT. W. GREEN [pp133/134]

WILKINS TANNEHILL, cashier & ROBERT W. GREENE
19 Aug. 1823   Assignment
I, Robert W. Greene, assign to Wilkins Tannehill, cashier of the Nashville Bank 43 shares of said Bank, in trust, to secure the payment of my notes. 16 July 1823   ROBT W. GREENE [pp134/135]

JAMES GORDON of NICHOLAS B. PRYOR
19 Aug. 1823   Bill of Sale
I sell to James Gordon a negro girl named Julia. [a previous
conditional bill of sale was given] 26 June 1823   N. B. PRYOR
Test: C. COOPER, Jas. WALKER   [p135]

ROBERT ARMSTRONG of HENRY RUTHERFORD
19 Aug. 1823   Bill of Sale
I, Henry Rutherford, of Madison County, TN, hereby sell to Robert
Armstrong a negro man, Sam, aged about twenty eight years.
31 June 1823   H. RUTHERFORD
Test: A. MORRISON, J. P. CLARK [p136]

BRYANT BOON of WILLIAM BRAY
19 Aug. 1823   Bill of Sale
I, William Bray, have sold & delivered to Bryant Boon one negro girl
named Sarah, about thirteen years old.11 Feb. 1823
                         WILLIAM BRAY
Test: Jno. DAVIS   [pp136/137]

DANIEL BUIE of CALL McNEILL
19 Aug. 1823   Bill of Sale
I, Call McNeill, have sold to Daniel Buie a negro girl, Elly, thirteen
years old. 19 May 1823   CALL McNEILL
Test: Hardy S. BRYAN, A. JUSTICE [p137]

CAREY FELTS of RICHARD DREWRY
19 Aug. 1823   Bill of Sale
I, Richard Drewry, have sold & delivered four negroes to Cary Felts:
Mimy, a negro woman thirty eight years of age; Silvy, a negro girl
eight years of age; Wiat, a negro boy two years of age & Rainey, a
negro girl one year of age.16 July 1823   RICH'D DREWRY [p138]

WILLIAM EDMISTON of MALLORY & CRADDOCK
21 Aug. 1823   Bill of Sale
We, Philip G. Mallory & Henry Craddock, both of Nottoway County,
VA, have sold and delivered to William Edmiston the following negro
slaves: Tishy, a girl about sixteen years old; Hannah, a girl about eight
years of age; Saul, a boy about eight years of age. 15 May 1823
 PHILLIP G. MALLORY HY CRADDOCK
Test: Sion HUNT, John EDMISTON [p139]

WILLIAM PARKER of JOHN LANIER
21 Aug. 1823   Bill of Sale
I, John Lanier, have sold to William Parker a negro man, Tom.
30 June 1823   JNO LANIER
Test: Lewis EARTHMAN, Jesse PARKER   [pp139/140]

LEWIS EARTHMAN of RODNEY EARHART
21 Aug. 1823   Mortgage Deed
I, Rodney Earhard, have sold to Lewis Earthman one negro man
named Alexander, about thirty seven years of age. Earthman is to
retain said man for six months, then if I have paid my debt, Earhart is
allowed to redeem. Nov. 26, 1822
Test: N. H. ROBERTSON, Wm BROOKS [p140]

HARDING & WHARTON of JOHN NICHOLS
21 Aug. 1823   Deed of Trust
John Harding & Jesse Wharton are my endorsers on note to the
Branch Bank of Tennessee at Nashville, to secure them from loss, I
assign 25 shares of the capital stock of said bank to them. 29 July 1823
JOHN NICHOLS   [p141]

R. McLAURINE & others to WM McLAURINE
21 Aug. 1823   Deed of Trust
William McLaurine of Powhattan County, VA and his sons, Robert
McLaurine, Willis McLaurine & George McLaurine of the state of
Tennessee. William McLaurine is desirous to make provision for the
support of Nancy McLaurine, wife of his son, William, of the state of
Tennessee, and for the children of Nancy by William. For this purpose
William McLaurine does sell to Robert, Willis & George McLaurine -
In Trust - two slaves, a man by the name of Richard, and a negro boy
named John, together with one bay horse & carryall & harness; also
desiring to secure a home for Nancy McLaurine, has deposited five
hundred dollars to purchase a piece of land for the use of Nancy and
her children to be used by them and divided at her death, or her
ceasing to be the wife or widow of said William, when the eldest of
them shall arrive at the age of twenty one years.
20 Feb. 1823   WM McLAURINE
proved in a court of Monthly sessions - Powhattan Co., VA on 20
Feb. 1823 and ordered to be recorded and certified to the State of
Tennessee.   Wm. S. DANCE, Clerk
Geo WILLIAMSON, Justice, Powhattan Co., VA
Edward MOSELEY, Pres. Jus., Powhattan Co., VA [pp141/144]

THOMAS HILL of PATRICK H. DARBY
21 Aug. 1823   Deed of Mortgage
Thomas G. BRADFORD purchased on 1 Sept. 1821 from John H.
WILKINS, the establishment & materials of the "*Clarian*" now the
"*Constitutional Advocate*" printing office & conveyed the same to
Moses NORVELL, in trust, for the benefit of Thomas Hill ... Thomas
Hill sold to Patrick H. DARBY and John H. WILKINS.
27 June 1823   PATRICK H. DARBY
Wit: Solomon CLARK   [pp145/146]

ROBERT T. WALKER of LEWIS STURDIVANT
22 Aug. 1823   Deed of Mortgage
Lewis Sturdivant is in debt to James GORDON & Robert T. Walker &
to the executors of Wm TAIT, dec'd - to secure debt does assign the
following property: two feather beds & bedsteads, one cherry bureau,
one cherry desk, 3 sorrell mares, one dun colored horse, thirteen head
of cattle, one cotton gin , one cotton press, one loom, about 20 acres
of corn standing. 9 Oct. 1822   LEWIS STURDIVANT
Test: John C. COOPER, Jas. WALKER   [pp146/148]

JOHN CATRON, Adm. of JNO CHILDRESS of S. C. ROBERTSON
18 Oct 1823   Bill of Sale
I, Stirling G. Robertson, have sold to John Catron, administrator of
John Childress, a negro man named Guinia Jack, aged about 26 or 28
years. - debt due by mortgage dated in 1822 & witnessed by John
BURGES & Wm GILL.5 May 1823   STERLING C. ROBERTSON
Wit: Nathan EWING, Joseph W. HORTON [pp148/149]

SARAH ROBERTSON of S. C. & E. B. ROBERTSON
18 Oct. 1823   Deed of Mortgage
We, Eldridge B. & Sterling C. Robertson do sell unto our Mother,
Sarah Robertson, six negro slaves; Betty, Jesse, Lucy & her child,
Dave; Tony, a boy about ten years old & Roderick, about twenty two
years old. Eldridge & Sterling are indebted to Sarah; also a note to
Richard C. NAPIER. 29 Apr. 1823   E. B. ROBERTSON
STERLING C. ROBERTSON SARAH ROBERTSON
Wit: Henry EWING [E. B. & S. Robertson]
     John CATRON, Sam'l B. MARSHALL [Sterling C. Robertson]
Joseph W. HORTON, Nathan EWING [pp149/150]

N. C. HALL of E. H. FOSTER
13 Nov. 1823   Agreement

On 21 July 1821 Thomas TALBOT made me a bill of sale for two slaves; Charles, a negro man and Judith, a negro woman to secure debt due to Elihu F. HALL to McDONALD & RIDGELEY of Baltimore ... claim on Walter H. OVERTON [suit in the district court of the district of Louisiana ... obligation on Montgomery BELL ... I obllidge my heirs to convey above named slaves to Nicholas HALL ... on account of said slaves being raised by Elihu F. Hall he may have the refusal of said slaves at whatever value is placed on them. ... they are to remain in the possession of Elihu F. Hall but not to be removed from Nashville without my consent.
18 Jan. 1822 EPHRAIM H. FOSTER [pp150/151]

SAMUEL SEAY of THOMAS TALBOT
24 Nov. 1823   Bill of Sale
I, Thomas Talbot, have sold to Samuel Seay a negro man, Dave (commonly called 'Little Dave'), about twenty years of age.
22 July 1823   THOMAS TALBOT
Test: Th. HILL, E. TALBOT [p152]

WILLIAM OGILVIE of STEPHEN BRYAN
24 Nov, 1823   Bill of Sale
I, Stephen Bryan, have sold & delivered to William Ogilvie a negro man slave named Richard, about seventeen years old, of black complexion. 29 Nov. 1822 STEPHEN BRYAN
Wit: Jos.W.HORTON, Elihu MARSHALL [pp152/153]

THOMAS WASHINGTON of G. G. WASHINGTON
24 Nov, 1823   Mortgage Deed
I have conveyed to Thomas Washington a negro man slave named F/Jarrell, about sixteen or eighteen years old; a negro girl, Frances, about twenty years old and her child, Edwin, about one year old; one bay mare, 10 yrs old, 1 bay colt, 3 yrs old; 1 sorrel horse, 8 yrs old; one side board, two tables & dozen chairs.... debt owed Thomas Washington - also Thomas Washington is security for me in suit of SMITH & wife against me in the circuit court for West Tennessee.
18 Oct. 1823   G[ILBERT] G. WASHINGTON [pp153/154]

MICHAEL GLEAVES of OLIVER S. CONNELL
24 Nov. 1823   Bill of Sale
I, Oliver S. Connell, of Robertson County, TN, have sold to Michael Gleaves a negro boy about sixteen years of age, named Locher.
13 Sept. 1823   OLIVER S. CONNELL
Wit: Jac. McGAVOCK, Joseph W.HORTON [pp154/155]

EDWARD DANIEL of PETER DOUGLASS
24 Nov. 1823   Bill of Sale
I hereby sell to Edward Daniel a negro woman, named Lydia, age
unknown. 10 Dec. 1822   PETER DOUGLASS
Wit: W. W. BERRYHILL, Joseph S. HAMILTON [p155]

EDWARD DANIEL of BENJAMIN DRAKE
24 Nov. 1823   Bill of Sale
I, Benjamin Drake, have sold to Edward Daniel a negro man slave,
named Handy, about twenty two years of age. 4 Sept. 1823
        BENJAMIN(X) DRAKE
Wit: Nathan EWING, Henry EWING [pp155/156]

BENJAMIN HYDE of STUMP & COX
24 Nov. 1823   Bill of Sale
We, Stump & Cox, have sold to Benjamin Hyde a negro woman,
named Sealey. 17 Nov. 1817   STUMP & COX
Wit: Jas. LOVELL   [p156]

DUKE W. SUMNER of EXUM P. SUMNER
24 Nov. 1823   Mortgage Deed
I, Exum Philip Sumner, have sold to Duke W. Sumner three negro
slaves; David, between thirty & forty years of age; his wife, Nancy,
about twenty seven years of age, and her child, Eliza, about one year
old.   Exem P. Sumner did purchase at the sale of Absalom PAGE,
dec'd, the above named negro woman & child and Duke W. Sumner
became his security. 10 June 1823   EXUM P. SUMNER
Wit: Jos. J. SUMNER, Jas. W. SUMNER   [p157]

JOSEPH GREER of JOS. W. HORTON, Shff
24 Nov. 1823   Bill of Sale
Whereas Peter PEYRAUX recovered a judgment [circuit court - May
term 1822 - Davidson County] against Thomas TALBOT - due to writ
the sheriff levied against the following negroes, the property of
Thomas Talbot; negro man, named Joe, about 47 years of age; negro
woman, Fanny, the wife of Joe, about 45 years of age; one negro
woman, Jenny, about 22 years of age, and her two children, Loyd, 4
years old, and Peter, 2 years old; Martin, a negro man about 50 years
old and Silla, his wife, about 40 years old; Jefferson, a negro boy about
18 years old; Luke, a negro boy about 20 years old - Joseph Greer, of
Lincoln County, TN, being the last and highest bidder.
8 Nov. 1823   Joseph W. HORTON, Sheriff

Wit: Thomas TALBOT, J. TALBOT, P. W. BARCLAY [pp158/159]

MARTIN BANCIE of HAYNES & STEELE
15 Dec. 1823   Bill of Sale
We, William Haynes & John Steele, of Montgomery County, TN, have
sold to Matthew one negro man slave, named Bobb, about twenty
eight years of age. 26 Nov. 1823 WM HAYNES   JOHN STEELE
Wit: Alpha KINGSLEY, Jno. N. POLLOCK [p160]

ALVAREZ FISK of ANDREW HAYS
23 Jan. 1824   Mortgage Deed
I, Andrew Hayes, have sold to Alvarez Fisk, of Natchez, Mississippi,
the following described negro men: Peter, of dark complexion, about
thirty one years old; Jack, dark complexion, about thirty four years of
age; Davy, dark complexion, about sixteen years of age. Hayes has
executed his note to Fisk - if debt is paid, this deed to be void.
1 Aug. 1823   ANDREW HAYS
Wit: Ephraim H. FOSTER, David HORNEL [pp160/161]

WILLIAM H. MACON of WILLIAM TEMPLE
9 Feb. 1824
I, William Temple, of the County of New Kent, VA, have in my
possession the twelve following negroes: Squire, a man about twenty
years old; Absalom, about eighteen; Huke, about thirty five; Sally, a
woman about twenty; Dilsey, about thirteen; Patty, about twentyfive
and her two children, Eliza & Isaac; Anna, about nine; Easter, six;
Julius, four; Richard, four. All of which are the property of William H.
MACON, of the County of New Kent, and are only lent to me and are
to be delivered to William H. Macon, or his heirs, with all their
increase, when demanded. 24 Oct. 1816   WILL TEMPLE
Wit: Wm MACON, Selden C. MACON
- proven in court for New Kent - 10 Apr. 1817 - B. DANDRIDGE,
CC
- produced in court by William H. Macon & ordered to be certified to
the proper court in the town of Nashville, TN. 12 Dec. 1823
                                                    [pp162/163]

EPHRAIM H. FOSTER of ASHLEY STANFIELD
12 Feb. 1824   Bill of Sale
I, Ashley Stanfield, of Galletin, TN, have sold to Ephraim H. Foster a
negro of dark complexion, about twenty one years of age, named
Aaron. 26 Apr. 1823 ASHLEY STANFIELD
Test: William COOPER, Andrew HUNT   [p163]

41

THOMAS BUCHANON of ANTHONY FOSTER
12 Feb. 1824   Bill of Sale
I, Anthony Foster, have sold to Thomas Buchanon a negro girl by the name of Lucy, dark complexion, about thirty years of age and her youngest child, now at her breast, name not remembered.
Jan. 17, 1824   A. FOSTER
Wit: Ephraim H. FOSTER, E. H. EAST   [p164]

CARY FELTS, trustee of ARTHUR BLAND
17 Feb. 1824   Deed of Trust
 This Indenture of five parts now surviving together with all the future lawfully begotten heirs of Arthur Bland & Polly O. Bland. Arthur Bland, for the natural love & affection he bears toward Polly O. Bland, his lawful wife, Elizabeth J G W Bland Len--d Mary Ann W Bland {*no punctuation and all shaded letters*} and conveys to Cary Felts, Trustee, a certain negro woman, Molly, aged nineteen years, also one negro girl by the name of Hariot, aged two years, together with their increase. 25 Nov. 1823
                A. BLAND   CARY FELTS   MARY O. BLAND
Wit: Joseph BURNETT, Sr., Battersby BALLOW, Sr., Joseph BURNETT, Jr.   [pp165/166]

JOHN ALFORD of WILLIAM HOLLINGSWORTH
17 Feb. 1824   Deed of Trust
I have conveyed to John Alford the following property: a girl slave named Cela, aged 17; Nance, aged 12 years.
John Alford is security for William Hollingworth on debt to John WATSON, State Bank of Tennessee, Thomas SAMPLE, Mrs. WILLIAMS. 5 Jan. 1824   WM (X) HOLLINGSWORTH
Wit: J. P. ERWIN, E. H. FOSTER   [pp166/167]

JOHN HAYWOOD of THOMAS HAYWOOD
17 Feb. 1824   Bill of Sale
Whereas I, Thomas Haywood, have boarded and studied law with my father, John Haywood from 15 Feb. last to this day 30 Sept. 1823, being seven months; have also boarded my wife and two children... John Haywood has engaged to pay in whiskey to the firm of DUNCAN & KEYS, in the town of Mooresville, Ala. ... I hereby sell to said John one negro man slave named Elijah and one small sorrel horse. 30 Sept 1823   THOMAS HAYWOOD
Test: Gideon JOHNSON, W. C. TURBEVILLE   [pp168/169]

42

JOHN McCASLAND of JAMES DAVIS
17 Feb. 1824   Bill of Sale
I, James Davis, of Warren County, KY, sell to John McCaslin a negro
girl slave, named Mary, about four years old.
13 Dec. 1823   JAMES DAVIS
Test: Samp. L. WHARTON, Edwin W. BEDFORD [p169]

JOHN HAYWOOD of THOMAS HAYWOOD
17 Feb. 1824   Bill of Sale
I, Thomas Haywood, have sold to John Haywood, Sr., a negro girl
named Nancy, twelve years old. I am indebted to Elisha BORDEN, of
Huntsville, Ala., deputy sheriff of the county of Maddison, for an
execution against me and John Haywood has agreed to advance to me
300 gallons of whiskey, 150 gallons of brandy.
 2 Feb. 1823   THOMAS HAYWOOD
Test: E. HAYWOOD, Benj. TURBEVILLE   [p170]

RICHARD H. BARRY of PHILIP SHUTE, trustee
17 Feb. 1824   Bill of Sale
On 25 Nov. 1819 there was a Deed of Gift made by Frederick STUMP
to Thos. J. Stump, Philip S. Stump and Tennessee M. Stump and to
Christopher Stump, now dec'd, and his wife, Rachel Stump, in trust to
me, for their use & benefit. ... among which property is a negro girl by
the name of Eliza, a negro boy, Amos, and a boy, Washington - all of
which I do now sell to Richard H. Barry for the purpose of paying
claims for which the property is liable.
6 Sept. 1823   PHILIP SHUTE   [p171]

LEMUEL TINNIN of WILLIAM HACKNEY
17 Feb. 1824   Bill of Sale
I, William Hackney, have sold to Lemuel Tinnin all interest I have in
and to one fourth part of the negroes & their increase my father,
Daniel HACKNEY, died possessed of, willed to my mother, Jemmina
Hackney, during her lifetime. The names of the said negroes as
follows: Jack, Moses, James, Lewis, Lans, Nancy, Abbady, Milly,
Hiday?, Ritty, Mersy, David, Malvina, Moses, Reinal?, Ned, Jack,
Evalina. 20 Dec. 1823   WM HACKNEY
Test: Isaac WALTON, E. P. CONNETT   [p172]

JESSE EVERETT of FREDERICK STUMP Exrs.
21 Feb. 1824   Bill of Sale

43

We, the undersigned executors of Frederick Stump, dec'd, have sold to Jesse Everett a negro boy, named Dick.
28 Aug. 1823   PHILIP SHUTE   JNO. CRIDDLE
Test: John JOHNS, Isaac EARTHMAN, Jr. [p173]

MONROE CANNON of JNO COCKRILL
4 March 1824   Bill of Sale
I, John Cockrill, have sold to Monroe Cannon a negro girl, named Mariah, of yellow complexion, about twelve years of age. 23 Feb. 1824   JOHN COCKRILL
Wit: Ephraim H. FOSTER, W. S. COMPTON, John RINKLE
                                                       [pp173/174]
HENRY HART of JOHN OVERTON
25 March 1824   Agreement
Henry Hart, a young man of colour, son of Samuel & Charlotte HART, who lives on a 4 acre lot of mine, near Mr. Bass's tanyard adjoining Nashville, contemplates to marry a coloured slave of mine, named Rachel, and being willing that said marriage take place, I promise to Henry to make provision in my last Will, that said girl, Rachel, with any children she may have by Henry, be emancipated and set free. 1 Oct. 1823   Jno. OVERTON
Wit: E. S. HALL, J. OVERTON   [pp174/175]

DAVID BARROW of ANDREW HAYS
13 May 1824   Deed of Trust
I have this day sold to David Barrow a negro girl, named Maria, aged seventeen years - In Trust - I am indebted to Henry CRABB and if debt is paid this deed to be void - Andrew Hays to keep possession.
3 May 1824   ANDREW HAYS   [pp175/176]
Test: Aaron READY, Jas. COLLINSWORTH

MATTHEW H. QUINN Of JAS. GRIZZARD
17 May 1824   Bill of Sale
Whereas on 2 Feb. 1822 several judgments were rendered by George WILSON, against Nicholas B. PRYOR, in favor of *Quinn, Elliston & Co.*, with Thomas PATTERSON, security. Debts remained unpaid and executions were levied on a negro boy, named Gilbert, property of Nicholas B. Pryor, and he was exposed for sale - Matthew H. Quinn being highest bidder. 22 Feb. 1824   JAS. GRIZZARD, Constable
Test: A. W. JOHNSON, Meritt S. PHILCHER   [pp176/177]

JAMES GOULD of HENRY P. LOYD
17 May 1824   Bill of Sale

I sell to James Gould all the household goods, implements & furniture in the schedule annexed: 1 Sideboard, 1 Bureau, 2 tables, 1 candlestand, 1 press, 1 cupboard, 1 sugarchest, 12 Windsor chairs, 2 bedsteads, 2 beds, 1 suit bedcurtains, 12 pr sheets, 10 pr pillowcases, 3 pr Blankets, 2 bed quilts, 1 Baize carpet, 6 Tableclothes, 1 doz. towels, 1 set Queensware, dining plates, dishes, etc., 1 Tea set, 1 coffeeset, 1 doz. knives & forks, 1/2 doz small knives & forks, 6 silver Tablespoons, 9 teaspoons, 1 set castors, plated, 3 decanters, 1/2 doz Tumblers, 1/2 Doz wine glasses, 2 waiters, 2 small waiters, 1 pr brass andirons, 1 pr common andirons, 2 pr brass candlesticks, 1 gold watch and all my kitchen furniture. 30 March 1824   HENRY P. LOYD
Wit: E. TALBOT, Williard MANCHESTER [pp178/179]

JAMES GOULD of WILLIARD MANCHESTER
17 May 1824   Bill of Sale
I, Williard Manchester, sell to James Gould all my accounts now standing on my account book marked "Watch Book" and to collect in my name; all items listed in attached schedule: 8 chairs, 1 rag carpet, 1 large bed, bedstead & furniture, 1 Bureau, 2 Tables, 2 silver tumblers, 2 Tea trays, 1 poplar bedstead, 1 coffee pot, 2 tea pots, 1 castor, cups & saucers & other table furniture, 9 pieces cut & ornamented glassware, 1 set desert silver spoons, 1 set silver teaspoons, 1 small looking glass, 1 pr shovel & tongs, 1 trunk, 1 pr firedogs, 1 wooden clock, 1 meal chest, 1 coarse waggon & all my kitchen furniture. 2 doz knives & forks, 1 small desk & contents.
23 March 1824   WILLARD MANCHESTER
Test: E. TALBOT, Ben. R. HOWLAND   [pp179/181]

MARY A. & MARTHA S. WHIRLEY of E. MILLER
18 May 1824   Bill of Sale
I, Elizabeth Miller, in consideration of the natural love & affection I bear unto my beloved children; Mary Ann Whirley & Martha Savilla Whirley, and also because of me moving, do give the following goods & chattels now in my dwelling house in Nashville: one Jackson press, 1 Bureau, 2 breakfast tables, 1 small worktable, 1 candlestand, 1 crib & bed & furniture, 1/2 doz Windsor chairs, 1 armed chair, 2 small chairs, 3 bed steads, 2 beds with furniture, 2 looking glasses, 10 pictures & frames, 1 set castors, 2 decanters, 1 case bottle, 3 pitchers, 9 bowls, 4 teapots, 3 sugar bowls, 3 cream jugs, 1 doz glass tumblers, 6 wine glasses, 4 doz earthen plates, 1/2 doz dishes, 1 set knives & forks, 1 set tablespoons, 8 silver teaspoons, 5 waiters, 1 Bread tray, 3 tea cannisters, 2 sugar boxes, 2 trunks, 1 copper teakettle, 1 copper stew kettle, 1 large iron pot, 1 dinner pot, 1 large oven, 1 skillet, 1

frying pan, 2 washing tubss, 1 water pail, 1 teakettle, 1 doz earthen jars, 1 pr shovel & tongs, 1 pr cast andirons.
April 1824   ELIZABETH (X) MILLER
Test: Eli TALBOT   [pp181/182]

PHILIP HURT of EDMUND LANIER
18 May 1824   Deed of Mortgage
I deliver to Philip Hurt 8 feather beds & their furniture, 8 bedsteads, 1 bureau, 1 bookcase, 1 sideboard, 24 windsor chairs, 1 sugar chest, 4 large tables with table furniture including plates, dishes, cups & saucer, etc., 3 walnut tables - Edmund Lanier is indebted to Philip Hurt - notes from 1819 - if Edmund pay the money and interest, this to be void.
2 Sept. 1823   EDMUND LANIER
Test: R. A. HIGGINBOTHAM, S. C. McDANIEL [pp182/183]

THOMAS COLLINS of A. M. DEGRAFFENRIED
18 May 1824   Bill of Sale
I, Abraham Maury Degraffenried, sell to Thomas Collins, a negro girl named Maria, sometimes called Murrier.
22 Dec. 1823   A. M. DeGRAFFENRIED
Test: John BELL, Benj. LITTON   [p184]

EPHRAIM H. FOSTER of WILLIAM B. DRAKE
18 May 1824   Bill of Sale
I, William B. Drake, of Wilson County, TN, have sold to Ephraim H. Foster, for the use of *Adams, Knox & Nixon*, of Philadelphia, a negro boy of light colour, about 18 years of age, named Jim. I warrant his title to said negro except against any one claiming said boy by virtue of a sale of said boy by sheriff sale on 19 Dec. 1820 on an execution of *Adams, Knox & Nixon* vs *Echols & Drake*.
28 Apr. 1824   WM. B. DRAKE   [pp184/185]

JOHN SHUTE of J. M. STUDEVANT
18 May 1824   Bill of Sale
I have sold to John Shute a negro boy named Joe.27 March 1824
JOSIAH M. STURDIVANT
Test: S. B. MARSHALL   [p185]

JOHN EARHART of JEREMIAH SADLER
18 May 1824   Bill of Sale
I have sold to John Earheart a negro boy by the name of David, now in the possession of my mother, Mary Sadler, who during her lifetime is

the proper owner of said slave and at her death the right of said slave is vested in me. 2 March 1824   JEREMIAH SADLER
Test: Hardeman HARMON   [pp185/186]

SARAH ROBERTSON OF S. C. & E. B. ROBERTSON
19 May 1824   Bill of Sale
We, Sterling C. Robertson and Eldridge B. Robertson sell to Sarah Robertson the following negroes: Washington, called Little Washington, aged about six years; Mingo, about forty years; Jim, about forty years; Peter, about forty five years; Harry, about forty five years; Washington, about thirteen years; Stephen, about eight years; Hager, about twenty years; Nancy, about twenty years. We warrant them to be sound & sensible, Harry & Peter excepted as to soundness. 15 Jan. 1824
ELDRIDGE B. ROBERTSON   STERLING C. ROBERTSON
Test: Nathan EWING, E. S. HALL   [pp186/187]

PATRICK W. CAMPBELL of JESSE WHARTON
23 May 1824   Bill of Sale
I, Jesse Wharton have this day sold to Patrick W. Campbell a certain negro man named Armistead, supposed to be about 42 years old...note on Duncan ROBERTSON. 22 Feb. 1823   J. WHARTON
Test: R. STOTHART   [p187]

JANE M. FOSTER of M. BARROW, Commissioner
25 May 1824   Bill of Sale
By virtue of a decree the the Court of Equity for the 4th Judicial Circuit - Jan. Term 1824 - Bank of the State of TN vs Thomas WHITESIDE & others; heirs of Jinken WHITESIDE, dec'd. Matthew Barrow, the commissioner appt. by the decree, exposed for sale the negro slaves - Slave, Mary, was purchased by Jane M. Foster.
20 March 1824   M. BARROW
Test: William S. COMPTON, L. P. CANTRELL[p188]

GORDON & WALKER of WILLIAM TEMPLE
31 May 1824   Deed of Trust
William Temple executed notes to Stephen Cantrell with Boyd McNAIRY & Duncan ROBERTSON as securities - to save McNairy & Robertson from harm, Temple executes this Indenture to Robert T. WALKER & James GORDON. - the following slaves: Patty & her three children, Eliza, Isaac & Caroline; Sally and her four children, Sarah, Amy, Norborn & Amos; Dilsey and her two children, Lilly & Maria; Anny; Esther; Squire; Absalom; Hickey; Richard; Julius. - the

following personal chattels: one waggon & gear, one ore cart, one Gig & Harness, one Dearborn & Harness, 9 horses, 2 yokes or pair of oxen & yokes; 30 head cattle, 50 head sheep, 75 head hogs, 4 featherbeds & furniture, 3 mattresses, 1 set dining tables, 1 round stand, 1 small table, 4 bedsteads, 2 doz chairs, 4 pr brass andirons, 2 pr brass candlesticks, 2 sets shovel & tongs, 1 bureau, 1 looking glass, 1 doz silver tablespoons, 1/2 doz silver teaspoons, 4 doz ivory handled forks & knives, all my crop of corn, 400 barrels; my crop of cotton, about 8000 lbs, my fodder & oats, my farming utensils and kitchen furniture.
WILL TEMPLE
Wit: Ephraim H. FOSTER, Benjamin W. BEDFORD [pp189/191]

BAYLOR & WALKER of FRANCES WALKER
31 May 1824   Deed of Trust
Frances Walker of Logan County, KY, being of full & proper age and for divers good reasons, thereunto moving, and the more particular cause, being about to change her single for the married state, has chosen her friends, Robert T. BAYLOR, of Todd County, KY, and James Volney WALKER, of Logan County, KY, to be her trustees for the following purposes: convey a negro man, named Lincoln, and Vinice, his wife, together with their children, Peggy & Joe, for the use of her, Frances Walker; also conveys all title she may have by virtue of inheritance as the daughter and heir of David WALKER, dec'd, for her only use & benefit. 28 Oct. 1820
FANNY WALKER ROBT. T. BAYLOR, JAMES V. WALKER
Test: Jacob W. WALKER, George W. TEMPLE
          Logan County - I, Spencer CURD, clerk of the county court of Logan, certify the within Deed of Trust ... proven by oath of Jacob W. Walker & George W. Temple. 1 Dec. 1820   [p192]

DANIEL BUIE of HARRIS DOOLIN
31 March 1824   Bill of Sale
I, Harris Doolin, of Robertson County, TN sell to Daniel Buie a negro boy, Fil, ten years old.
26 Jan. 1824   HARRIS DOOLIN
Test: Hardy S. BRYAN, J. McBRIDE, Thomas FARMER [p193]

ISAAC SITLER of JOHN M. HILL
31 May 1824   Deed of Trust
Duncan ROBERTSON, Andrew MORRISON & Daniel BRIM have become securities for John M. Hill on notes in favour of Richard DREWRY - Mary BUCKNER - Matthew H. QUINN - SHUTE & CRIDDLE and to protect them from harm, convey the following to

Sitler: two yoke oxen, 2 ox carts, 1 keel boat, oars & poles, one feather bed, bolster, pills, Bedspread, sheets & bedstead, 6 brown windsosr chairs, 2 writing desks, 3 split bottom chairs, 3 tables, 1 cupboard, 2 trunks, 1 small Japanned trunk, 1 Tea box, 1 spice box, 1 small looking glass, 2 pitchers, 3 bowls, 3 stoneware pickling crocks, 1 coffee mill, 2 dishes, 6 plates, 1 set coffee cups, 4 tumblers, 1 Salt sellar, 3 teaspoons, 4 large spoons, 1 pepper box, 2 large iron pots, 2 skillets, 1 oven & lid, 1 Inkstand & sand box, 3 tin pans, 2 pails, 6 axes, 1 broad axe, 2 augers, 1 Iron square, 20 claret bottles, 30 stone jugs, 1 tin Quart measure, 1 pint measure, 2 funnels, one hand saw, 4 iron wedges, 1 Logchain, 1 shuffle board& weights, 9 pin alley & balls, 1 candlestand & snufflers, 1 garden hoe; the frame building I now occupy, the time I have to 2 acres of ground and the Landings for this year, leased to Hill by Alfred BALCH; 1 large gallon bottle, 2 boxes segars, 2 barrels whiskey, 1 Slate, a parcel of beef & bacon, 1 brown mare, saddle, bridle & blanket; the time & hire of five negro men and one woman for this year (John, Emanuel, Bill, Toney, Gilbert & Amey); demands I have against Stephen CANTRELL. If debt is paid, this to be void. 20 February 1824

JNO. M. HILL   ISAAC SITLER

Test: Henry P. LLOYD, H. ELLIOT [pp193/194]

THOMAS W. TALBOT & others of ROBERT WOODS

12 June 1824   Bargain & Sale
Robert Woods, in consideration of the regard he has for the children of Eli TALBOT and five dollars in hand paid, hath given unto Thomas Waters Talbot, James Lawrence Talbot, William Charles Talbot, Mary Ridgley Talbot and George Washington Talbot and their heirs forever the following property: one oval table with folding leaves, one large dining table, one dozen chairs, one looking glass, one doz knives & forks, one doz. large china coffee cups & saucers, one doz. teacups & saucers, 1 doz. plates, 4 dishes, 4 cut glass goblets, 1 doz. wine glasses, (cut), 3 cut glass tumblers, 1 large tumbler, cut, 2 glass dishes, 2 cut glass decanters, 1 large glass bowl, one doz. silver tablespoons, 1 doz. silver teaspoons, 1 silver soup ladle, 1 cream spoon, 1 pr. sugar tongs, 1 large carpet, one stair carpet with rods, 2 small carpets, a lot of books containing Shakespears plays in 6 vols., Rob Roy in 2 vols., The Book of Common Prayer, Musical Grammar, Vicar of Wakefield, Walkers Dictionary and sundry school books, one family Bible, one large bedstead, mattress & bolsters, one bureau, one cradle & bed, one fire fender, one tin roaster, one candle stand, one wash stand, one dressing table, one trucke bedstead & bed, 1/2 doz. chamber pots, 3 trunks, 1 kitchen table, one cooking stove, 2 tubs, 1 pail, 1 tray, 1

brass kettle, 1 pr. waffle irons, 2 ovens, 1 skillet, 1 gridiron, 1 pr. castors, 2 Japanned boxes, 1 pr. salts, 3 brushes, 1 clarionet, 1 violin & case, 1 large teaboard, 4 waiters. ... if either of the above die, their share to pass to the survivors as tenants in common.
ROBERT WOODS
P.S. ...Eli TALBOT, and Delia, his wife, shall hold and enjoy the use of the goods conveyed above for their natural lives.
Wit: Alexander RICHARDSON   [pp195/196]

WILLOUGHBY WILLIAMS of JOHN HAMILTON
19 June 1824   Mortgage
I, John Hamilton, convey to Willoughby Williams the following property: Charles, a negro man slave aged about 30; Prudence, aged about 40; Henry, aged about ten; Suckey, aged about ten.   John Hamilton owes to Willoughby Williams & Solomon CLARK. If debt is paid, this mortgage to be void.
24 Feb. 1824   JOHN HAMILTON
Wit: Wm HAMILTON, Joseph B. GRIZAN, L. NALL [pp197/198]

NATHANIEL A. McNAIRY of M. BARROW
19 June 1824   Bill of Sale
By virtue of a decree of the court of equity for the 4th Judicial District - Jan. Term 1824 - Bank of the State of TN vs Thomas WHITESIDE & others, heirs of Jinkin WHITESIDE, dec'd. I, Matthew Barrow, commissioner, exposed for sale the negro slaves specified in said decree: Charlotte and her two children Minty & Ned; also Sally & John, Daniels children, were purchased by Nathaniel A. McNairy.
20 March 1824 M. BARROW   [pp198/199]

NATHANIEL A. McNAIRY of F. STUMP'S Exrs.
21 June 1824   Bill of Sale
We, John CRIDDLE, Philip SHUTE & Thomas SHUTE, executors of the Will of Frederick STUMP, dec'd, have sold to McNairy the following negro slaves, belonging to the estate: Zilphy, a negro woman about 26 years of age, dark complexion and her children, Ishmael, about 7, Emily, about 1 year old, & Shade, about 5 years old, all of dark colour. 9 Sept. 1824 PHILIP SHUTE   JNO CRIDDLE
Test: Solomon CLARK, E. H. FOSTER   [p199]

BETSEY JACKSON of JOHN STAMPS
21 June 1824   Bill of Sale
I, John Stamps, have given to my daughter, Betsey Jackson, a negro girl named Winney. 10 Nov. 1815   JOHN STAMPS

Test: Josiah MULLIN, John T. HAYES [p200]

ENOCH PRITCHARD of SALLY PRITCHARD
21 June 1824   Bill of Sale
I, Sarah Pritchard, have sold to Enoch Pritchard a negro boy about
four years old, named Jack.21 Sept. 1823   SALLY PRITCHARD
Test: Elias DODSON, John HARBISON   [p200]

JOHN HARMON of EDWARD D. HOBBS
22 June 1824   Mortgage
I sell to John Harmon one negro woman, named Susan, about thirty
six years old, also her daughter, Mary, aged six. If debt is paid, this
deed to be void. 1 Oct. 1823   E. D. HOBBS
Test: M. H. QUINN   [pp201/202]

JOHN COCKRILL of FRANCIS M. DEAN
6 July 1824   Bill of Sale
Francis Dean, of the town of Franklin, TN, has sold to John Cockrill a
negro woman, named Armon and her two children, Koziah and Mary.
15 Dec. 1813   F. M. DEAN
Test: James H. MAURY, James C. SHULTZ, William HEWLETT
        [pp202/203]

JOHN OLDHAM of JAMES STEWART
9 July 1824   Bill of Sale
I have this day sold & delivered to John Oldham, of New Orleans, for
the use and benefit of the late firm of *William Kenner & Co.*, a negro
woman, named Fanny, about thirty three years old - said Fanny has
been unwell but is now recovering and should soon be well.
1 June 1824   JAMES STEWART
Wit: William B. WILSON, David CROCKETT   [p203]

LUCIUS J. POLK of MATTHEW BARROW
13 July 1824   Bill of Sale
By virtue of a decree from the Court of Equity for the 4th Judical
Circuit in Bank of Tennessee vs Thomas WHITESIDE & others, heirs
of Jinken WHITESIDE, dec'd, Matthew Barrow, Commissioner,
having exposed for sale the negro slaves in said decree - the negro
slave, Armstead, was purchased by Lucius J. Polk.
30 March 1824   M. BARROW   [p205]

NATHANIEL A. McNAIRY of C. STUMP
16 July 1824   Bill of Sale
I have this day sold to Nathaniel A. McNairy a negro girl about seven
years old, named Aggy.
14 July 1824 CATHERINE STUMP   [p206]

WILLIAM B. DRAKE of EPHRAIM H. FOSTER
26 July 1824   Bill of Sale
By virtue of a decree from the County Court of Wilson County, 27
Nov. 1820, suit of ADAMS, KNOX & NIXON vs ECHOLS &
DRAKE the sheriff sold to me a negro woman, called Mack, about 36
years of age; children - Furgerson, Henry, Lucy & Patsy - for all of
which negroes suit was brought against me and is now pending by
Wm. B. DRAKE in the Circuit Court of Williamson County - Lucy,
since purchase departed life and Mack has had two other children,
Alexander & Eveline. Drake & I have compromised and I transfer to
Drake all my title & interest to the foregoing negroes; Mack and her
children, Henry, Ferguson, Patsey, Eveline & Alexander. 28 Apr. 1824
EPHRAIM H. FOSTER   [pp206/207]

THOMAS KIRKMAN to DUNCAN ROBERTSON
12 August 1824   Bill of Sale
Duncan Robertson has this day sold to Thomas Kirkman a negro
woman, named Nancy, about twenty nine years old.
21 July 1824   DUNCAN ROBERTSON
Wit: Alexr. BLACK   [p207]

JOHN CUNNINGHAM of JOEL WALLER
12 August 1824   Deed of Mortgage
I have sold to John Cunningham two negroes, Seth & Mary. If debt is
paid this deed to be void. 26 June 1824   JOEL WALLER
Test: Samuel BELL, Joseph WALLER   [p208]

SUSANNAH PERKINS of JOEL WALLER
12 August 1824   Mortgage
I have this day sold to Susannah Perkins two negroes, Sarah, aged five
years, and Phillis, three years old. If debt is paid, this deed to be void.
9 June 1824   JOEL WALLER
Test: Th. EDMISTON, Samuel BELL   [pp208/209]

LETITIA COOTS of JOEL WALLER
12 August 1824   Mortgage

I have sold to Letitia Coots one negro boy, named Anthony, aged thirteen years. If debt is paid, this deed to be void.
3 July 1824   JOEL WALLER
Wit: John CUNNINGHAM, Samuel BELL   [pp209/210]

WILLIAM EDMISTON of LUCINDA EARHART
12 August 1824   Bill of Sale
I, Lucinda Earhart, have sold to William Edmiston a negro boy slave, named James, about thirteen years old.
12 June 1824   LUCINDA EARHART
Test: Jno. H. SMITH, Jos. McCUTCHEN   [p210]

MARK R. COCKRILL of JONAS MENEFEE's Adm.
12 August 1824   Bill of Sale
I, Jonas Menefee, administrator of Jonas Menefee, dec'd, have sold to Mark R. Cockrill two negro boys, Joseph, about fourteen years and Jeffrey, about nine or ten. Said slaves belonged to the heirs of Jonas Menefee, dec'd.31 May 1824   JONAS MENEFEE, adm.
Wit: Benjamin W. BEDFORD, L. P. CHEATHAM, W. H. BEDFORD   [p211]

ZACHEUS GERMAN of ENSLEY & ARNOLD
12 August 1824   Bill of Sale
We, Joseph Ensley, Jr. and Milley ARNOLD sell to Zacheus German, of Williamson County, TN, a negro woman, named Deb, supposed to be eighteen years of age. 2 Jan. 1824
    JOSEPH ANSLEY   MILLY (X) ARNOLD
Test: James COOPER,David CARTWRIGHT   [pp211/212]

JOHN F. ANEAL of THOMAS WILSON
12 August 1824   Bill of Sale
I, Thomas Wilson, have sold to John F. Aneal three negroes; one girl named Hester, 10 years old; one mulatto boy named Harvey, two years old; one mulatto boy, Emanuel, nine months old.
25 Jan. 1824   THOS. WILSON
Test: Geo. W. HELAND   [p212]

HENRY CRITCHLOW of BENJAMIN BIBB
12 August 1824   Bill of Sale
I have sold to Henry Critchlow a negro man, Jacob, about twenty six years of age. 8 Nov. 1822   BENJAMIN BIBB
Test: John BLACKMAN, Robert C. OWIN   [p213]

JOHN SHELBY of SAMUEL DAVENPORT
12 August 1824   Bill of Sale
I, Samuel Davenport, of Mercer County, KY, have this day sold to
John Shelby a negro man, John, about twenty five years of age.
14 June 1824   SAMUEL DAVENPORT
Test: L. BELL, L. G. CRIDDLE   [pp213/214]

WILLIAM OGILVIE of ELIZABETH OGILVIE
12 August 1824   Bill of Sale
I, Elizabeth Ogilvie, for one dollar and love & affection I have for my
son, William Ogilvie, convey to him the following negroes: a man,
George, about 27 years old; a woman, Franky, 32 years old, and her
child.13 July 1824   ELIZABETH (X) OGILVIE
Test: Alexander BUCHANON, David CUMMINS   [p214]

JONATHAN DRAKE of JOHN DRAKE
12 August 1824   Bill of Sale
I, John Drake, in consideration of the natural love & affection I have
for my son, Jonathan Drake, give him a negro man, George, about 28
years of age, in full satisfaction for any claim he would otherwise have
to any part of my personal estate in the event of my death without first
making a will together with what he has already had.
29 July 1824   JOHN (X) DRAKE
Test: Th. CLAIBORNE   [p215]

SAMUEL EDNEY of WILLIAM & JAS. DILLAHUNTY
12 August 1824   Bill of Sale
We, William Dillahunty and James Dillahunty have sold to Samuel
Edney on negro girl named Naomi. 8 Dec. 1818
    WM DILLAHUNTY   JAMES DILLAHUNTY
Test: B. Russell HOWLAND, Edmond EDNEY   [pp215/216]

GEORGE HANDY of GEORGE W. MARTIN
13 August 1824   Deed of Mortgage
George W. Martin has sold to George Handy, of Philadelphia, PA, the
following negroes: a negro man named George; one woman, Jenny &
child; Beck & child; Escelia; Phireby; Nancy; Elijah; Claiborne; Eliza &
Betsy. If debt is paid, this deed to be void. 16 July 1824   GEO. W.
MARTIN   [pp217/218]

McNAIRY & SHELBY of ELIHU MARSHALL
13 August 1824   Bill of Sale

I, Elihu Marshall, have sold to Boyd McNairy & John Shelby the following negroes; Annis, about twenty; Nancy, about the same age; Fanny, about sixteen; Matilda, about twenty two; Judy, about twenty five; Harriet, about nine; Hal, about four.
27 March 1822   ELIHU MARSHALL
Test: William BROOKS, B. F. CURRY   [p218]

JOHN SHELBY of ISAAC SITLER
15 August 1824   Bill of Sale
I, Isaac Sitler, have sold to John Shelby one negro woman between twenty eight and thirty, named Amy. 28 May 1822   ISAAC SITLER
Test: Isaac DAVIS, Henry FOX   [pp218/219]

DANIEL CAMERON of JOHN F. STUMP
15 Nov. 1824   Bill of Sale
John F. Stump has this day sold to Daniel Cameron a negro boy named Isaac, about nine years old. 15 Nov. 1824   JOHN F. STUMP
Test: Duncan ROBERTSON, P. W. BARCLAY   [p214]

WILLIAM B. GLEAVES of JOHN C. HAYS
15 Nov. 1824   Bill of Sale
I have this day sold to William B. Gleaves one sorrel mare. 31 March 1821   CAMPBELL HAYS
Test: Thomas GLEAVES, Hollis (X) RIGHT   [p220]

JOHN SHELBY of JAMES P. CLARK
15 Nov. 1824   Bill of Sale
I have sold to John Shelby a negro man, mulatto colour, aged about twenty five, named Joshua.
27 Oct. 1824   J. P. CLARK   [p220]

ELI CHERRY of JOSHUA HOOKER
15 Nov. 1824   Bill of Sale
I, Joshua Hooker, of Wilson County, TN, sell to Eli Cherry a negro woman, named Suckey, about thirty years old and her two children, Harriett, aged three years old next Jan. 1825 & Marion, about six weeks old. 15 Sept. 1824   JOSHUA   HOOKER
Test: Frederick BINKLEY, Richard DRAKE   [p221]

JOSEPH HERNDON of JAMES B. HOUSTON
15 Nov. 1824   Bill of Sale

I, James B. Houston, sell to Joseph Herndon, of Maury County, TN, the following two negroes; a boy named Harry and a negro woman named Mary. 15 Apr. 1824   J. B. HOUSTON
Test: W. HOUSTON   [pp221/222]

HAYS BLACKMAN of WILLIAM PILLOW
15 Nov. 1824   Bill of Sale
I, William Pillow, of Maury County, TN have sold to Hays Blackman a negro woman slave named Fanny and her six children, Jinny, Green, Ruth, Mary, Addison & Alice. 25 June 1824   WM PILLOW
Test: J. EZELL, Charles HAYS, M. PILLOW   [p222]

MARTIN SMITH of ROGER B. SAPPINGTON
2 Dec. 1824   Deed of Trust
Roger B. Sappington has sold to Martin Smith the following named negroes: Binkley, a man aged 26 years; Abraham, about 30; Isham, about 33; Mingo, 50 years; Penny, 25; Mary, 14; Phillis, 12; Daniel, about 9; Robert, aged 6 years. Roger B. Sappington has borrowed from the State Bank at Nashville with notes to Thomas HICKMAN & Martin SMITH. If notes are paid this deed to be void.
18 Dec. 1823   ROGER B. SAPPINGTON
Test: J. P. ERWIN, And. HYNES   [p223]

JANE BIRDWELL of ISAAC BIRDWELL
6 Dec. 1824   Bill of Sale
I, Isaac Birdwell, sell to Jane Birdwell a negro girl child called Claracey. 28 Feb. 1824 ISAAC BIRDWELL
Test: Andrew BIRDWELL, Samuel BIRDWELL   [p224]

THOMAS CRUTCHER for the benefit of LYTLE, HICKMAN & SMITHS of R. B. SAPPINGTON
8 Dec. 1824   Deed of Trust
Roger B. Sappington has conveyed to Thomas Crutcher the following negroes: Penny & her four children, Mary, Phillis, Daniel & Robert... for the following purpose: whereas William LYTLE, Thomas HICKMAN, Martin SMITH, Jacob C. SMITH & Andrew Ewing are securities of Roger B. Sappington to John SHUTE.
18 July 1823   ROGER B. SAPPINGTON
Test: H. VanPELT, Thomas C. SMITH   [pp224/225]

HENRY CRABB of JOSEPH W. HORTON
11 Dec. 1824   Bill of Sale

I, Joseph W. Horton, have sold to Henry Crabb a negro woman, named Amy, of black color, about twenty seven years of age.
27 Nov. 1824 JOSEPH W. HORTON [p226]

MARY J. H. & SUSANNAH B. MENEFEE of W. N. MENEFEE
14 Dec. 1824   Bill of Sale
I, William N. MENEFEE, do give to Mary J. H. Menefee and Susannah B. Menefee, daughters of James N. MENEFEE, my brother, in consideration of the love and respect I have for him and one dollar to me paid, three beds, bedsteads & furniture, one pair large looking glasses, one pair of candlesticks, one table and secretary, one cupboard and contents and one dozen chairs.28 Oct. 1823   WM N. MENEFEE
Wit: E. W. B. NOWLAND, Wm NICHOL   [pp226/227]

JOHN N. MENEFEE of JOHN NICHOLS
14 Dec. 1824   Bill of Sale
I, John Nichols, for and in consideration of John Nichols Menefee, son of James N. Menefee, in consideration of the respect I have for his father, and for the further consideration of being named after me, give him one bay stud colt, three years old; one black mare, another black mare with a mule colt. 1 Sept. 1823   JOHN NICHOLS
Test: Harris COBBLER, Robert L. DUFF   [p227]

WEAKLEY, CANTRELL & NAPIER of JOHN BOSLEY
4 Jan. 1825   Mortgage
John Bosley has executed his note and Robert STEPHEN & Richard C. NAPIER have become his joint security and to secure against any hazard sell to Stephenson & Napier the following named slaves; Tom, aged about 26 years; Richard, about 24 years; Mary, about 11 years; Philip, about 5 years; Hannah, about 4 years; Rachel, an infant girl.
3 Dec. 1824
JOHN BOSLEY R. WEAKLEY S. CANTRELL R. C. NAPIER
Test: Was. L. HANNUM, Wm HOUSTON [pp227-229]

JOEL PARRISH of ANDREW HAYS
6 Jan. 1825   Deed of Trust
James C. HAYS has borrowed from the Bank of TN, for me, and George W. GIBBS & Thomas CLAIBORNE are securities with him and to secure them from harm sell to Joel Parrish the following slaves; Flora, aged seventeen years; Sylva, aged fifteen; Franky, aged ten; Alfred, aged fourteen; Reuben, aged eleven; Jackson, aged five years. ... said slaves to remain in possession of Andrew Hays.
27 Dec. 1823 ANDREW HAYS [p230]

JOSEPH & ROBERT WOODS of LAKE & GILBERT
16 Feb. 1825   Bill of Sale
We, John A. LAKE, and Thomas GILBERT, have sold to Joseph
Woods & Robert Woods two thirds parts of the steamboat *Emerald*,
now lying in Cumberland River near Nashville. John A. Lake &
Thomas Gilbert are indebted to Joseph & Robert Woods - if debt is
paid this deed to be void. 12 Feb. 1825
    JOHN A. LAKE   THOS. GILBERT   JOS. & ROBERT
WOODS
Test: Tho. J. READ, John PATTIE   [pp230/231]

JAMES OVERTON of WILLIAM BRYANT
18 Feb. 1825   Mortgage
I, William Bryant, have sold to Jas. Overton all the hogs I own, 15
geese, 20 barrels of corn, 2 stacks of fodder, I have on the place I now
live on; one bed & furniture, one barshear plough & gear for one
horse, one large pot, two horses ... I have this day purchased a horse,
barshear plough & gear, and also rented from James Overton, the
plantation on which I now live, containing 20-25 acres. If I pay the
debt - this deed to be void. 24 Dec. 1821   WM BRYANT
Wit: Wm HARRIS   [p232]

JANE READ of JONES READ
19 Feb. 1825   Bill of Sale
In consideration of the love & affection I bear to my granddaughter,
Jane Read, daughter of Thomas J. Read, I convey to Jane Read a
negro girl, named Angelina, about ten years of age.
25 March 1823   JONES READ   [p233]

BASS & SPENCE of JAMES C. HAYS
19 Feb. 1825   Bill of Sale
I, James C. Hays have sold to Bass & Spence a negro boy, named
Bob. 21 Nov. 1824   JAS. C. HAYS   [p233]

ALEXANDER LOVE to IRWIN & PEARL
21 Feb. 1825   Mortgage
I, Alexander Love, convey to Dyer Pearl & James Irwin, a negro girl
slave, named Milley, about fifteen. I am indebted to Irwin & Pearl and
if debt is paid this deed to be void.20 Jan. 1825   A. LOVE
Test: Philip HOOVER, A. M. OSBORN   [p234]

ANN M. HEWLETT of HENRY WADE
21 Feb. 1825   Bill of Sale
I have sold to Ann M. Hewlett and her children a negro girl named
Edey. 11 Jan. 1825   HENRY WADE
J. H. LANEAR   [p235]

EPHRAIM H. FOSTER of AARON STOCKTON
21 Feb. 1825   Bill of Sale
I have sold to Ephraim H. Foster the following negro slaves, lately
purchased by me of Andrew WAGONER, of VA: Dick, Harry, John,
Molly, Betsey, Mary, Margaret, Sinte, Lydia & Mace.
17 Jan. 1825   A. STOCKTON   [pp235/236]

JOSEPH W. HORTON of SOLOMON CLARK
21 Feb. 1825   Deed of Trust
Solomon Clark has conveyed to Joseph W. Horton two negroes; Wat,
about twenty five years old and Edwin, about the same age - Solomon
is indebted to William E. WATKINS, if debt is paid, this deed to be
void. 19 Dec. 1824   SOLOMON CLARK
Test: W. H. BEDFORD, Benjamin W. BEDFORD   [pp236/237]

EPHRAIM H. FOSTER of ANDREW HAYS
21 Feb. 1825   Deed of Trust
Andrew Hays has conveyed to Foster the following negroes: Louisa,
about 15 or 16 years old; Patsey, about 12 or 13; Madison about 8 or
10 years old; James about 5 or 6; Mary about 5 or 6; and an old man
named Henry.   Andrew HAYS, with John B. HAYS & James C.
HAYS his securities, is indebted to Joseph W. HORTON. If debt is
paid, this deed to be void. 5 April 1824   ANDREW HAYS
Test: John SHELBY, John SAUNER [pp237/238]

ROBERT WHYTE of WILLOUGHBY WILLIAMS
21 Feb. 1825   Bill of Sale
I have sold to Robert Whyte one negro man named Claiborne, about
twenty nine years old and one woman, named Charity, wife of
Claiborne, about twenty five years old.20 Dec. 1824 W. Williams
Test: Joseph SHAW, Jos. D. MURRAY   [pp238/239]

JOHN SHELBY of JAMES C. HAYS
21 Feb. 1825   Bill of Sale
I have sold to John Shelby a negro man named Sanco, about thirty
years old. 17 Jan. 1825 JAS. C. HAYS   [p239]

HENRY GRAVES of CHARLES CLARK
21 Feb. 1825   Deed of Mortgage
For bond due Henry Graves, I convey one cow & calf, two
featherbeds & furniture, three sows & pigs, one saddle & bridle, two
hoes, two axes, one set drawing chain, one spinning wheel, two chests,
three trunks, tubs, pail, and all other household furniture, likewise of
crop of all description. 20 Sept. 1824   CHARLES CLARK
Test: Edward FICK, Abel NANNEY [pp239/240]

JOHN LYLE of JNO M. TILFORD
21 Feb. 1825   Acknowledge & Agreement
I hereby acknowledge that John Lytle, of Rutherford County, has
loaned to me and placed in my possession for the use of my family the
following negroes: Elsey, Stephen, Perry, Amy, Jude. I agree to
return said negroes upon demand ... am not to be made accountable
for any that may die in my possession.
18 Dec. 1824   JNO. M. TILFORD
Test: Wm. L. COMPTON, W. M. SMITH   [p240]

JAMES W. WRIGHT of JAMES WRIGHT
21 Feb. 1825   Deed of Gift
I, James Wright, have this day given unto my son, James W. Wright, a
negro boy named Peter, a negro girl named Winney and a negro girl
named Mary, and sundry articles, it being part of his legacy.
23 Oct.1824   JAMES (X) WRIGHT
Test: Adam HOPE   [p241]

CHARLES & DAVID BALLENTINE of L. BALLENTINE
22 Feb. 1825   Bill of Sale
I, Lemuel Ballentine, in consideration of the natural love & affection I
bear to my two sons, Charles Ballentine and David Ballentine, and in
consideration that David Ballentine has undertaken as my attorney in
fact, and to transact all my worldly business, give to my son Charles,
of Davidson County, TN, and to my son, David, of Christian County,
KY, the following negro slaves; one woman named Dicey, one boy
named Billy; one boy named Sam; one girl named Violet; one boy
named Alen; one boy named Hampton; two negro girls, Melinda &
Emeline; two head of horses, 9 head of cattle. I shall continue to have
use and possession during my natural life and if my wife, Aleah
Ballentine, the said property shall remain in her possession for her
natural life. 15 Nov. 1824   LEMUEL BALLENTINE
Test: David CRAIGHEAD   [pp241/242]

MARK YOUNG of JOHN KENNEDY
22 Feb. 1825   Bill of Sale
I, John Kennedy, have sold to Mark Young one negro woman, named
Nancy, about forty years old. 13 Nov. 1824   JOHN KENNEDY
Test: John F. STUMP   [p242]

SAMUEL SHANNON of JOHN SHUTE
22 Feb. 1825   Bill of Sale
I have sold to Samuel Shannon a negro woman slave by the name of
Mariah, about twenty six years old. 16 Aug. 1823   JOHN SHUTE
Test: W. McALONES, Wm. ALLEN[p243]

JAMES W. HOGGATT of ANTHONY CLOPTON
22 Feb. 1825   Bill of Sale
I have sold to James W. Hoggatt a negro man named Wyatt, about
nineteen years old. 4 Jan. 1825   A. CLOPTON
Test: James M. WALKER   [p243]

JAMES W. HOGGATT of ANTHONY CLOPTON
22 Feb. 1825   Bill of Sale
I have sold to James W. Hoggatt a negro girl by the name of Malinda,
about six years old. 4 Jan. 1825   A. CLOPTON
Test: James M. WALKER   [p244]

GEORGE STULL of NANCY STULL
22 Feb. 1825   Bill of Sale
I have sold to George Stull one negro woman named Easter, about
fifty years old. 30 Dec. 1824 NANCY (X) STULL
Test: John McGAVOCK, Ambrose UBANKS   [p244]

THOMAS SMITH of MARTIN SMITH
2 March 1825   Bill of Sale
I have this day transfered and released unto Thomas Smith, of Bedford
County, all that part of the personal estate and negroes which
belonged to my father at his death and which I may be intitled to
according to provision made in the will of the said Thomas, deceased,
as to the distribution of his estate. 25 Dec. 1824   MARTIN SMITH
Test: Jno. F. SMITH, Martin ADAMS   [p245]
- proven in Williamson County, TN County Court - Jan. 1823

THOS SMITH & others of MARTIN SMITH
2 March 1825   Deed of Mortgage

61

I, Martin Smith, have this day sold to Stephen WEST & Elizabeth, his wife, and Jacob CRITZ, all of Williamson County and Thomas Smith, of Bedford County, the following negroes: Peter, a man about thirty; Uria, a negro girl about ten. I am indebted to Stephen & Elizabeth West, Jacob Critz & Thomas Smith - Martin Smith is to retain possession. 4 Dec. 1824   MARTIN SMITH
Test: J. FARRINGTON, Mark W. SMITH   [pp245/246]
- proven in Williamson County Court - January Sessions 1825

WILLIAM HOMES of JOHN EARTHMAN
9 March 1825   Bill of Sale
I have sold to William Homes a negro man slave, named Jack. 11 Aug. 1824   JOHN EARTHMAN
Test: L. EARTHMAN, John GULLIDGE   [pp246/247]

HARRY L. DOUGLASS and JOHN CRIDDLE
11 Apr. 1825   Bill of Sale
Received payment in full for negro man, Jack, sold as the property of Henry DOUGLASS, on an execution from the county court of Davidson County on 10 Dec. 1821.   T. BRADLEY, shff
Rec'd of Col. John Criddle, redemption money for the slave named Jack. 6 Nov. 1825   H. L. DOUGLASS
- Circuit Court of Wilson County - Oct. Term 1824 - personally appeared Thomas Bradley, sheriff of Wilson County.
27 Oct. 1824 John S. TOPP, clerk of Wilson Circuit Ct.   [p247]

WILLIAM P. FRENCH of JOHN STILLWELL
11 May 1825   Bill of Sale
I, John Stillwell, of the County of Spencer, KY, sell to William P. French and John KELLER the undivided half of the Steamboat *Riego*, now in the Cumberland River together with 1/2 of her furniture, riging, boats and apparel, said Boat was enroled in the City of New Orleans on 2nd Nov. 1824 No 52 by John KELLER of Shippingport, KY, James B. DANSFORTH, of Louisville, KY, John AUSTIN, of Charleston, Ind., S. S. LEWIS, of Boston, and Edmund H. LEWIS, of Louisville, KY, as owners at the time of enrolment. 10 May 1825
JOHN STILLWELL, by his Atty in fact   DAVID MERIWETHER [pp248/249]

JOHN STILLWELL & DAVID MERIWETHER of WM P. FRENCH
11 May 1825   Deed of Trust
I, William P. French, formerly of Boston, but now at Nashville, TN, have purchased of John Stillwell, of Spencer County, KY, one

undivided half of the steamboat *Riego*, with John KELLER as my
security - I convey all my right to David Meriwether, of Louisville, in
trust to secure this note. 10 May 1823 WM P. FRENCH [pp249/250]

GEORGE & BENJAMIN PIERCE of TYREE RODES
17 May 1825   Bill of Sale
I, Tyre Rodes, of Giles County, TN, have sold to George & Benjamin
Pierce a negro man by the name of Jim, twenty four years of age.
17 May 1824   TYREE RODES
Test: R. WEAKLEY   [p251]

JOHN SHELBY of JOHN SHUTE
18 May 1825   Bill of Sale
I have sold to John Shelby a negro man named Daniel, about thirty
four years old. 27 March 1825   JOHN SHUTE   [p251]

JAMES H. HOOPER and ELIZABETH HOOPER
18 May 1825   Deed of Gift
I, Elizabeth Hooper, in consideration of the natural love and affection I
have for my son, James H. Hooper, have conveyed the following
negro slaves to him: Bes, Nat, Hetta, Drewry, Peter, Jacob, Jim, Robin
& Pat, together with their future increase; all my household & kitchen
furniture, plantation utensils, and all my cattle, sheep, hogs & poultry,
together with my stock of horses.
9 March 1825   ELIZABETH (X) HOOPER
Test: Joab HARDEN, Edmund CHARLTON, Amariah B. EVERETT,
David PARKER
   I agree that Elizabeth Hooper, my mother, shall enjoy the above
mentioned property during her natural life. J. H. HOOPER
Test: [same listed above]   [p252]

WILLIAM O. DONNELLY of JOHN ROOK
18 May 1825   Deed of Gift
for the love and affection I have for William O. Donnelly, a relation of
mine, do give one sorrel mare, one bay mare, one featherbed &
furniture. 17 March 1825 JOHN ROOK
Test: James (X) A Donnelly   [p253]

WILLIAM FINNEY of J. H. HOWLETT, constable
18 May 1825   Bill of Sale
I have sold, by virtue of an execution in favor of Wm Finney against
Tandy L. KEY, all the right, title & interest Key has into the following

six negroes; Jim, Milley, Dick, Polly, Allen & Chans & William Finney was highest bidder.29 March 1825 J. H. HOWLETT, constable[p253]

ROBERT LANIER of SNEED & HUNT
18 May 1825   Bill of Sale
We, Absalom D. SNEED and Solomon HUNT, both of Montgomery County, TN, have sold to Robert Lanier a negro boy named Windsor, about eleven or twelve years old.
25 April 1825 H. D. SNEED SOLOMON HUNT
Test: J. EARTHMAN Jr., Lewis EARTHMAN   [p254]

SAMUEL L. WHARTON of M. BARROW, commissioner
18 May 1825   Bill of Sale
By virtue of a decree of the court of Equity, 4th Judicial Circuit, Bank of the State of TN vs Thomas WHITESIDE & others, heirs of Jinken WHITESIDE - negro slave, Sindy, was exposed for sale and Samuel L. Wharton was highest bidder.20 March 1824   M. BARROW
Test: J. WHARTON, Thos. WHITESIDE   [pp254/255]

WILLIAM GRUBBS of CHARLES N. M. MERIWEATHER
18 May 1825   Bill of Sale
I, Charles N. M. Meriweather, of Todd County, KY, confirm the sale of a negro woman named Mary, sold by Alexander BLUE to William Grubbs. 22 April 1825 CHAS. N.M. MERIWEATHER
Test: C. JOHNSON   [p255]

JAMES W. McCOMBS of F. STUMP'S Exrs.
18 May 1825   Bill of Sale
We, the executors of Frederick Stump dec'd, have sold to J. W. McCombs a negro girl, named Louy, about twelve years old.
1 May 1824 PHILIP SHUTE   JOHN CRIDDLE   [p256]

MICHAEL GLEAVES of DREWRY MAYS
18 May 1825   Bill of Sale
I, Drury Mays, of Halifax County, VA, have sold to Michael Gleaves a negro girl named Melissa, fifteen or sixteen years of age.
12 March 1825   DRURY MAYS
Test:Joseph W. HORTON, David B. LOVE[pp256/257]

ELIZABETH KING of WILLIAM TAYLOR
18 May 1825   Bill of Sale

For value received of Elizabeth King, widow of William King, dec'd, I assign all my right and interest in William Kings estate to said Elizabeth. 7 Sept. 1822   WILLIAM TAYLOR
Test: Philip SHUTE   [p257]

ROBERT WEAKLEY of THOMAS HICKMAN
18 May 1825   Bill of Sale
I have sold to Robert Weakley a negro woman, Mary, about eighteen years old, born on my property and raised by me.
18 April 1825   THO. HICKMAN [pp257/258]

SIMON GLENN of THOMAS CLAIBORNE
18 May 1825   Bill of Sale
I have sold to Simon Glenn a negro man slave named Albert, a shoemaker by trade, twenty four years old.
1 Sept. 1824   TH. CLAIBORNE
Wit: A. MORRISON, Dyer PEARL [p258]

DAVID ABENATHY of M. SMITH & W. LYTLE
18 May 1825   Bill of Sale/Warranty
Roger B. SAPPINGTON did on 18 Dec. 1823, convey to Martin Smith the following negroes: Bentley, aged 26 years; Abraham, about 30; Isham, about 33; Mingo, 50; Penny, 25; Mary, 14; Phillis, 12; Daniel, about 9; Robert, 6 years - note to the Bank of the State of Tennessee for which Martin SMITH, Thomas HICKMAN, Joseph W. HORTON & Andrew EWING were securities and said note was unpaid and as directed by the Deed of Trust on 18 Jan. 1825, were exposed to public auction - negro man, Mingo, was purchased by David Abenathy. 24 Feb. 1825   WILL LYTLE
Test: Henry EWING, Nathan EWING [pp259/260]

THOMAS SAMPLE, SARAH SAMPLE & HUGH F. BELL
18 May 1825   Articles of Agreement
Sarah Sample is the owner of three negro slaves named Joe, Squire & Sall, and also shares of bankstock in the Nashville Bank to which she is entitled in her own right and as heir of her deceased father, Robert SAMPLE ... whereas a marriage is shortly intended to be between Hugh T. Bell, of Montgomery County, TN, and Sarah Sample and it is agreed that the property of Sarah shall be secured for the sold use & benefit of Sarah during her life ... does convey unto Thomas Sample the negro slaves and all shares of stock, to be held In Trust - for the benefit of Sarah Sample. 14 April 1825
HUGH T. BELL   SARAH SAMPLE   THOMAS SAMPLE

Test: J. N. BLACKBURN, J. S. BUCHANON   [pp260-262]

WILLIAM LYTLE of THOMAS HICKMAN
30 May 1825   Deed of Mortgage
Thomas Hickman has conveyed to William Lytle the following negro
slaves; one woman, Winney, about forty five and her two daughters;
one named Kitty, about seventeen and the other, Sally, about fourteen;
also a child, Minerva, about three years old. Slaves shall remain in
possession of Thomas Hickman until April 1827 - if debt is paid, this
deed to be void. 20 April 1825   THOS. HICKMAN
Test: J. P. CLARK, Geof. YERGER [pp262/263]

JOHN CURRIN of ROBERT LANIER
13 June 1825   Bill of Sale
I have sold to Jno. Currin two negroes, a boy named Windsor, aged
twelve, and a girl named Juda, aged twelve.
28 April 182   ROBERT LANIER
Wit: R.H.BARRY, Jno. H. SOMMERVILL [pp263/264]

ARON STOCKTON of JOHN AUSTIN
13 June 1825   Bill of Sale
I, John Austin, of Charleston, Indiana, have sold to Aron Stockton, of
Virginia, one undivided fourth of the Steam Boat *Rugo*, as she now
rides in Cumberland River; enroled in New Orleans on 2 Nov. 1824 -
one hundred and one feet, seven inches in length, eighteen feet, seven
inches in breadth, one hundred and one tons 56/95.   20 May 1825
JOHN AUSTIN   [p264]

THOMAS HICKMAN of JOS. HORTON, shff.
6 July 1825   Bill of Sale
due to a judgment against Edmond LANIER, Thomas HICKMAN &
James GRIZZARD by the Nashville Bank, May 1823, levied on the
followiwng negroes: Billy, a man; Nancy, a woman and her two
children, Jim & Nelson; Patsey and two children, Ben & Susan, all the
property of Edmond Lanier, and sold at public auction on 16 Sept.
1823, with Thomas Hickman being the high bidder, therefore, by
virtue of my office, convey them to Thomas Hickman.   10 Oct. 1823
JOSEPH W. HORTON, Shff   [p265]
Test: R. E. FOSTER, Francis CAMPBELL

DAVID VAUGHN of JOHN NEWNAN
12 July 1825   Bill of Sale

Due to my deed of Trust, recorded in 1824, on several negroes and a portion remaining unpaid, hereby convey negroes Ned, aged 23 years, and Sylvia, aged 24 years, to David Vaughn.
4 June 1825   J. NEWNAN
Wit: E. S. HALL, Was. L. HANNUM   [pp265/266]

JOHN BOYD of J. HORTON, shff
16 July 1825   Bill of Sale
writ issued July 1821 against Joseph H. McEWIN, levied on a negro woman, Abby, and her child, Maria, for debt owed John BOYD, at public sale Ephraim H. FOSTER was high bidder, and Foster has directed Horton, as sheriff, to convey said negroes to John Boyd.
29 Aug. 1821   J[osiah] HORTON
W. H. BEDFORD, Edwin W. BEDFORD   [pp266/267]

AARON STOCKTON of JOHN KELLAR
26 July 1825   Bill of Sale
I, John Kellar, of Shippingport, KY, have sold to Aaron Stockton, of Virginia, one undivided fourth of the steamboat *Rega*, now in the Cumberland River. 13 May 1825   JOHN KELLAR
Test: N. PATTESON, I. J. SUMMER   [pp267/268]

DEMPSEY COOK of GEO. STULL
26 July 1825   Bill of Sale
I have sold to Dempsey Cook a negro woman named Caster, between forty & fifty years old. 26 July 1825   GEO STULL   [p269]

JOHN SHUTE of WILLIAM SHUTE
16 Aug. 1825   Bill of Sale
I have sold to John Shute a negro man, Benjamin, about twenty five years of age. 19 July 1825   WM SHUTE
Wit: John GUNNING, Patk. COLLINS [p269]

JOHN BOYD of HARVEY D. PARRISH
16 Aug. 1825   Bill of Sale
I have sold to John Boyd a negro man slave named Joe, about twenty two years of age. 16 Sept. 1824   HARVEY D. PARRISH
Test:Philip PIPKIN, Enos PIPKIN [p270]

THOMAS WASHINGTON of PETER DOUGLAS
16 Aug. 1825   Bill of Sale
I, Peter Douglas, convey to Thomas Washington, a negro man slave, Moses, about 30 years old. I am about to file a bill in equity again

Felix GRUNDY, James CARRUTHERS, and the executors of James TRIMBLE, dec'd; Thomas Washington is my security. 1 Oct. 1824
PETER DOUGLAS
Test: Was. L. HANNUM   [pp270/271]

JOHN COLE of JAMES WOODWARD
16 Aug. 1825   Mortgage Deed
James Woodward conveys to John Cole two sorrel mares, two heifer yearlings, two sows & pigs, twelve shoats and one feather bed. If debt is paid, this deed to be void. 11 June 1825 JAS. WOODWARD
Test: Saml L. WHARTON, M. GLEAVES [p271]

WILLIAM PARKER of DAVID HAYS
16 Aug. 1825   Bill of Sale
I, David Hays, of Robertson County, TN, have sold to William Parker a negro man by the name of Cupid, between the ages of twenty eight and thirty. 2 Jan. 1824   DAVID HAYS
Test: Robert LANIER, John LANIER [p272]

BRAXTON LEE of WILSON SANDERLIN
17 Aug. 1825   Bill of Sale
I, Wilson Sanderlin, of Montgomery County, TN, and sold to Braxton Lee one negro girl, Tansey, about fourteen years old.
13 June 1825   WILSON SANDERLIN
Test: Burrel LEE, James M. LEE [p272]

ENOCH P. CONNELL of WILLIAM HACKNEY
17 Aug. 1825   Bill of Sale
I have sold to William Hackney the following negroes and their future increase which Jemima HACKNEY has a lifetime estate in: Jack, Moses, Jim, Lewis, Laris, Nanny, Matilda, Milley, Ally, Maretta, Artimicey, David, Jack, Eveline, Misina, Ned, Jefferson, Manerva & Moses and warrant against my interest.
28 May 1825   WM HACKNEY
Test: LEMUEL TINNIN   [p273]

WILLIAM HACKNEY of SPENCER PIERCE
17 Aug. 1825   Bill of Sale
I, Spencer Pierce, of Sumner County, transfer to William Hackney all claim I have in the named negroes now in the possession of Jemina Hackney: Jack, Moses, Jim, Lewis, Laris, Nan, Matilda, Milley, Alley, Maritta, Artimeca, David, Jack, Eveline, Marina, Ned, Jefferson, Malvina & Moses and their future increase; also the one fourth part of

the money Rachel sold for - my title being founded on article of agreement entered into between William Hackney, Jesse HUSK, Robert PIERCE, for his children, and Charles PIERCE, in behalf of myself. 26 July 1824   SPENCER (X) PIERCE
Test: E. P. CONNELL, Lemuel TINNEN   [pp273/274]

FOSTER & FOGG of A., J. C. & J. B. HAYS
17 Aug. 1825   Deed of Trust
We, Andrew Hays, John B. Hays and James C. Hays, all of TN, being indebted to William DICKINSON & Joel SHREWSBERRY, trading under the name of *Dickinson & Shrewsberry*, of Virginia, have executed our notes to them and to secure the payment convey to Ephraim H. FOSTER and Francis B. FOGG the following slaves: Harry, aged 42; Peter, aged 34; Tom, 23 years; Sam, 20 years; David, 17 years; Albert, 15 years; Reubin, 14 years; Jack Allen, 36 years; Madison, 12 years; James, 8 years; Jackson, 7 years; Maria, 18 years & her infant child, Violet; Louisa, 16 years and her infant child, Martha; Patsey, 14 years; Mary 10 years; Flora, 18 years and Sylvia, 16 years. The possession of the slaves is to be with Andrew HAYS and not to be taken out of West Tennessee. The consideration for which the notes are give is the delivery of six thousand bushels of salt by *Dickinson & Shrewsberry* to Joseph & Robert WOODS at the price of one dollar per bushel in Tennessee paper. 2 April 1825
ANDREW HAYS JOHN B. HAYS JAS. C. HAYS EPHRAIM H. FOSTER F. B. FOGG
Test: N. PATTESON, Jas BARRETT, N. B. PRYOR, Felix W. ROBERTSON as to J. B. HAYS; James SWANSON, Jr. as to J. B. HAYS; Wm. L. COMPTON as to F. B. FOGG; Samuel SEAY [pp274/276]

ALEXANDER C. EWING of SMITH CRIDDLE
18 Aug. 1825   Deed of Trust
I have sold to Alexander C. Ewing, of Williamson County, TN, two negro fellow slaves named Ben, aged 50 years, and Peyton, aged about 27 years. In trust - to secure debt and if debt is paid with interest this deed to be void. 3 Jan. 1825   SMITH CRIDDLE
Test: R. S. HIGHTOWER, Wm. B. EWING [pp276/277]

WILLIAM LYLE of LYLE & WINTERS
18 Aug. 1825   Power of Attorney
State of Georgia Jackson County. Know that we, John Lyle and Albert Winters, the former an heir in his own right of Levi LYLE, dec'd, and the latter an heir in right of his wife, Amelia WINTERS

formerly Amelia Lyle, daughter of Levi Lyle, dec'd, because we are moving, do make William Lyle, of the state of Mississippi, and Claiborne county, our Lawful Attorney, to sell & convey our claim in three negroes: Jinney, Dicey & Willis, now in the possession of Deborah Lyle, the mother of the said Levi Lyle, dec'd. 30 June 1825
JOHN LILE   ALBERT WINTERS
Test: Samuel WATSON, George SHAW J.J.C.
- I, Edward ADAMS, clerk of the Inferior court of Jackson County, GA, certify that George Shaw is an acting Justice of the Inferior court. 30 June 1825   Edward Adams, Clk
- I, William D. MARTIN, Senior Justice of the Inferior court, certify that Edward Adams is clerk of the said court.
30 June 1825 W. D. MARTIN J.J.C [pp277/278]

ELIJAH LAKE of LEVI LYLE'S heirs
18 Aug. 1825   Bill of Sale
We, William LYLE, of Claiborne County, Mississippi, John Lyle & Albert WINTERS, of Jackson County, GA, all heirs at law, Albert in right of his wife Amelia, formerly Amelia Lyle, have sold to Elijah Lake the following negroes: Jane, a woman about 56 years; Willis, a boy about 15; Dice, a woman about 19 and her boy child, named Jesse, about five months. The slaves decended to us as heirs at Law of Levi Lyle, dec'd. 12 July 1825   WILLIAM LYLE
John Lyle by Atte. in fact William Lyle
Albert Winters, by Atte in fact William Lyle
Test: Nathan EWING, Henry EWING   [pp278/279]

WILLIAM HUGGINS of GEORGE C. BOOTHE
18 Aug. 1825   Bill of Sale
I, George C. Boothe, of Rutherford County, TN, have sold to William Huggins one negro boy about twenty years old, named Jordan.
18 Jan. 1825   G. C. BOOTHE
Test: John HUGGINS, Samuel BOOTH [p279]

SEVIER DRAKE of JOHN DRAKE
18 Aug. 1825   Bill of Sale
I, John Drake, in consideration of the natural love & affection I bear to my son Sevier Drake, and divers other consideration, me hereunto moving, convey to my son a negro man, named Charles, about twenty six years old.
30 March 1825   JOHN (X) DRAKE
Test: Hiram WELLS, Joab HARDEN [p280]

JOHN M. & MARTHA WILSON of M. & J. PURKINSON
18 Aug. 1825   Bill of Sale
I, Martha Purkinson, formerly Martha TAIT, for the natural love &
affection I have for John M. Wilson & Martha Wilson and any other
child which may be begotten of the body of my daughter Jane, convey
to them a negro girl, Polly, about twelve years of age...subject to the
payment of seventy three dollars sixty two cents when paid by James
Wilson or any other person to Richard B. TAIT and whenever
Zachariah Tait and Robert think proper for the interest of the above
named children. 10 Dec. 1824   MARTHA (X) PURKINSON
Test: Robert S. TAIT, Thomas WRIGHT, Robert T. WILLIAMSON
-Know that I, Jackman PURKINSON, relinquish all interest to the
above negro girl. 10 Dec. 1824   JACKMAN PURKINSON
Test: John WILLIAMSON, James WILSON [pp280/281]

ROBERT S. TAIT of M. & J. PURKINSON
18 Aug. 1825   Bill of Sale
I, Martha Purkinson, for the natural love & affection I have for my
beloved son, Robert S. Tait, give to him a negro woman, named Priss,
about thirty six years old. 1 April 1814   MARTHA (X) PERKINSON
Test: William JACKSON, John WILLIAMSON, James WILSON
- Know that I, Jackman Perkinson, relinquish all my interest to the
described negro woman and all her increase since the within Deed of
Gift was signed by my wife, Martha Perkinson.
10 Dec. 1824 JACKMAN PURKINSON
Test: John WILLIAMSON, James WILSON [pp281/282]

JAMES CLEMMONS of WILLIAM RALSTON, constable
8 Sept. 1825   Bill of Sale
I have this day sold at public sale the following property of Miles B.
ARRINGTON: two negro girls, Nancy & Malinda, one bay mare &
colt, one bed, two ploughs & gear, to James Clemmons - to satisfy a
judgment in favour of C. Y. HOOPER of Chas. M. BROOKS. 23 June
1825 Wm RALSTON, constable   [p282]

JOHN CATRON of ROBERTSONS
12 Oct. 1825   Bill of Sale
We, Sarah ROBERTSON, Sterling C. ROBERTSON, & Eldridge B.
ROBERTSON, have sold to John Catron a negro woman, Nancy,
about twenty three years of age. 18 Jan. 1825
   SARAH ROBERTSON   STERLING C. ROBERTSON   E. B.
ROBERTSON

Wit: A. G. EWING, Henry EWING   [p283]

SAMUEL & JOHN MARSHALL of ALEXANDER LOVE
22 Oct. 1825   Deed of Trust
To secure a debt to Samuel & John Marshall, merchants of Nashville, I
convey a negro girl, Milley, aged thirteen years. If debt is paid this
deed to be void.
7 June 1825 A. LOVE SAML & JNO MARSHALL [by Sam'l B.
MARSHALL
Test: Was. L. HANNUM, Saml HOPKINS [pp283/284]

LANIER & LOVE of CYRUS CAMPBELL
7 Nov. 1825   Mortgage
I, Cyrus Campbell, convey to Isaac H. Lanear & Charles I. Love, the
following goods to secure debt: one four horse waggon, one ore
waggon, seven head of oxen, three head of horses, one sorrell mare,
50 cord of Tanbark hay, chestnut, oak & sone black oak, quantity not
known, 3 milch cows & calves, one pair Smiths bellow, one anvil, and
all my tools, however all is to remain in my possession. 2 Sept. 1825
CYRUS CAMPBELL Bernard VANLEAR [pp284/285]

THOMAS MATTHIAS of STEPHEN MATTHIAS
7 Nov. 1825   Bill of Sale
I have sold to Thomas Matthias the following property: one negro girl,
Delilah, about 12 years old, one mare & colt, three sows & pigs, six
head of sheep, one bed, bedstead & furniture, one table, one cupboard
and contents, all household & kitchen furniture.
17 Aug. 1825   STEPHEN MATTHIAS
Test: Nathan EWING, Henry EWING [p285]

JOHN O. EWING of BARRY & SHUTE
7 Nov. 1825   Bill of Sale
We, Richard H. Barry & Philip Shute, have sold to John O. Ewing a
negro woman named Eliza, about nineteen years of age.
23 Sept. 1825 R. H. BARRY   PHILIP SHUTE
Test: W. W. GOODWIN, Seymour PLUMMER [p286]

JOHN BUCHANON of RICHARD DREWRY
7 Nov. 1825   Bill of Sale
I have sold to Major John Buchanon a negro man, named Edmond,
about thirty five years of age. 19 July 1825 Richard DREWRY
Test: Wm. DILLAHUNTY, Jas. CARTER [pp286/287]

HENRY CRABB of JOSEPH & ROBERT WOODS
7 Nov. 1825   Bill of Sale
We, Joseph & Robert Woods, have sold a negro man named Caswell,
about twenty five years of age, to Henry Crabb.10 April 1825
ROBERT WOODS, JOS. WOODS by Robert Woods
Plaquemine, Louisiana
Test: James G. WASHINGTON,Wm.M.BERRYHILL [p287]

HENRY CRABB of JAMES M. ELLISTON
7 Nov. 1825   Bill of Sale
I have sold to Henry Crabb a negro woman named Rachel, of black
colour and stout aged about twenty. 6 Aug. 1825
                                    JAMES M. ELLISTON
Test: Jas. TILFORD, Jos. WOODS   [pp287/288]

HENRY CRABB of WILLIS WHITE
7 Nov. 1825   Bill of Sale
I, Willis White, have sold to Henry Crabb a negro girl named Judy, of
black colour, aged twenty two.7 Sept. 1825   WILLIS WHITE
Test: Charles M. NICHOLS, Alen H. SOMMERVILLE   [p288]

HENRY CRABB of ROBERT BAXTER
7 Nov. 1825   Bill of Sale
I, Robert Baxter, of Dickson County, TN, have sold to Henry Crabb a
negro man named Lige, about forty years of age.
 5 July 1825   ROBERT BAXTER
Test: Bernard VANLEER, J. H. LANEAR [pp288/289]

HENRY CRABB of WILLIAM E. WATKINS
7 Nov. 1825   Bill of Sale
I have sold to Henry Crabb a negro man named Kerr, about twenty
two years old, black colour, and a negro boy named Lewis, about
twenty, of yellow colour. 31 Aug. 1825 W. E. WATKINS
Test: J. H. MARTIN, Th. S. DUNCAN   [p289]

HENRY CRABB of GEORGE AMENT
7 Nov. 1825   Bill of Sale
I have sold to Henry Crabb a negro man named Sam, black colour,
stout made, about twenty nine. 20 June 1825   GEORGE AMENT
Test:John H. SMITH, Robert J. MOORE [pp289/290]

HENRY CRABB of JOHN C. McLEMORE
7 Nov. 1825   Bill of Sale

I have sold to Henry Crabb a negro woman named Maria, about sixteen, and her child, Monroe, about six weeks old.
6 Dec. 1824   JNO. C. McLEMORE
Test: Willo. WILLIAMS, Jo. D. MURRAY [p290]

HENRY CRABB of EDWARD DANIEL
7 Nov. 1825   Bill of Sale
I have sold to Henry Crabb a negro man sllave, black, named Handy, about twenty five years old. 20 July 1825   EDWARD DANIEL
Test: R. C. FOSTER, Jno. S. CON   [pp290/291]

HENRY CRABB of BERNARD VANLEER
7 Nov. 1825   Bill of Sale
I have sold to Henry Crabb a negro girl named Cynthia, about fifteen years old. 4 July 1825   BERNARD VANLEER
Test: Benjamin W. BEDFORD, R. BRADY [p291]

HENRY CRABB of FRANCIS McKAY
7 Nov. 1825   Bill of Sale
I have sold to Henry Crabb a negro man slave named Randall, forty two years old. 26 July 1825   FRANCIS McKAY [p291]

HENRY CRABB of THOMAS CLAIBORNE
7 Nov. 1825   Bill of Sale
I have sold to Henry Crabb a negro boy slave named Madison, about sixteen years old. 30 May 1825   Th. CLAIBORNE
Test: Wm COMPTON   [p292]

HENRY CRABB of JAMES C. HAYS
7 Nov. 1825   Bill of Sale
I, J. Campbell Hays, have sold to Henry Crabb three negroes - Chloe and her two children, Jane & Anne. The first a woman about thirty, Jane about nine, Anne about three - all black. 18 July 1825
JAMES C. HAYS by L. P. CHEATHAM
Test: E. S. HALL, Jno. R. BURKE [p292]

HENRY CRABB of JOS. & ROBERT HAMILTON
7 Nov. 1825   Bill of Sale
I, Joseph Hamilton, Jr., of Jefferson County, TN, by my Attorney in fact, Robert Hamilton, of said county, have sold to Henry Crabb a negro man slave named Dave, about thirty two years, black colour; a negro boy slave named Larry, about seventeen, same colour. 4 July 1825   JOSEPH HAMILTON, JR. by Robert Hamilton

Test: Geo. S. YERGER, Wm. W. LEA   [p293]

HENRY CRABB of CHRISTOPHER G. COX
8 Nov. 1825   Bill of Sale
I, Christopher G. Cox, of Warren County, KY, city of Bowling green, have sold to Henry Crabb a negro girl named Suckey, about 19 or 20, black colour. 16 June 1825   C. G. COX
Test: William COMPTON, Duncan ROBERTSON
                                              [pp293/294]

HENRY CRABB of PHILIP SHUTE
8 Nov. 1825   Bill of Sale
I have sold to John BELL, agent for Henry Crabb, a negro girl, aged sixteen years. 25 Ap. 1825   PHILIP SHUTE
Test: W. TANNEHILL, S. CANTRELL [p294]

EDWARD DANIEL of EDWARD SANDERSON
8 Nov. 1825   Bill of Sale
I have sold to Edward Daniel a negro woman, named Caroline, about twenty three years of age. 18 Aug. 1825   EDWARD SANDERSON
Test: D. CAMERON, Wm D. DORRIS [pp294/295]

MARTHA A. R. JONES of JOHN COCKRELL
8 Nov. 1825   Bill of Sale
I, John Cockrell Senr., have sold to Martha A. R. Jones and her heirs three negro slaves; Milley, about twenty five years old; boy named Simon, about twelve years old; one boy named Jerry about five years old. 15 Dec. 1821   JOHN COCKRELL
Test: Henry EWING, Nathan EWING [p295]

WILLIAM PARRADISE of ALLEN KNIGHT
8 Nov. 1825   Bill of Sale
I have sold to William Parradise a negro woman slave by the name of Drusilla, about seventeen years old. 1 Oct. 1825   ALLEN KNIGHT
Test: S. SHANNON   [pp295/296]

ALLEN KNIGHT of PETER KNIGHT
8 Nov. 1825   Bill of Sale
I, Peter Knight, have sold to Allen Knight a negro girl, named Motira, fourteen years old. 24 Oct. 1825   PETER KNIGHT
Test: B. H. LANEAR, Garrison LANEAR   [p296]

EPHRAIM H. FOSTER of THOMAS HICKMAN
8 Nov. 1825   Deed of Trust

Bernard VANLEER recovered judgments against Thomas HICKMAN, Andrew EWING and Oliver WILLIAMS in July 1825 - to secure payment, Thomas Hickman agrees to convey to Ephraim H. Foster three negro slaves; Theresa, aged twenty years; Lucy, aged twenty two; Lydia, aged thirty five years and John, aged eleven years.
17 Aug. 1825   THO. HICKMAN
Test: Francis B. FOGG, R[oswell] P. HAYES   [p297]

LINSEY C. HALL of CHARLES M. HALL
8 Dec. 1825   Bill of Sale
I have sold to L. C. Hall a negro woman and female infant at her breast. The woman, named Diley, about twenty two years of age.
1 Aug. 1823   CHARLES M. HALL
Test: John BRAUGHTON, John B. HALL
- Bill of Sale proven in open court - Nov. Term 1825 - John Braughton states that John B. Hall witnessed at the time he signed but now lives beyond the bounds of this state. [p298]

FRANCIS McKAY of WILLIAM WHITE
29 Dec. 1825   Bill of Sale
I have sold to Francis McKay a negro man, named Randall, supposed to be between forty & fifty years old.
1 Jan. 1824   WILL. WHITE   [p298]

GREEN BERRY GREER of JACOB FUDGE
7 Feb. 1826   Mortgage Deed
Jacob Fudge has borrowed from Green Berry Greer and to secure debt conveys a wagon & gear plus several horses if debt is not paid.
9 Aug.1825   JACOB (X) FUDGE
Test: J. W. GREER, Elizabeth P. BURTON, George W. BURTON
[p299]

THOMAS J. STUMP of RACHEL STUMP
7 Feb. 1826   Deed of Relinquishment
I, Rachel Stump, in consideration of being permitted to hold and enjoy the portion of negroes conveyed by Frederick Stump, dec'd, to Philip SHUTE, by deed dated 25 Nov. 1819...trusts allotted to me by Samuel WEAKLEY, Richard HYDE & Edwin SMITH, do release to Thomas J. Stump negroes Peggy, George & Silvey (Chanys child), they being set apart by commissioners to Thomas J. Stump.
15 Oct. 1825   RACHEL STUMP
Test. H. W. McGAVOCK, I. J. SUMNER [pp299/300]

EDWARD DANIEL of PETER DOUGLAS
7 Feb. 1826   Bill of Sale
I, Peter Douglas, have sold to Edward Daniel a negro boy, named
Robert, about seven years old.3 Dec. 1825   PETER DOUGLAS
Test: Jac. McGAVOCK, M[ichael] GLEAVES   [p300]

SALLY LEWIS of THOMAS L. SPIECE
7 Feb. 1826   Bill of Manumission
I, Thomas L. Spiece, manumit and forever discharge from slavery and
from my service a negro woman named Sally Lewis, formerly the
property of Col. Joel LEWIS, from whose heirs she came to be my
property ... bind myself, my heirs, executors & administrators not to
obstruct said Sally Lewis in the full enjoyment of her liberty and right
to go and do as she may please. 14 Nov. 1825   THOS. L. SPIECE
Test: A. LOMAN, Floyd HURT   [pp300/301]

BEAL BOSLEY of JOHN BOSLEY
7 Feb. 1826   Bill of Sale
I have sold to Beal Bosley four negro boys; Wesley, about ten years
old; Ben, about nine; Mark, seven; and Abraham, five years old.
2 Dec. 1825   JOHN BOSLEY
Test: John M. HOLLINSWORTH, Abraham WHITSON   [p301]

JOHN SHELBY of WILLIAM F. COLLINS
7 Feb. 1826   Bill of Sale
I have sold to John Shelby a negro man named Peter, about twenty
five years of age. 14 Dec. 1825   WM. F. COLLINS
Test: J. C. BENSON, Kendal WEBB   [p302]

WILLIAM WILLIAMS of JAMES H. TURNER
7 Feb. 1826   Bill of Sale
I have sold to William Williams a negro girl named Melinda, sixteen
years of age. 4 Jan. 1826   JAMES H. TURNER
Test: J. PHILLIPS, C. COOPER   [p302]

RACHEL, PHILIP & TENNESSEE STUMP of   THOMAS J.
STUMP
7 Feb. 1826   Deed of Release
I, Thomas J. Stump, release all title and claim I have to negro slaves
Silvey, Ben, Minerva, Harry, Quaker & his wife, Lovy, Lucy, Minty,
Mariah, Polly, Louisa, Nathan, James and Zealous and their future
increase to Rachel Stump, Tennessee M. Stump and Philip S. Stump.
VIZ - I relinquish my right to negro slaves Quaker and his wife Lovy,

Lucy, Minty & Mariah to Rachel Stump during her life; Negroes Polly, Laura, Nathan, James & Zelous to Tennessee M. Stump, her heirs & assigns forever; negroes Silvey, Ben, Minerva & Harry to Philip S. Stump...in pursuance of an agreement for the partition of the property conveyed by the late Frederick Stump.
15 Oct. 1825   THOS. J. STUMP
Test: J. J. SUMNER, H. W. McGAVOCK   [p303]

JOHN THOMAS of JAMES C. HAYS
7 Feb. 1826   Bill of Sale
I have sold to John Thomas a negro boy named Alick. 14 May 1825
JNO. C. HAYS
Test: Samuel BURNETT, Wallace DIXON   [pp303/304]

STEWART and LAKE of THOMAS GILBERT
7 Feb. 1826   Deed of Transfer & Assignment
I transfer to James Stewart and John A. Lake the 1/3 of the steamboat *Emerald* - they having paid me according to contract. They are to pay a debt owned by me originally to *Breedlow, Bradford & Robinson*, now to *Banks, Miller & Kincaid* of New Orleans.
8 June 1825   THOS. GILBERT
Test: John F. DISMUKES, R. ARMSTRONG   [p304]

REUBEN PAYNE of MARTIN SMITH & others
7 Feb. 1826   Bill of Sale
Roger B. SAPPINGTON, by indenture dated 18 Dec. 1823, did convey to Martin Smith the following slaves: Bentley, a negro man about 26 years; Abraham, about 30; Isham, 33; Mingo, 50; Penny, 25; Mary, 14; Phillis, 12; Daniel, about 9; Robert, 6 years. Martin SMITH, Thomas HICKMAN, Andrew EWING, & Joseph W. HORTON were securities for a debt to the Bank of Tennessee ... debt was unpaid so after advertisement in the *Nashville Whig*, were sold at public auction and Reuben Payne was buyer of Isham, Penny & Robert, Mary, Phillis & Daniel. 2 March 1825
 MARTIN SMITH   ANDREW EWING   THO. HICKMAN   J. W. HORTON
Test: Jacob C. SMITH   [pp304/306]

DAVID VAUGHN of JOHN NEWNAN
7 Feb. 1826   Articles of Agreement
John Newnan has borrowed of *Yeatman & Woods* and David Vaughn is his security and to secure to Vaughn, I convey my present crop of cotton growing on my plantation on the Cumberland, about 80 acres,

as well as the cotton picked and when picking is completed David is to send the same to Michael CAMPBELLS Gin and is authorized to sell the same. I also Mortgage the following negro slaves to Vaughn: Ned, 28 years old; Silvia, 24 years; Peggy, about 45; Charles, about 10; Jack, 18; Flora, aged 44. The negroes are to remain in my possession. 22 Sept. 1825 J. NEWMAN   D. VAUGHN
Test: Was. L. HANNUM, J. L. PRIESTLEY[p307]

SAMPSON KEY of TANDY KEY
7 Feb. 1826   Deed of Gift
I, Tandy Key, for the love and affection I bear to my son, Sampson Key, convey to him all claim I have by virtue of the will of my deceased father, William W. KEY, to the following negroes: Dick, about twenty two years; Chany, about nine years; Allen, about eleven years; Polly, about twenty four years; Milley, about fifty years old.
16 Jan. 1826   TANDY (X) KEY
Test: William ALFORD, John ALFORD [p308]

EDWARD DANIEL of PHILMER WHITWORTH
8 Feb. 1826   Bill of Sale
I, Wilmer Whitworth, of Montgomery County, TN, have sold to Edward Daniel one negro man, named Nat, about forty two years of age. 7 Jan. 1826   PHILMER WHITWORTH
Jas. GRIZZARD, Allen S. HALL   [pp308/309]

WILLIAM WHITE of THE STATE BANK
8 Feb. 1826   Deed of Relinquishment
The Bank of the State of Tennessee made a loan on 25 May 1822 to William White and took a lien against the following negroes: Billy, Jack, Carter, Washington, Jackson, Randal, Delphia, Betsey, Hannah; Mima, Franky, Anne, Little Anne, Nancy, Daniel, Nelson, Ned, Jinney, Mary, Hassty & Isabell. Due to the discharge of the said loan the Bank has this day released the said slaves. 17 Jan. 1826 J. PHILIPS, Pres.
Wit: C. COOPER   [p309]

JOSEPH W. HORTON of THOMAS HICKMAN
8 Feb. 1826   Bill of Sale
I have sold to Joseph W. Horton a negro boy slave named Randall, about sixteen years old. 14 Feb. 1825   THO. HICKMAN
Test: Benjamin W. BEDFORD, Lurnan HAIL   [p310]

MATTHEW BARROW of JOSEPH H. TALBOT
8 Feb. 1826   Deed of Trust
Joseph H. Talbot, of the county of Madison, TN, has conveyed to
Matthew Barrow a negro woman, named Hannah, about twenty years
of age. In Trust - Joseph H. Talbot sold to John JOHNS a negro boy
slave, named Benjamin, warrenting the title - suit has commenced
against Johns for negro boy Benjamin, by John MORRISON.
25 Jan. 1826   JOS. H. TALBOT   [pp310/311]

BENJAMIN TURBIVILLE of HARTWELL WALLACE
14 Feb. 1826   Deed of Trust
Hartwell Wallace and Effy, his wife, late Effy Turbiville, spinster, of
the first part and Benjamin Turbiville of the second part: Hartwell
Wallace is possessed of the following property - negro slaves Nancy,
Louisa & Hilliard; household goods, chattels & furniture and in
consideration of the love and affection he bears to Effy, his wife, and
to make provision for her and for her children after his death, does
transfer the slaves, furniture, etc., to Benjamin In Trust - that slaves &
furniture are to be for her seperate use during her life, and for her
children, lawfully begotten by her husband, & not subject to debts of
her husband. 18 Jan. 1826 HARTWELL WALLACE
Test: Thomas HAYWOOD, E. HAYWOOD   [pp312/313]

JOHN CHAPMAN of RICHARD DABB's Adm.
3 March 1826   Bill of Sale
We, Elizabeth DABBS & John R. Dabbs, adm., on the estate of
Richard Dabbs, dec'd, sell to John Chapman the following negro
slaves; a negro woman named Maria, about twenty two years of age, a
negro girl named Emily, about four years old, and a negro boy,
Charles, about two years old. 18 Jan. 1826
ELIZABETH DABBS   JNO R. DABBS
Test: Elizabeth HAMLET, John WILLIS, E. H. EAST, Thos.
BUCHANON   [p313]

McNAIRY, McLEMORE, FOSTER & LEWIS
3 March 1826   Deed of Trust
John CHAPMAN has executed a note to John R. DABBS, and Boyd
McNairy, John C. McLemore, Ephraim H. Foster & William B. Lewis
are his securities - to secure same, he conveys the following negro
slaves, a woman, Maria, aged 22; girl, Emily, 4 years; boy, Charles,
two years. 18 Jan. 1826   J. CHAPMAN
Test: W. TANNEHILL   [pp314/315]

HENRY CRABB of ROBT SCALES
9 March 1826   Bill of Sale
I sell to Henry Crabb a negro man slave, Benn, about twenty eight
years of age. 15 Aug. 1825   ROBT SCALES
Test: J. GORDON, Jas. WALKER   [p315]

SALLY SHELBY of JOHN SHELBY
10 May 1826   Bill of Sale
I, John Shelby, in consideration of the affection I have for my niece,
Sally D. Shelby, daughter of A. B. SHELBY convey to Sally a negro
girl, Polly, about twelve years of age.
26 April 1826 JOHN SHELBY   [p316]

SALLY SHELBY of ORVILLE SHELBY
10 May 1826   Bill of Sale
I, Orville Shelby, of Sumner County have conveyed to Sally Shelby a
negro girl, Charlotte, about ten or twelve years old.
20 March 1826   O. SHELBY
Test: John SHELBY, Chas. PUGSLEY   [p316]

JOHN SHELBY of JOHN EARTHMAN's Adm.
11 May 1826   Bill of Sale
We, Lewis EARTHMAN, Polly Earthman & Isaac Earthman, adms. of
John Earthman, sell to John Shelby a negro man named George (now
running). 10 Dec. 1825
  LEWIS EARTHMAN   POLLY EARTHMAN   I. EARTHMAN
Wit: Boyd McNAIRY, John J. HINTON   [p317]

JOHN SHELBY of D. & H. GARDNER
11 May 1826   Bill of Sale
We, Dempsey Gardner & Henry Gardner, both of Robertson County,
TN, sell to Doctor John Shelby a negro man, Isaac, about twenty six
years of age. We made known to Dr. Shelby that Isaac some years
ago sustained a rupture and also a defect in the sight of one eye in an
injury. 27 March 1826 D. GARDNER   H. GARDNER
Wit: Joshua GARDNER, Edwin GRIFFIN   [pp317/318]
- proven in Robertson County Circuit Court - April 1826.   SAM
KING, Clerk
  DOCTOR CHARLES PUGSLEY is entitled to 1/2 of the interest in
negro man, Isaac.
14 April 1826   JOHN SHELBY   [pp317/318]

CHARLES BOSLEY of JOS. W. HORTON, sheriff
11 May 1826   Bill of Sale
The Bank of the State of TN recovered a judgment against Richard C.
NAPIER, Stephen CANTRELL & Robert WEAKLEY, Jan. 1826 and
was levied on by sheriff on the following negroes as the property of
John BOSLEY: Tom, a man about thirty; Rachel, a woman about
thirty and her three children, Mary, about twelve, Philip, about five,
and Vice, about two years old. Said negroes were exposed to public
sale with Charles Bosley being highest bidder. 17 April 1826
JOSEPH W. HORTON, sheriff [pp318/319]
CHARLES BOSLEY of JOHN BOSLEY
11 May 1826   Bill of Sale
I have sold to Charles Bosley three negroes; Anthony, about twenty
five; Samuel, twenty five; Peter, about twenty years old.
2 Dec. 1825   JOHN BOSLEY
Test: John M. HOLLINSWORTH, Abraham WHITSON   [p319]

STEPHEN CANTRELL of THOMAS HICKMAN
11 May 1826   Mortgage
I have sold to Cantrell a negro boy named George about fifteen years
of age - if debt to Cantrell is paid, this deed to be void.
5 Jan. 1826   THO. HICKMAN
Test: M. GLEAVES, Robt. STOTHART   [p320]

STEPHEN CANTRELL of THOMAS HICKMAN
11 May 1826   Mortgage
I have sold to Stephen Cantrell, Jr. two negro men; Alfred, aged about
twenty one, and Bill, about nineteen years old. Stephen Cantrell to
have possession and the benefit of their time and labour - if any
accident by death or otherwide the loss to be the loss of Thomas
Hickman. If debt is paid, slaves are to be given up.
5 Jan. 1825   THO. HICKMAN
Test: I. P. CLARK   [pp320/321]

WILLIAM DOCKERTY of JOHN GUNNING
12 May 1826   Deed of Trust
I have sold to William Dockerty a sorrel mare and her colt and one
double case plain gold watch - if debt is paid this deed to be void. 14
Sept. 1825   JOHN GUNNING
Test: Ephraim H. FOSTER   [pp321/322]

JOHN McMURRY of LEONARD KEELING
12 May 1826   Bill of Sale

I have sold to James McMurrey, of Lauderdale County, Alabama, a negro man, John. 3 Aug. 1825   L. KEELING
Test: Ellen (X) CASON   [p322]

JOHN C. HOUSE of NIMROD HOOPER
12 May 1826   Bill of Sale
I, Nimrod Hooper, of the County of Humphrey, TN, have sold to John C. House a negro girl slave named Sophia, aged twelve years old.
23 Oct. 1824   N. HOOPER
Test: John HOOPER, Thomas L. BROWN, James HOOPER
[pp322/323]

WILLIAM JAMES of ENOCH P. CONNELL
12 May 1826   Bill of Sale
I have sold to William James a negro boy named Spurlet, about twelve years old. 17 Feb. 1826   E. P. CONNELL
Test: W. M. WINBOURN, Thos. W. GWINN
- I certify above named boy, Spuelet, is a mulatto.   [p323]

WILLIAM B. LEWIS of WILLIAM C. EMMETT
12 May 1826   Deed of Trust
I have conveyed my 1/2 interest in the furniture in the *Nashville Inn and Mansion House*, inventory signed by Duncan ROBERTSON and myself and Overton SEAWELL as partners; also the following negro slaves; Arthur, Rainey, Minerva, Joe, Carlos, and their increase, to William B. Lewis - In Trust - I have rented the *Nashville Inn* from William B. Lewis - as long as I pay rent I retain the use and possession.   2 March 1826   WM C. EMMETT
Test: A. P. MAURY, Tho. CRUTCHER [p324]

WILLIAM JAMES of WILLIAM PAGE
12 May 1826   Bill of Sale
I have sold to William James a negro girl named Penny, about eleven years old. 23 Dec. 1825   WM PAGE
Test: D. B. LOVE, Isaac BIRDWELL [p325]

UMPHREY B. DUNNAVANT of THO & E. NOLIN
12 May 1826   Mortgage
We, Thomas Nolin and Elizabeth Nolin, his wife, formerly Elizabeth OWENS, convey to Umphrey B. Dunnavant a negro boy named Abram. If debt is paid this deed to be void.   14 Oct. 1825
THOMAS NOLIN   ELIZABETH (X) NOLIN
Test: Smith CRIDDLE, Abraham (X) DUNNAVANT [pp325/326]

JOSEPH ANDERSON of SAMUEL YOUNG
12 May 1826   Mortgage
Samuel Young, of Pittsburg, PA, has sold to Joseph Anderson,
surviving partner of the late firm of *Anderson & Knox*, the Steamboat
Lafayette, now in the trade between New Orleans, Nashville,
Louisville & Pittsburg - In Trust - if payments are made this deed to be
void. 7 Apr. 1826   SAMUEL YOUNG
Test: Wm ALLEN, Patterson B. WEST   [pp326/327]

BENJAMIN WILLIAMS of NATHAN BENNETT
15 May 1826   Deed of Trust
Nathan Bennett has sold to Benjamin Williams a negro man named
Joshua, about twenty one; a negro boy slave named Jack, about nine -
In Trust - Bennett is indebted to Jesse J. EVERETT and if debt is not
paid Williams is to sell the above slaves, if debt is paid, this bill to be
void. 30 Jan. 1826   NATHAN BENNETT
Test: Isaac MAYFIELD, Henry(X)LADY [pp328/329]

HENRY O. DONOLY of WILLIAM & MARTHA GOODE
16 May 1826   Mortgage
William Goode and his wife, Martha Goode convey the following
negro slaves to Henry O. Donoly: a negro woman named Pat, one
negro woman named Peggy, one negro man named Alick; negro man
named Albert; negro boy named Isaac; negro boy named Dick; negro
girl named Harriet; negro boy named Harry and negro boy named
Jackson; one sorrel mare, bed, bedstead and furniture.   The above
negro slaves formerly belonged to Benjamin MOODY, dec'd, and have
descended to William & Martha as his heirs.   William Goode is
indebted to Henry O. Donoly and if debt is paid, this deed to be void.
15 Apr. 1826 WILLIAM GOODE MARTHA (X) GOODE
Test: Thomas VAUGHN, William G. WESTMORELAND
[pp329/330]

SALLY SHELBY of ORVILLE SHELBY
10 May 1826   Bill of Sale
I, Orville Shelby, of Sumner County, have conveyed to Sally Shelby a
negro girl, Charlotte, about ten or twelve years old.
20 March 1826   O. SHELBY
Test: John SHELBY, Chas. PUGSLEY   [p316]

JOHN SHELBY of JOHN EARTHMAN's Adm.
11 May 1826   Bill of Sale

We, Lewis Earthman, Polly Earthman & Isaac Earthman, adms. of John Earthman, sell to John Shelby a negro man named George (now running). 10 Dec. 1825
LEWIS EARTHMAN   POLLY EARTHMAN   I. EARTHMAN
Wit: Boyd McNAIRY, John J. HINTON   [p317]

JOHN SHELBY of D. & H. GARDNER
11 May 1826   Bill of Sale
We, Dempsey Gardner & Henry Gardner, both of Robertson County, TN, sell to Doctor John Shelby a negro man, Isaac, about twenty six years of age. We made known to Dr. Shelby that Isaac some years ago sustained a rupture and also a defect in the sight of one eye in an injury. 27 March 1826   D. GARDNER   H. GARDNER
Wit: Joshua GARDNER, Edwin GRIFFIN   [pp317/318]
- proven in Robertson County Circuit Court April 1826.   SAM KING, Clerk
   DOCTOR CHARLES PUGSLEY is entitled to 1/2 of the interest in negro man, Isaac. 14 April 1826   JOHN SHELBY [pp317/318]

CHARLES BOSLEY of JOS. W. HORTON, sheriff
11 May 1826   Bill of Sale
The Bank of the State of TN recovered a judgment against Richard C. NAPIER, Stephen CANTRELL & Robert WEAKLEY, Jan. 1826 and was levied on by sheriff on the following negroes as the property of John BOSLEY: Tom, a man about thirty; Rachel, a woman about thirty and her three children, Mary, about twelve, Philip, about five, and Vice, about two years old. Said negroes were exposed to public sale with Charles Bosley being highest bidder.   17 April 1826   JOSEPH W. HORTON, sheriff   [pp318/319]

CHARLES BOSLEY of JOHN BOSLEY
11 May 1826   Bill of Sale
I have sold to Charles Bosley three negroes; Anthony, about twenty five; Samuel, twenty five; Peter, about twenty years old.
2 Dec. 1825   JOHN BOSLEY
Test: John M. HOLLINSWORTH, Abraham WHITSON   [p319]

STEPHEN CANTRELL of THOMAS HICKMAN
11 May 1826   Mortgage
I have sold to Cantrell a negro boy named George about fifteen years of age - if debt to Cantrell is paid, this deed to be void.
5 Jan. 1826   THO. HICKMAN

Test: M. GLEAVES, Robt. STOTHART   [p320]

STEPHEN CANTRELL of THOMAS HICKMAN
11 May 1826   Mortgage
I have sold to Stephen Cantrell, Jr. two negro men; Alfred, aged about
twenty one, and Bill, about nineteen years old. Stephen Cantrell to
have possession and the benefit of their time and labour - if any
accident by death or otherwide the loss to be the loss of Thomas
Hickman. If debt is paid, slaves are to be returned to Hickman.
 5 Jan. 1825   THO HICKMAN
Test: J. P. CLARK   [pp320/321]

WILLIAM DOCKERTY of JOHN GUNNING
12 May 1826   Deed of Trust
I have sold to Dockerty a sorrel mare and her colt and a double case
plain gold watch. I am in debt to him and the mare & colt shall remain
at the farm of John SHUTE at the expense of Gunning but as the
property of Dockerty until debt is paid.
14 Sept. 1825   JOHN GUNNING
Test: Ephraim H. FOSTER   [pp321/322]

JAMES McMURRY of LEONARD KEELING
12 May 1826   Bill of Sale
I have sold to James McMurry of Lauderdale County, Alabama, a
negro man named John. 3 Aug. 1825 L. KEELING
Test: Ellen (X) CASON   [p322]

JOHN C. HOUSE of NIMROD HOOPER:
12 May 1826   Bill of Sale
I, Nimrod Hooper, of Humphrey County, TN, have sold to John C.
House a negro girl, named Sophia, aged thirteen years.
23 Oct. 1824   N. HOOPER
Test: John HOOPER, Thomas L. BROWN, James HOOPER
[pp322/323]

WILLIAM JAMES of ENOCH P. CONNELL
12 May 1826   Bill of Sale
I have sold to William James a negro boy named Spurlet, about twelve
years of age. 17 Feb. 1826   E. P. CONNELL   [p323]
Test. W. M. WINBOURN, Thos. W. GWINN

WILLIAM B. LEWIS of WILLIAM C. EMMETT
12 May 1826   Deed of Trust

I convey to William B. Lewis my 1/2 interest in the furniture in and about *The Nashville Inn & Mansion House*; being on the inventory certified by Duncan ROBERTSON on 23 Jan. 1826; also the interest I have in the following negro slaves: Arthur, Rainey, Minerva, Joe & Carloz. I, William C. Emmett, in partnership with Overton SEAWELL, have rented the *Nashville Inn* from William B. Lewis. If the rent is paid this deed is to be void.
2 March 1826 WM. C. EMMETT
Test: A. P. MAURY, Thos. CRUTCHER   [p324]

WILLIAM JAMES of WILLIAM PAGE
12 May 1826   Bill of Sale
I have sold to William James a negro girl named Penny, about eleven years old. 23 Dec. 1825 WM PAGE
Test: D. B. LOVE, Isaac BIRDWELL   [p325]

UMPHREY B. DUNNAVANT of THO. & E. NOLIN
12 May 1826   Mortgage
We, Thomas Nolin & Elizabeth Nolin, his wife, formerly Elizabeth OWENS, have conveyed to Umphrey B. Dunnavant a negro boy named Abram to secure loan. If debt is paid, this deed to be void. 14 Oct. 1825 THOMAS NOLIN ELIZABETH (X) NOLIN
Test: Smith CRIDDLE, Abraham (X) DUNNAVANT [pp325/326]

JOSEPH ANDERSON of SAMUEL YOUNG
12 May 1826   Mortgage
Samuel Young, of Pittsburg, PA, conveys to Joseph Anderson, surviving partner of the late firm of *Anderson & Knox*, the Steamboat, *Layfayette*, now in the trade between New Orleans, Nashville, Louisville & Pittsburg. If mortgage is paid this deed to be void.
7 April 1826   SAMUEL YOUNG   [pp326/327]
Test: Wm ALLEN, Patterson B. WEST

BENJAMIN WILLIAMS of NATHAN BENNETT
15 May 1826   Deed of Trust
Nathan Bennett conveys to Benjamin Williams a negro man slave named Joshua, about twenty one years of age and a negro boy slave named Jack, about nine years old. Bennett is indebted to Jesse J. EVERETT. When debt is paid this deed shall become void.
30 Jan. 1826   NATHAN BENNETT
Test: Isaac MAYFIELD, Henry (L) LADY [his mark] [pp328/329]

HENRY O. DONOLY of WILLIAM & MARTHA GOODE
16 May 1826   Mortgage
William Goode and his wife Martha convey to Henry O. Donoly all the interest in the following named slaves: a negro woman named Pat, negro woman named Peggy, negro man named Alick, a negro man named Albert, negro boy named Isaac, negro girl named Harriet, negro boy named Dick, negro boy named Harry, negro boy named Jackson; also a sorrel mare, Bed, Bedstead & furniture. The above named slaves formerly belonged to Benjamin MOODY, dec'd, and descended to William & Martha as his heirs. William & Martha shall remain in possession until default be made on the payment.
18 April 1826 WILLIAM GOODE MARTHA (X) GOODE
Test: Thomas   VAUGHN,   William   G.   WESTMORELAND
[pp329/330]

WILLIAM MURPHEY of FOSTER, HICKMAN & Sheriff
16 May 1926   Bill of Sale
Whereas in July Sessions 1825 of the Court of Pleas & Quarter Sessions, Bernard VANLEER recovered judgments against Thomas HICKMAN, Andrew EWING & Oliver WILLIAMS.   Hickman conveyed the following negro slaves to Ephraim H. Foster In Trust: a negro woman named Theresa, twenty years old; negro woman named Lucy, twenty two years old; negro woman named Lydia, thirty five years old; negro boy named John, eleven years old. Hickman failed to pay and a writ was issued and Michael GLEAVES, deputy under Joseph W. HORTON, sheriff, did levy the same on negro woman named Theresa and her child, Miranda; negro woman named Lucy and her child named Toney [the said children Miranda & Toney being the increase since the date of the Deed of Trust] and on 2nd Feb. 1826 proceeded to sell at auction.   Negro woman named Theresa a her child, Miranda, to William Murphey.
14 Feb. 1826   JOSEPH M. HORTON, sheriff of Davidson County
Test: Henry EWING, Walter SIMS   [pp330/332]

ALEXANDER C. EWING of SMITH CRIDDLE
16 May 1826   Deed of Trust
I have sold to Alexander C. Ewing, of Williamson County, TN, two negro fellow slaves named Ben, aged about 50 years, and Peyton, about 27 years.   I have borrowed from Ewing and if debt is paid this deed to be void. 7 Jan. 1826   Smith Criddle
Test: R. S. HIGHTOWER, G. W. ERWIN   [pp332/333]

NATHANIEL A. McNAIRY of MARSHALL B. MUMFORD
26 May 1826   Deed of Trust
I, Marshall B. Mumford, in consideration of the natural love and
affection I bear to my wife, Sally Mumford, and my children, Mary
Mumford, Elizabeth Mumford, Martha Mumford, Maria Mumford,
Jane Page Mumford & William Mumford, convey the following negro
slaves to Nathaniel A. McNairy: Mary, about twenty years old and her
child Martha, about two years old; Fanny, about sixteen; Sally, about
fifteen years old. In trust for my wife and children and such other
children I may have, share and share alike. 17 May 1825   M. B.
MUMFORD   [p334]

ROBERT WEAKLEY of THOMAS HICKMAN
5 June 1826   Deed of Trust
I, Thomas Hickman, convey a negro man named Moses, about twenty
two years old, to Robert Weakley to secure my debt to him. If debt is
paid, this deed is to be void. 3 Sept. 1825   Thos. Hickman
Test: William BROOKS, Wm BALL   [pp334/335]

RICHARD B. OWEN, dec'd Heirs
14 June 1826   Agreement
We, Robert B. CURRY and Jane his wife, formerly Jane OWEN,
Franklin L. OWEN, William E. OWEN, John H. OWEN, by his
guardian, Franklin L. OWEN, and Robert B. OWEN, by his guardian,
William E. OWEN, children of Richard B. OWEN, late of Monroe
County, Alabama, have this day made a division of the negroes, the
property of Richard B. Owen in his lifetime, except that portion
bequeathed to George W. OWEN by the last Will of Richard B. Owen.
We have taken into consideration advancements made to Robt. Curry
& his wife and William E. Owen. We have had negroes valued by three
disinterested persons: Matthew BARROW, D. A. DUNHAM & I. H.
SMITH. Negro Polly and child Albert were assigned to Wm. E. Owen.
Nelson, Patty & Margaret were assigned to Franklin L. Owen. Ned,
Mary & child, and Russia Anne were assigned to John H. Owen by the
consent of his guardian. Mumford, Alsey & child & Fanny & Sam
were assigned to Robert B. Owen by the consent of his guardian.
Davey, Melissa & Celion assigned to Franklin L. Owen. Freem? was
assigned to Robert B. Curry & wife. Horace & Louisa assigned to
Wm E. Owen. Anaca & Jackson assigned to John H. Owen by consent
of his guardian. 18 Jan. 1826   WILLIAM E. OWEN   F. L. OWEN
ROBT B. CURRY   WM E. OWEN, Guardian for ROBT B. OWEN
F. L. OWEN, Guardian for JOHN H. OWEN   [pp335-337]

FRANCIS LINCK of JOHN SCHERER
14 August 1826   Deed of Trust
I have conveyed two stills, one containing forty two gallons, the other
containing about one hundred and fifty gallons and worm and other
apparatus belonging to it. If debt is paid this deed to be void.
6 March 1826   JOHN SCHERER
Test: John WALKER   [p338]

JOHN SHELBY of JOHN HAMILTON
14 August 1826   Bill of Sale
I have sold to John Shelby a negro man named Charles, about thirty
three years old.   JOHN HAMILTON
Test: Chas. PUGSLY, Geo. WILSON   [pp338/339]

EDWARD DANIEL of JOHN CRAIN
14 August 1826   Bill of Sale
I,John Crain of Pulaski County, KY, have sold to Edward Daniel a
negro girl named Polly, aged eleven years and two months.
21 June 1826   JOHN CRAIN
Test: Samuel SEAY, C. J. F. WHARTON [p339]

ENOCH P. CONNELL of JESSE HACKNEY
14 August 1826   Bill of Sale
I, Jesse Hackney of Maury County, TN, have sold to Enoch P. Connell
the following named negroes and their future increase; Jack, Moses,
Jim, Lewis, Lares, Nanny, Matilda, Milley, Alley, Marella, Astimecy,
David, Jack, Evaline, Merina, Jefferson, Manerva, Moses and two
infants, now in the possession of Jemina Hackney. 10 June 1826
JESSE HACKNEY
Test: W.P. CONNELL, A. HENING, ROBERT (X) BATES   [p340]

UPHOMY WALLACE of BENJAMIN J. TURBIVILLE
14 August 1826   Bill of Sale
I have sold a negro man slave by the name of Goff to Uphomy
Wallace. 23 Feb. 1826   BENJAMIN J. (X) TURBIVILLE
Test: Wm RAMSEY, Benj. TURBIVILLE   [p340]

ROBERTSON & FAULKNER of OBEDIAH JINKINS
14 August 1826   Mortgage
I have conveyed to N. H. Robertson & James Faulkner one waggon,
one sorrel mare, one bay mare, three cows, three calves, two
steers...to secure note payable to J. EARTHMAN, Jr.

90

25 July 1826   OBEDIAH JINKIN   [p341]

MARK YOUNG of NATHANIEL A. McNAIRY
21 August 1826   Bill of Sale
I have sold to Mark Young a mulatto negro man named Nathan, about
twenty years of age. 17 July 1826   N. A. McNAIRY [pp341/342]

JAMES RIDLEY of THOMAS MOOREFIELD
24 August 1826   Bill of Sale
To secure payment of judgments rendered in the Circuit Court of
Davidson County, I convey to James Ridley a negro woman named
Polly Walker and Letha, her child; William & Anthony, also her
children; girl named Mariah. Negroes are now in possession of W.
BARROW. 12 May 1821 THOS MOREFIELD
Test: G. W. GIBBS, C. COOPER   [p342]

JOHN HAMILTON of OAKLEY JONES
24 August 1826   Bill of Sale
I have delivered to John Hamilton a negro man slave by the name of
Charles, about twenty eight years old. 26 Aug. 1819   OAKLEY
JONES
Test: Jno. CHILTON, Jno. BOYD   [pp342/343]

JOHN W. & ROBERT C. CAMPBELL of CYNTHIA A.
CAMPBELL
24 Aug. 1826   Bill of Sale
I have sold to John W. & Robert C. Campbell the following negroes:
Nancy, about thirty two; William, about thirteen; Jack, about eight;
Anne, about five months, all children of Nancy. Lewis, about twelve,
child of Hannah. Randal, about twenty eight; Pascal, about twenty.
--- April 1826 CYNTHIA A. CAMPBELL
Test: Francis B. FOGG, John McDANIEL [p343]

WILLIAM CAMPBELL, CYNTHIA A. CAMPBELL & GEORGE
W. McGEHEE
Oct 3, 1826   Marriage Agreement
Whereas a marriage is about to be had between George W. McGehee
& Cynthia A. Campbell and Cynthia is possesed of divers parcels of
real estate, notes, slaves, etc. ...note due from John W. Campbell and
Robert C. Campbell ... hereby agreed between George W. McGehee,
Cynthia Campbell & William Campbell, her father, that William shall
as Trustee, receive & collect said note ... interest shall be due Cynthia

for her natural life, and after her death, shall belong equally to the children of George W. McGehee & Cynthia. 6 Apr. 1826
    GEORGE W. McGEHEE   CYNTHIA A. CAMPBELL   W. CAMPBELL
Test: A. BALCH, R. C. CAMPBELL [p344]

FRANCES R. CANNON's heirs of SAMUEL CHAPMAN
15 Nov. 1826   Relinquishment
James A. Cannon by his Indenture dated 23 April 1821, conveyed to Samuel Chapman sundry articles and also his right to the estate of Thomas ROYLE, dec'd, consisting of land, negroes and other property.
    "Now I the said Samuel Chapman release ... unto the heirs of Frances R. Cannon, dec'd all right I have to the property mentioned in the Deed above ..." [reg. Book 'P', pp17/18]
13 July 1826 SAM (X) CHAPMAN
Test: Henry EWING, Nathan EWING [p345]

ENOCH P. CONNELL of JEMIMA HACKNEY
15 Nov. 1826   Bill of Sale
I convey to Enoch P. Connell all right I have to the following negroes: Nancy, about sixty two years of age; Jack, about sixty; Moses, about fifty seven; Jim, about forty; Lewis, about thirty five;' Laves, about twenty two; Ritty, about thirty; Ally, about thirty; Milley, about twenty five; Matilda, about twenty five; Niece, about thirteen; David, about ten; Mareny, about eight; Ned, about six; Jefferson, about four; Eveline, about four; Minerva, about five; Moses, about four; Jim, about two; Jack, about three; Westley, about nine months; which negroes I have a reversionary interest in during my natural life. 4 July 1826 JEMIMA (X) HACKNEY
Test: Aquilla RANDALL, Isaac HARRIS [pp345/346]

ENOCH P. CONNELL of ROBERT PEARCE & others
15 Nov. 1826   Bill of Sale
We, Robert Pearce, Daniel Pearce, Joseph Pearce, for himself and as Guardian for Jesse Pearce, Lucinda Pearce, have this day sold our right, title & interest to the following negroes and their increase; Nancy, Jack, Moses, Jim, Louis, Ally, Ritty, Laris, Milley, Matilda, Artimesa, David, Marina, Ned, Jefferson, Jim, Moses, Westley, Jack, Eveline, & Malvina. 4 Aug. 1826 ROBERT (X) PEARCE, DANIEL (X) PEARCE, JOSEPH (X) PEARCE, JOSEPH PEARCE as Guardian for JESSE PEARCE,LUCINDA (X) PEARCE

Test: J. P. CLARK, Geo S. YERGER, Aquila RANDALL, Rolla HARRISON, Isaac HARRISON   [p346]

ANDREW MORRISON of WILLIAM PITTMAN
15 Nov. 1826   Bill of Sale
I have sold to Andrew Morrison my negro man slave by the name of Jerry, a carpenter. 13 Feb. 1826   WILLIAM PITTMAN
Test: A. DUNCAN, J. H. MARTIN   [p347]

BENJAMIN W. BEDFORD of JAMES W. McCOMBS
15 Nov. 1826   Bill of Sale
I have sold to Benjamin W. Bedford a negro female slave named Mary, about nine years of age. 22 Aug. 1826   JAS. W. McCOMBS
Test:W. H. BEDFORD, J. W. HORTON   [p347]

THOMAS L. WILLIAMS, Trustee of LEONARD P. CHEATHAM
15 Nov. 1826   Bill of Sale
I have sold to Thomas L. Williams, of Knoxville, TN, the use of the heirs of JOHN P. & FRANCES L. ERWIN, one negro man, named Lewis, aged about forty years. 26 Nov. 1826   L. P. CHEATHAM [p348]

THOMAS L. WILLIAMS of THOMAS YEATMAN
15 Nov. 1826   Deed of Trust
Indenture made 19 April 1823 between Thomas Yeatman and Thomas L. Williams, of Knox County, TN, whereby Yeatman conveys to Thomas L. Williams a negro woman, Claret, now in possession of John P. ERWIN, being the same negro purchased as the property of John P. Erwin at Marshalls sale on 28 Nov. 1821, also the other goods and property purchased ...In Trust - for the use and benefit of the children of John P. Erwin and his present wife, Frances L. Erwin. TH. YEATMAN   [pp348/349]

JOHN MORGAN of ROBERT WEAKLEY
16 Nov. 1826   Bill of Sale
I have sold to John Morgan a negro woman, Mary, about nineteen years of age; which negro was born and raised the property of Thomas HICKMAN,Esqr. 29 July 1826   R. WEAKLEY
Test: Thomas R. MORGAN   [p349]

ENOCH WELBORN of MILLSAPS & McCUTCHEN
16 Nov. 1826   Bill of Sale

We, William Millsaps & John McCutchen, of Robertson County, TN, have sold to Enoch Welbourn a negro girl and her future increase. 13 Sept. 1826   WILLIAM MILLSAP by Jno. McCutchen, his Attorney in fact   [p350]

PEACOCK and WILLIAMS copartnership
16 Nov. 1826   Articles of Copartnership
We, Edward Peacock and Thomas Williams have entered into copartnership in the Tayloring business for the period of four years. 28 Aug. 1826   EDWARD (X) PEACOCK   THOS. WILLIAMS
Test: eorge CROCKETT, James SCOTT   [pp350/351]

JOHN C. HOUSE of S. DAVIDSON
16 Nov. 1826   Bill of Sale
I have sold a negro woman by the name of Pil, twenty four years of age to John C. House. 18 July 1826   S. DAVIDSON
Test:Elisha GARLAND, Gilliam KING   [p351]

YEATMAN & WOODS of ALPHA KINGSLEY
16 Nov. 1826   Mortgage
Alpha Kingsley has sold to Thomas Yeatman, Joseph & Robert Woods the following to secure debt: eight cherry posts Bedsteads complete, eight featherbeds, bolsters & pillows, two hair mattrasses, one dozen rush bottom chairs, one dozen stump back fancy chairs; one settee, one cherry wardrobe, one Jackson press, one Secretary & bookcase, three Bureaus, three dozen common windsor chairs, one mantle glass, three ingrain carpets, three hearth rugs, four large elegant dining tables, six small cherry chamber tables, six toilette glasses, one Service of Silverplate, consisting on one coffee, one tea and one water pot, one sugar dish, one wash bason, one cream pot, two dozen large spoons, one dozen desert spoons, two dozen and one half teaspoons and one soup spoon, four dozen large ivory handled knives & forks, four small ivory handled knives & forks, three ivory handled carvers & forks, one steel carver, twelve buck handled knives & forks, six dozen liverpool dining plates, six dozen liverpool twifflers, four dozen small twifflers, two dozen dishes, assorted sizes, four small tureens, six covered dishes, one set edged Castors, three pair brass andirons, 4 pair iron andirons, six pair steel andirons (brass mounted), shovels & tongs, four fenders, eight decanters, three dozen tumblers, six goblets, two dozen wine glasses, eight china & glass pitchers, eight damask tablecloths, two dozen fine towels, two dozen coarse towels, six washstands, basons & ewers to each, eight mosquito bars, twenty four

sheets, twenty four large & best blankets, two dozen pillowcases, twelve counterpanes, one dining room carpet, sundry pieces of carpet for passage, four fancy settees for use of passage, one passage lamp, four plated candlesticks and snuffers, eight brass snuffers, eight snuffer trays, seven tea waiters, two pair looking glasses, one eight day clock & case, six poplar tables, one copper wash kettle, one copper teakettle, one iron kettle, 4 iron pots, 4 iron ovens, 1 gridiron, kitchen shovel & tongs, ten stone & clay jars, 6 glass jars, four dimijons, one poplar safe. 5 Oct. 1826   ALPHA KINGSLEY
Test: Nathan EWING, Henry EWING   [pp352/353]

THOMAS WASHINGTON of EDWARD BARKER
17 Nov. 1826   Bill of Sale
I, Edward Barker, of Todd County, KY, have sold to Thomas Washington a mulatto boy slave named William Sursen?, aged nineteen years. 22 March 1826   EDWARD BARKER
Test: A. W. JOHNSON, John DECKER   [pp353/354]

ROBERTSON & EARHART of JOHN B. HALL & others
17 Nov. 1826   Bond of Indemnity
Eldridge B. Robertson & Abraham Earhart have become securities for John B. Hall, William Hall, B. SHROPSHIRE, John C. NEELY & Maclin CROSS, legatees of Charles M. Hall, dec'd, for an appeal from the judgment of the County Court and we relinquish to Robertson & ARHART our interest in said estate. 28 Oct. 1826
JOHN B. HALL   WILLIAM HALL by John B. Hall, Atto in fact
B. SHROPSHIRE, by J. G. Neely, Atto in fact JOHN G. NEELY
MACLIN CROSS   [p354]

JOSEPH CRIGHTON of NANCY DOSSELL
18 Nov. 1826   Bill of Sale
I have sold to my grandson, Joseph Crighton, infant son of Robert Crighton, for natural love & affection and one dollar, one mare & saddle, two cows & calves, two steers, two heifers, thirty head of hogs with their increase, two feather beds & furniture, one cupboard and a pair of andirons now in my possession and so to remain until I die or Joseph comes of age.10 May 1824   NANCY (X) DOSSELL
Test: Andrew J. DONELSON, John DONELSON, Jr.   [p355]

DANIEL YOUNG & others of JOHN L. YOUNG
18 Nov. 1826   Deed of Gift
John L. Young, for love & affection for his children, has conveyed to Daniel Young, Napoleon B. Young, John B. Young, Ferdinand Jones

Young, William F. L. B. Young, Amanda Malvina F. Young and Amelia Elizabeth Ann Young the following property: to my son, Daniel Young, my negro man, Laurence; to my son, Napoleon B. Young, my negro woman, Nelly; to my son, John B. Young, my negro girl, Mary; to my son, Ferdinand Jones Young, my negro girl, Betsey; to my son, William F. L. B. Young, my negro boy, Randall; to my daughter, Amanda Malvina F. Young, my negro girl, Harriet; to my daughter, Amelia Elizabeth Ann, my negro child, named Ailcey. 18 Oct. 1826   J. L. YOUNG
Test: J. HINTON, W. M. HINTON   [pp355/356]

BROOKS & STEELE of NANCY B. HALL, Adm.
18 Nov. 1826   Power of Attorney
I, Nancy B. Hall, Adm. PM on the goods & chattels of Charles M. Hall, dec'd, for divers reasons, me moving, appoint Christopher Brooks and Samuel Steele my true & lawful attorneys to and in my name to take possession of all the estate of Charles M. Hall, dec'd and handle all affairs necessary, proper & lawful.
17 Oct. 1826 NANCY B. (X) HALL   [pp356/357]

ALLEN MATTHIS of EPHRAIM PEYTON
18 Nov. 1826   Bill of Sale
I have sold to Allen Matthis a negro man named Jesse, about twenty five years old. 25 July 1826   EPHRAIM PEYTON
Test: E. P. CONNELL, Wm P. BYRN   [p357]

ORR & WATSON of O. SEAWELL
Nov. 1826   Deed of Trust
I have conveyed to Robert Orr and Matthew Watson the following property: 36 new feather beds & bedsteads, ten new dining tables, one mahogany dining table, twelve tablecloths, four large gilt looking glasses, fourteen carpets, six fire fenders, six pairs brass andirons, one secretary, two bureaus, one handsome work stand, one new sideboard, twelve dozen chairs, six candlestands, fifty pairs linen sheets, forty pair blankets, all my table china of every description, sixteen small tables, thirty six pairs of new marseilles counterpanes, fifteen bedcurtains, sixteen pairs brass candlesticks, six dozen knives & forks, two dozen silver tablespoons, two copper coffee urns, sixteen washstands, two new stables and a carriage house, erected by me on the lot belonging to the estate of James TRIMBLE, dec'd with liberty to remove two pairs cutglass decanters, twenty five pairs of plain decanters, six dozen glass tumblers, plain & cut, six dozen wine glasses, one pair elegant window curtains, six pairs common curtains, one clock together with

all the household & kitchen furniture of the Mansion House, all of which I own individually. I am indebted to Orr & Watson and James P. CLARK & Moses NORWELL are my securities. 24 Dec. 1826 OVERTON SEAWELL
Test: Geo. WILSON, G. Duncan RAINEY [pp358/359]

JOSIAH CLARK of ROBERTSON & ELLIOT
5 Dec. 1826   Bill of Sale
We, Duncan Robertson & Hugh Elliot have sold a negro girl about nine years of age to Josiah Clark, of Washington County, PA. 10 Nov. 1826 DUNCAN ROBERTSON HUGH ELLIOT
Test: Joseph H. LANING, Alex. McINTOSH   [p360]

RACHEL STUMP of POLLY BRADSHAW heirs
5 Dec. 1826   Bill of Sale
We, the undersigned children & heirs of Polly Bradshaw, convey to Rachel Stump a negro woman by the name of Zelph [now in the possession of Nathaniel A. McNAIRY] together with all the children she has had or hereafter may have.
16 Jan. 1826 SPENCER R. WYATT MARTHA M. WYATT
TABITHA W. BRADSHAW J. F BRADSHAW
Test: Philip SHUTE   [p360]

ELLEN KIRKMAN of LAUGHLIN, LEDBETTER, WENDEL & others
6 Dec 1826   Bill of Sale
We, Samuel H. Laughlin, George A. SUBLETT, John R. Laughlin & William Ledbetter, all of Rutherford County, TN, have sold to Ellen Kirkman a negro woman named Harriet. 9 Oct. 1826
SAMUEL H. LAUGHLIN   JOHN R. LAUGHLIN   GEO. A. SUBLETT WM LEDBETTER
Test: James FALLS, Silas LOCKE
- Whereas on 2 Jan. 1821, Samuel H. Laughlin, of Rutherford Co., TN executed a Deed of Trust to secure a mortgage, proved by the oaths of Hugh D. NIELSON and Samuel P. BLACK, registered in Rutherford County Book O, page 10, and including the above named negro woman slave, Harriet. S. ANDERSON   DAVID WINDEL
Test: James FALLS, Silas LOCKE   [pp361/362]

HENRY CRABB of WILLIAM COMPTON
22 Dec. 1826   Bill of Sale

I have sold to Henry Crabb two negroes, one a woman aged thirty three, named Henny, black colour, the other a negro girl, Tilda, aged about twelve, black colour.2 Oct. 1826   WM COMPTON
Test: W. BARROW, John MARSHALL   [p362]

HENRY CRABB of JAMES OVERTON
22 Dec. 1826   Bill of Sale
I have sold to Henry Crabb a negro boy named Jeff, light yellow colour, aged about fifteen. 12 March 1826 J. OVERTON [p362]

HENRY CRABB of JOSEPH ANDERSON
22 Dec. 1826   Bill of Sale
I have sold to Henry Crabb a negro woman, named Phoeby. 15 Nov.
1826   JOSEPH ANDERSON, Surviving Partner
  of *Anderson & Knox*   [p363]

THOMAS A. DUNCAN of LAWSON W. JOHNSON
22 Dec. 1826   Bill of Sale
I, Lawson W. Johnson, of Hopkins County, KY, have sold to Thomas A. Duncan a mulatto negro girl named Betsey, eleven years of age.
9 May 1823   LAWSON W. JOHNSON
Test: P. M. LONG, Thos. LONG   [p363]

WILLIAM B. LEWIS of JAMES McLAUGHLIN
9 Jan. 1827   Transfer
I transfer to William B. Lewis all title and claim I have to the furniture in the *Nashville Inn*, it being 1/3 part.
10 Oct. 1826   JAS. McLAUGHLIN
Test: Thos. LONG   [p364]

WM. B. LEWIS of WM. C. EMMITT
9 Jan. 1827   Bill of Sale
I have sold to William B. Lewis my right, title & claim to all the furniture in the *Nashville Inn & Mansion House*. I also transfer the following negro slaves: Arthur, a boy aged twenty five; Rainey, a woman about twenty; Joe, a boy aged about three years; Carlos, a boy about one year of age. 16 Oct. 1826   WM. C. EMMIT
Test: P. M. LONG, W. E. ANDERSON   [pp364/365]

PHILIP LINDSLEY of ALEX BELL
13 Jan. 1827   Bill of Sale
I have sold to Philip Lindsley a negro boy named John, about sixteen years of age, dark complexion. 2 Jan. 1827   ALEXANDER BELL

Test: F. B. FOGG, Spencer JARNAGEN, Nathan EWING
[pp365/366]

SAMUEL V. D. STOUT of ALEXANDER ALLISON
8 Feb. 1827   Bill of Sale
I, Alexander Allison, of Smith County, TN, have sold to Samuel V. D.
Stout a negro woman, Jenny, about twenty five years old, and her
child, Harry, about three years old.
19 March 1823   ALEX ALLISON
Test: M. M. MONOHAN   [pp366/367]

SAMUEL V. D. STOUT of H. H. WALLACE
8 Feb. 1827   Bill of Sale
I have sold to S. V. D. Stout a negro boy, Jack, about eighteen years
of age. 27 Aug. 1825   H. H. WALLACE
Test: M. M. MONOHAN   [p367]

HARRIET RICHMOND of BARTON RICHMOND
8 Feb. 1827   Bill of Sale
I have sold to Harriet Richmond, formerly of Littlecompton, Rhode
Island, a mulatto girl, Alice, about eighteen years of age, and her
infant child; my mulatto boy, Joseph, about seventeen years of age;
and my mulatto girl, Ann, about thirteen years of age.
4 Dec. 1826 BARTON RICHMOND   [p367]

HENRY EWING of CHRISTOPHER ROBERTSON
8 Feb. 1827   Bill of Sale
I, Christopher Robertson, of Dickson County, TN, have sold to Henry
Ewing a negro woman slave named Acry?, mulatto color, about 21
years of age. 1 July 1826   C. ROBERTSON
Test: A. G. EWING, L. H. TANNEHILL   [p368]

ALGERNON SIDNEY JONES of JOHN COCKRILL
10 Feb. 1827   Bill of Sale
John Cockrill, Sr. did under a Deed of Gift, dated 15 Dec. 1821, grant
to his Grandson, Algernon Sidney Jones, son of Martha A. R. JONES,
now Martha A. R. THOMPSON, two small negro boy slaves named
Thornton and Jack, now in the possession of Robert C. Thompson.
Said Deed of Gift has been mislaid and cannot be registered according
to law...I therefore confirm the Conveyance of Thornton & Jack.
29 Nov. 1826   JOHN COCKRILL
Test: Nathan EWING, Henry EWING   [pp368/369]

JOHN HARMON of JESSE WILLS
10 Feb. 1827   Bill of Sale
I, Jesse Wills, have sold to John Harmon a negro man named Bird,
about 33 years of age.
5 July 1825   JESSE WILLS
Test: N. B. PRYOR, William (X) TEACHER   [p369]

JOHN BUCHANON of R. C. DREWEY
12 Feb. 1827   Bill of Sale
I have sold to John Buchanon a negro girl slave, Maria, aged six years;
also a negro boy, Braddock, aged four years.
9 Dec. 1826   R[ichardson] C. DREWEY
Test: William YOUNG, Robert ELAM, James B. BUCHANON
[pp369/370]

JOHN BUCHANON of R. C. DREWRY
12 Feb. 1827   Bill of Sale
I have sold to John Buchanon a negro woman, Anarchy, aged about
twenty four; also a girl, her daughter, Malvina, two years of age.
4 Nov. 1826   R. C. DREWRY
Test: Washington PULLIAM, Wm BUCHANON   [p370]

MOSES F. BROOKS of POLLY HAYS
12 Feb. 1827   Bill of Sale
I have conveyed a negro woman, Fanny, and child, Ann Jane, to
Moses F. Brook. 18 Jan. 1827   POLLY HAYS
Test: Wm CREEL, John H. SEABORN   [pp370/371]

EDWARD MATTHEWS of HIRAM HITE & wife
12 Feb. 1827   Bill of Sale
We, Hiram Hite and Elizabeth Hite have this day sold to Edward
Mathews a negro girl named Rebecca. 27 Dec. 1825
HIRAM HIGHT   ELIZABETH (A) HIGHT
Test: Samuel (x) LINK, Ezra HOLSTEAD   [p371]

EWING, ANDERSON, PRICE & PATTERSON of THOS
PATTERSON
12 Feb. 1827   Mortgage
I, Thomas Patterson, to cover my debts to Nathan Ewing, Josh S.
Anderson, Thomas K. Price & Benjamin Patterson, convey the
following: one gray horse & gig, one cart and oxen, one brown horse,

ten head of cattle, and all my farming tools. 12 Jan. 1827
THOMAS PATTERSON
Wit: J. GINGRY, Martha DIBRELL [pp370/371]

JOHN MORGAN of JAMES NORMENT
12 Feb. 1827   Bill of Sale
I have sold to John Morgan a negro girl, Evelina, six years of age; a
negro girl, Virginia, four years old.
22 Sept. 1826 JAMES NORMENT
Test: Thomas R. MORGAN, Geo. GAMP?, Benj. MORGAN [p372]

STEPHEN JOHNSON to CHARLES R. JOHNSON
12 Feb. 1827   Bill of Sale
I have sold to Charles R. Johnson the following described personal
property: one sorrel horse, one bay horse, eight or ten head of cattle,
three sows & nineteen pigs, one cart & gear, one grind stone, all my
farming utensils, three beds, bedsteads & furniture, one table, seven
chairs, one chest, one trunk and all household & kitchen furniture.
23 Dec. 1826   STEPHEN JOHNSON
Test: Thomas MORRIS, John NEWLAND [pp372/373]

MARY NICHOL of SAMUEL BLAIR
12 Feb. 1827   Bill of Sale
For love and affection I have given to my daughter Mary Nichol, of
Carroll County, TN, a negro girl, Vina, nine years old. Said negro girl,
with all her increase, is to belong to my daughter and the heirs of her
body, and shall in no manner be liable to be sold for the debts of John
W. Nichol, her husband. 24 Jan. 1827 SAMUEL BLAIR [p373]

JOSEPH L. EWING of WILLIAM S. CABELL
12 Feb. 1827   Bill of Sale
I, William S. Cabell, of Nelson County, VA, have sold to Jos. L.
Ewing, a negro woman slave, Amy, about twenty years of age.
17 Jan. 1827   WM. S. CABELL [pp373/374]

WEAKLEY of MASTERSON HOOVER of WEAKLEY
12 Feb. 1827   Bill of Sale
I, William Masterson, of Mercer County, KY, have this sold to Robert
Weakley a negro man, John, a Blacksmith, twenty one years of age.
13 Jan. 1827 WILLIAM MASTERSON
Test: H. PETWAY, I. J. GILL
- Jan. 16, 1827 - for value received, I transfer the within Bill of Sale to
Michael Hoover.   A. WEAKLEY

Test: Jno SOMMERVILLE, M. GLEAVES   [p374]

ISAAC EARTHMAN of THOMAS HICKMAN
12 Feb. 1827   Mortgage Deed
I sell to Isaac Earthman the following negroes; a woman, Winney,
about forty five, and her two daughters, Kitty, about eighteen, and
Sally, about fifteen, and also a child, Minerva, about four years old. I
am indebted to Earthman and if debt is paid, this deed to be void.
 8 Dec. 1825 THO. HICKMAN
Test: J.P. CLARK, Lewis EARTHMAN [p375]

HARDY S. BRYAN of REUBEN CHICK
12 Feb. 1827   Deed of Trust
I hereby grant to Reuben Chick, of Robertson County, TN, two negro
slaves; one female, Charlotte, and one male, Peter. I am indebted to
Chick and if debt is paid, this deed to be void. 6 Jan. 1827
REUBEN CHICK
Test: C. BIDWELL   [pp376/377]

JOHN McCUTCHEN of JAMES BRUTON
5 Apr. 1827   Bill of Sale
I have sold to John McCutcheon a negro boy named William, about
nineteen years old.   JAMES BRUTON
Test: Wm. EDMISTON, Wm COMPTON [p377]

ROBERT WEAKLEY of WILLIAM MASTERSON
5 Apr. 1827   Bill of Sale
I, William Masterson, of Danville, Mercer County, KY, have sold to
Robert Weakley a negro man named George, about twenty years old.
18 Jan. 1827 WILLIAM MASTERSON
Test: S. H. BLYTHE, Thos. BROWN   [pp377/378]

HANNAH T. CHEWNING of JAMES CONDON
5 Apr. 1827   Bill of Sale
I, James Condon, for and in consideration of the love, good will &
affection I bear to my daughter, Hannah T. Chewning, I deliver unto
her a negro girl slave named Delilah, about the age of four years. this
---- day of   182 . JAS. CONDON   [p378]

SARAH J. CHEWNING of JAMES CONDON
5 Apr. 1827   Bill of Sale

I, James Condon, in consideration of the love, good will & affection I bear to my daughter, Sarah J. Chewning, deliver unto her a negro boy slave named John, about six years of age.this -- day of 182 .
JAS. CONDON   [p379]

STEPHEN CANTRELL of WILLIAM HEWLITT
5 Apr. 1827   Mortgage
Stephen Cantrell having become security on a note to *Bass & Spence*, Hewlitt conveys the following property: two beds, bedsteads & furniture complete, one Bureau, one press, one dining table, one tea table, one settee, one half dozen windsor chairs, one common carpet, one washstand with bowl & pitcher, one dressing glass and dressing table, one pair dog irons, shovel & tongs, kitchen table and all kitchen furniture.   If debt be paid, this deed to be void. 16 Jan. 1827
WILLIAM HEWLETT
Test: Allen COTTON, G.C.P.CANTRELL [pp379/380]

LEWIS EARTHMAN of I. & G. HUMPHREYS
10 May 1827   Bill of Sale
We, Isaac Humphries & George Humphries, of the County of Montgomery, TN, have sold to Lewis Earthman one negro girl of black complexion, named Valentrila, about fourteen years old.
17 Feb. 1827 ISAAC HUMPHRIES   GEORGE HUMPHRIES
Test: Isaac F. EARTHMAN, John H. EARTHMAN [pp380/381]

LEWIS EARTHMAN of RICHARD H. HICKS, constable
10 May 1827   Bill of Sale
I, Richard H. Hicks, by reason of sundry executions for collection against John L. YOUNG, have sold one negro girl, Mark, property of said Young, to Lewis Earthman. 6 Nov. 1826   R. H. HICKS, constable
Test: William GRUBBS, Hardy S. BRYAN [p381]

ISAAC EARTHMAN, Jr. of EXUM P. SUMNER
10 May 1827   Bill of Sale
I have sold to Isaac Earthman a negro boy slave named Riley, about fifteen years of age, to secure debt. 29 Jan. 1827   Exum P. Sumner
Test: I. EARTHMAN, Jr.,B.H.LANEAR [pp381/382]

MICHAEL GLEAVES of GEORGE W. L. MARR
10 May 1827   Bill of Sale

I have sold to Michael Gleaves three negroes: Toney, a man about thirty five years of age; Lucy, his wife, about twenty years of age; Toney, a boy child about one year of age.
23 Dec. 1826   G. M. L. MARR
Test: William NICHOLSON, N. H.ROBERTSON   [p381]

HENRY PERKINS of E. CHILDRESS' Admr.
15 May 1827   Bill of Sale
I, John CATRON, as administrator of Elizabeth Childress, have sold to Henry Perkins a negro woman named Sally and her female child named Tennessee. 16 Apr. 1827   JN CATRON
Test: Henry EWING, N. EWING   [p383]

BENJAMIN LITTON of E. CHILDRESS' Admr.
18 May 1827   Bill of Sale
I have this day delivered to Benj. Litton, as admr. of Elizabeth Childress, a negro man slave named Will. 16 Apr. 1827   JN CATRON
Test: Nathan EWING, Henry EWING   [p383]

GEORGE C. CHILDRESS of E. CHILDRESS' Admr.
18 May 1827   Bill of Sale
I, John Catron, as admr. of Elizabeth Childress, have sold to George C. Childress a negro woman and child, named Cresy & Gilbert, a boy about 1 year old. 16 Apr. 1827   JN CATRON
Nathan EWING, Henry EWING   [p384]

WILLIAM B. & THOMAS W. AMENT of JAMES GRIZZARD
18 May 1827   Bill of Sale
I have sold to William B. & Thomas W. Ament a negro woman, Kesiah, about twenty nine years of age. 21 April 1827
JAS. GRIZZARD [p384]

JAMES OVERTON of JOHN THOMSON
18 May 1827   Bill of Sale
I, George T. Thompson, of Christian County, KY, have sold to James Overton three negro slaves; one man & two girls by the names of Edmond, Phebe & Caroline; together with a set of blacksmith tools and a cart & oxen.
6 Oct. 1824 GEO. T. THOMSON, Atto. in fact for
        JOHN THOMSON
Wit: Simon BRADFORD, Jervis CUTLER [p385]

JAMES OVERTON of JOHN THOMSON
18 May 1827   Bill of Sale
I, George T. Thompson, of Christian County, KY, have sold to James Overton a wagon and gear for five horses, together with eight horses, two mares & six horses. 5 Nov. 1824   GEORGE T. THOMSON, Atto. in fact for JOHN THOMSON
Wit: John R. BURKE   [p385]

FREDERICK MITCHELL of JOHN B. FREEMAN
18 May 1827   Mortgage
To secure loan I hereby convey two wagons, with all the harness thereto and nine head of horses. 30 Dec. 1827   JOHN B. FREEMAN
Wit: J. H. MARTIN, J. M. MARTIN   [p386]

BARTHOLOMEW WALSH of JAMES BARRETT
18 May 1827   Bill of Sale
I have sold to Bartholomew Walsh a negro boy named Stephen, dark complexion, about eleven years old. 30 Jan. 1827   JAMES BARRET
Wit: John J. WALSH, Daniel CAMERON   [pp386/387]

ROBERT LANEAR of SMITH CRIDDLE
21 May 1827   Deed of Trust
I, Smith Criddle, being indebted to Robert Lanear, mortgage my negro man Ben, about fifty seven years old.
8 Jan. 1827   SMITH CRIDDLE
Test: L. G. CRIDDLE, Joseph ROWLAND 7 Apr. 1827 [pp387/388]

JANE HAYS of SARAH HAYS
21 May 1827   Deed of Gift
I, Sarah Hays, for the particular love & affection I bear to my Granddaughter, Jane Hays, daughter of James Hays, who I partly raised and who has a long time lived with me and waited on me in my old age, give a negro boy named Bird; having heretofore given her the same negro by deed of gift, which deed was not proved in time as the law directs. 25 Jan. 1827   SARAH (X) HAYS
Test: S. GREEN, Jesse STANCILL, B. GRAY   [p388]

JOHN PINKERTON of JOSEPH J. BRIDGES
21 May 1827   Mortgage Deed
I convey to John Pinkerton one bay mare, one Dearbon wagon & gear, one cow & calf, 2 beds & furniture, 3 bedsteads & eight barrels of corn, three axes & 2 pair of chain traces, haims & collars, one barshear

plow & 150 lbs Bacon. If debt is paid this deed to be void. 24 Apr. 1827   JOSEPH J. (&) BRIDGES {his mark]
Test: Lewis JOSLIN   [pp388/389]

JOHN BUTTERWORTH of THOMAS DILL
21 May 1827   Bill of Sale
I have sold to John Butterworth a negro girl named Ceila, about six or seven years old. 14 Apr. 1827 THOS. DILL   [p389]

WILLIAM HARRIS of JOHN MORGAN
21 May 1827   Bill of Sale
Received full payment from William Harris for a negro woman named Mary, about nineteen or twenty years of age and her child, Sandy.
1 Feb. 1827 JNO. MORGAN
Test: Wm L. NORMENT, James NORMENT   [p389]

MATTHEW BARROW of JOHN REEDER
21 May 1827   Bill of Sale
I, John Reeder, of Wythe County, VA, have sold to Matthew Barrow the following negro slaves: Solomon, aged about twenty seven years of age; Jesse, about twenty three; Rachel, about seventeen years, a good cook; Betsey, about twenty five years and her five children, three girls & two boys. Jane, about nine years old; Martha Ann, about seven; Oney, about five; Jack, about three; Sandy, about one year old. I warrant them all sound and healthy. *Jesse, one of the above negro men received a kick from a horse yesterday near to his left knee, I warrant him to recover and be free from any stifness from this hurt.
9 Apr. 1827   JOHN REEDER
Wit: Joel PARRISH, Joseph MEEK, Jr., C. COOPER   [p390]

EPHRAIN H. FOSTER of THOMAS H. FLETCHER
21 May 1827   Mortgage
I convey to Ephraim H. Foster the following: one complete set of dining tables, one Breakfast table, one Mahogony sideboard, 18 windsor chairs, three pier looking glasses, two carpets, two hearth rugs, 2 pair Brass & iron andirons, 2 pair iron andirons, three shovels & tongs, 1 pair card tables, two hand bellows, two hearth brushes, one portrait of Tho. H. Fletcher & frame, two high post bedsteads, two short post bedsteads, two Bureaus, three feather beds & furniture, one matrass & furniture, one pair flower pots, two wire fenders, two hearth rugs, one cow & calf, one horse, well known by the name of *Sea Serpent*, 68 volumes of Law & Miscellaneous Books in said Fletchers office, one office desk, table & 6 chairs, one set of tea

chests, one set of dining chairs, 18 tumblers, 12 wine glasses, 2 pair salts, 4 doz. plates, 10 dishes, one complete set of Ivory Handled knives & forks, two dozen common knives & forks, 4 Quart decanters, 4 free ladle, 1 kitchen table, two stands of Bed curtains, 10 window curtains, 2 tubs, 4 pails, 1 bucket, 3 pots, 3 ovens, 1 large iron kettle, 1 skillet, one frying pan, two skillets, one teakettle, one pair waffle irons, one candlestand, and two pairs mantle ornaments. If Fletcher pays his debt to Foster this deed to be void.
24 April 1827 THOS. H. FLETCHER [pp390/392]

DANIEL CAMERON of JOHN D. BUTLER
29 May 1827   Mortgage
I convey to Daniel Cameron the following property: 48 bottles of wine, six kegs, 12 Jars, one box of chocolate, one Shew bow, one dreaner for tumblers, 18 tumblers, 7 decanters, 1 bottle stand, 600 cigars, four waiters, one quarter box of St. Domingo and one quarter box of Spanish cigars, one set of measurers, 10 gallons of cherry bounce, one keg of Sloughtons bitters, one barrel of whiskey, two kegs of Tennerieffe wine, two pair of scales & weights belonging to each, one barrel of vinegar, two tables, all my baking utensils and the shelving & counter, all above are in the house which I now occupy -- six cots with furniture, a breakfast and dining table, two sets of chairs, one windsor, one split botton, two signs, one bureau, two featherbeds with the bedsteads and furniture, four trunks, all my table furniture, two cows, three heifers. Also a frame house I erected on the lot of Joseph T. ELLISTON upon which I live. I am indebted to Joseph T. Elliston and if debt is paid, this deed to be void. 8 May 1827   JOHN D. BUTLER
Test: Th. A. DUNCAN, Wm. ALLEN   [pp392/393]

ISAAC EARTHMAN of GARRISON LANEAR
2 June 1827   Bill of Sale
I have sold to Isaac Earthman, Jr., one negro boy named Peter, thirteen years old. 23 Jan. 1827 GARRISON LANEAR   [p393]

PHILIP LINDSLEY of HINCHEY PETWAY
5 July 1827   Bill of Sale
I have sold to Philip Lindsley a negro woman named Mell, about thirty five years old, dark complexion. 23 June 1827   H. PETWAY
Test: L. P. CHEATHAM, J. M. HORTON, A. CHEATHAM
[p394]

FRANCIS LINCK of WILLIAM S. CABELL
14 Aug. 1827   Bill of Sale
I, William S. Cabell, of Nelson County, VA, have sold to Francis
Linck a negro woman named Amy. 1 Jan. 1827   WM. S. CABELL
Test: Andrew GINGRY   [p394]

FRANCIS LINCK of ELIAS S. BOWMAN
14 Aug. 1827   Bill of Sale
I have sold to Francis Linck a negro girl named Jenette, about fourteen
years old.
1 Dec. 1826   ELIAS S. BOWMAN
Test: J. WALKER   [p395]

FRANCIS LINCK of HENRY QUESTENBURY
14 Aug. 1827   Bill of Sale
I have sold Francis Linck a negro woman named Anna, aged about
forty two years. 1 Dec. 1826 HENRY QUESTENBERRY
Test: J. WALKER   [p395]

PEYTON ROBERTSON of ELISHA DAVIS
14 Aug. 1827   Bill of Sale
I, Elisha Davis, of Williamson County, TN, have sold to Peyton
Robertson the three following negroes; Jim, about thirty years old, six
feet high, dark complexion; Lucy, twenty three years old, dark
complexion; Isaac, fifty years old and small size, dark complexion ...
all above slaves were sold to Elisha Davis by Peyton Robertson in
1819 or 1820. 25 May 1827   E. DAVIS
Test: Charles B. THOMPSON, F. D. ROBERTSON [pp395/396]

DAVID ABENATHY of SIMON EVERETT
14 Aug. 1827   Deed of Transfer & Power of Attorney
I, Simon Everett, one of the children and heirs of Nicey Everett, dec'd,
who was a daughter of Jesse & Martha JOLLY, both deceased, late of
Pitt County, NC, transfer to David Abenathy all claim I have to the
estate of Jesse & Martha Jolly. I hereby empower David Abenathy to
act as my agent. 9 July 1827 SIMON EVERETT
Test: Henry EWING, Nathan EWING   [pp396/397]

GODFRED SHELTON of WILLIAM GOODRICH
14 Aug. 1827   Mortgage
I, William Goodrich, have this day bought from Godfred Shelton one
waggon & gear. If payment is made this deed to be void. 29 Nov.
1826   WILLIAM (a) GOODRICH {his mark}

Test: Mat. C. CARITHERS [p397]

BEAL BOSLEY of OBIDIAH JINKINS
14 Aug. 1827 Mortgage
I am indebted to Beal Bosley for the rent of said Bosleys plantation,
formerly the plantation of Sappington, now dec'd. I convey to Bosley
all my household & kitchen furniture, together with about 40 head of
hogs, three head of horses and waggon & gears, two head of cattle. If
rent is paid this deed to be void.
9 Feb. 1827 HENRY (X) O'DONLEY
Test: John BROWN [pp397/398]

WILLIAM F. J. DAVIS of ALICE COLLINSWORTH
14 Aug. 1827 Deed of Gift
I, Alice Collinsworth, in consideration of the natural love & affection I
bear unto my beloved Grandson, William Franklin Jones Davis, grant
him a negro girl, Martha Louisa, aged five years.
25 Aug. 1826 ALICE (X) COLLINSWORTH
Test: A. COLLINS, Thomas FARROUGH [p398]

ANDREW WORK of MATTHEW PATTON
14 Aug. 1827 Deed of Trust
I, Matthew Patton, deliver the following to Andrew Work - one negro
slave named Violet, a female aged twenty three or twenty four, also
her three children - a boy named Stephen, about nine years old; a girl
named Celey, a mulatto about four years old; a boy named Jacob,
about two years old. Also all my household and kitchen furniture
consisting of three beds & furniture, tables, chairs, etc., all my stock of
horses, cows, hogs and other stock -- In Trust - he is to hold the slaves
and other property for the use & benefit of Matthew Patton and his
wife Mary Patton during their lives and during the life of the survivor
of them and for the use of the children now born or hereafter to be
born of them in equal shares. 23 July 1827
MATTHEW PATTON ANDREW WORK
Wit: J. W. CAMPBELL, Th. CLAIBORNE [p399]

HARDY S. BRYAN of REUBIN CHICK
15 Aug. 1827 Deed of Trust
I sell to Hardy S. Bryan, of Robertson County, TN, a negro man,
Uriah, aged twenty two years, two sorrel mares, one roan filley, one
cart & yoke of oxen, twenty head of cattle, one set of small tools,
twelve head of hogs, seven feather beds, bedsteads and furniture, two
folding tables, one bureau, one walnut and one poplar press, one

dozen and a half chairs, one writing desk, one harrow, four ploughs, one large kettle, two pots and two ovens and three skillets. I am indebted to Bryan and if the debt be paid this deed to be void.
5 June 1827   REUBEN CHICK
Wit: William ALLEN, Sam CLARK   [pp400/401]

DANIEL CAMERON of JOHN GRAHAM
30 Aug. 1827   Bill of Sale
I have sold a negro woman, named Catherine, about twenty five years old, and her son, three years old.
28 July 1827 JN. GRAHAM   [p401]

FREDERICK N. MITCHELL of JOHN B. FREEMAN
30 Aug. 1827   Bill of Sale
I have sold Frederick N. Mitchell a negro girl slave, about fourteen years old. 5 June 1827 JOHN B. FREEMAN   [p402]

PRETTYMAN M. BUCKNER of HOMER BUCKNER
8 Oct. 1827   Bill of Sale
I have sold Prettyman M. Buckner a negro boy, Jim, about six or seven years old. 13 July 1827 HOMER BUCKNER   [p402]
Wit: B. E. McCAULEY, Joseph GINGRY

ROBERT B. & McNAIRY NEWELL of JANE NEWELL
8 Oct. 1827   Bill of Sale
I, Jane Newell, for maternal love and affection and services rendered by my sons, Robert B. Newell & McNairy Newell, sell them the following slaves: Bob, aged thirty nine; Aaron, aged twenty eight; Henderson, fifteen years; Harriet, twenty one and her child, Daniel, aged two months. 21 May 1827   JANE (X) NEWELL
Wit: R. H. BARRY, Lev SHUTE   [p403]

HUGH F. & JOHN B. NEWELL of JANE NEWELL
8 Oct. 1827   Bill of Sale
I, Jane Newell, for maternal love & affection and services rendered me by my sons, Hugh F. Newell and John B. Newell, both of Harden County, the following negro boys: James, thirty nine; Watson, eighteen; & Joseph, seventeen years old. 21 May 1827   JANE (X) NEWELL
Wit: R. H. BARRY, Lev SHUTE [pp403/404]

JOHN PECK of JOSHUA GARDNER
10 Nov. 1827   Bill of Sale

I, Joshua Gardner, of Robertson County, have sold to John Peck a negro boy named Sip, about fifteen years old. 18 Nov. 1826 JOSHUA GARDNER
Wit: Henry GARDNER, Wm H. EARLE
I, Sam KING, clerk of the Circuit Court for Robertson County, certify the Bill of Sale from Joshua Gardner to John Peck & ordered to be certified for registration in Davidson County.   [p404]

JOHN PECK of JOSHUA GARDNER
10 Nov. 1827   Bill of Sale
I, Joshua Gardner, of Robertson County, TN, have sold to John Peck a negro woman named Milley, about 25 years old; also her child, named Sal, about two years old. 18 Nov. 1826   JOSHUA GARDNER
Wit: Henry GARDNER, Wm H. EARLE [pp404/405]

HUGH ROLAND of NATHAN EWING
16 Nov. 1827   Bill of Sale
I have sold to Hugh Roland a negro man slave named Casewell, about thirty one years old, of black colour. 27 Sept. 1827
                    NATHAN EWING
Wit: Henry EWING   [p405]

ENOCH WELBOURN of ZEBULON P. CANTRELL
16 Nov. 1827   Bill of Sale
I have sold and delivered to Enoch Welbourn a negro boy, named Chesterfield, about ten years old. 1 Oct. 1827 Z. P. CANTRELL
[p406]

ENOCH WELBOURN of ROYESTER & STEWART
16 Nov. 1827   Bill of Sale
We, George R. Royster of Davidson County, and John Stewart, of Sumner County, TN, have sold to Enoch Welbourn a negro boy slave named Richard, six years old. 1 Aug. 1827
        GEORGE R. ROYESTER   JOHN STEWART
Wit: Jno. L. BUGG   [p406]

JAMES CLEMMENTS of HENRY CRABB
16 Nov. 1827   Bill of Sale
I have sold James CLEMENTS a negro boy named Henry. 1 Jan. 1823
HENRY CRABB
Test: W. B. LEWIS, Jno. BELL   [p407]

CHARLES DUNCAN of JAMES CLEMMONS
16 Nov. 1827   Bill of Sale
I have sold to Charles Duncan a negro woman named Jane. 9 Oct.
1827   JAMES CLEMONS
Test: Samuel F. GREENE, Paul VAUGHN   [p407]

JACOB CARTWRIGHT of S. and B. WITHERS
16 Nov. 1827   Bill of Sale
We have sold to Jacob Cartwright two negro girls, one named Peg,
about fifteen years old; one named Kitty, about eight years old.
15 May 1827 SAMUEL WITHERS BERNARD WITHERS
Test: A. MATHIS, Isaac McCASLAND   [pp407/408]

SAMUEL V. D. STOUT of WATTERS ELAM
16 Nov. 1827   Bill of Sale
I have sold to Samuel V. D. Stout a negro boy named Collins, dark
complexion, about eight years of age. 16 Oct. 1827
                    WATTERS ELAM
Test: A. L. DONOVAN, Thos. CARAWAY   [p408]

JOSIAH C. HORTON of JOSIAH HORTON
16 Nov. 1827   Bill of Sale
I, Josiah Horton, in consideration of the natural love and affection I
have for my son, Josiah C. Horton, have transferred to him three negro
slaves: Isaac, a boy about thirteen years old; Billy, a yellow girl, twelve
years old; John, a boy of dark complexion, about seven years old.
25 May 1827   J. HORTON
Test: Jos. W. HORTON, H. W. HORTON   [p409]

JOSEPH W. HORTON of JOSIAH HORTON
16 Nov. 1827   Bill of Sale
I have sold to Joseph W. Horton four negro slaves: a negro woman of
yellow complexion named Dolly, about twenty five years old and her
three children; Aggy, about five years old, Jim, about three years old,
and Amanda, about eight months old. 25 May 1827   J. HORTON
Test:H. W. HORTON, Josiah C. HORTON   [p409]

EARTHMAN & HOOPER of LINDSLEY TINSLEY
16 Nov. 1827   Deed of Trust
Tinsley is indebted to C. Y. Hooper and to secure the debt deeds to
Lewis Earthman and C. Y. Hooper a negro girl slave, Mariah, about
eighteen years old. Hooper is to have possession until debt is paid. 23

Aug. 1827   Lindsley TINSLEY   C. Y. HOOPER   Lewis EARTHMAN
Test: Henry EWING, Nathan EWING   [p410]

THOMPSON & MARTIN of JOHN G. NEELY
16 Nov. 1827   Mortgage Deed
I, John G. Neely, of Wilson County, TN, have sold to William Thompson and John H. Martin three negroes; Chaney, a woman about twenty or twenty one years old, and her two children, Julia, a girl about six or seven, and Jackson, a boy about one year old. I am indebted to Ephraim D. MOORE, Charles M. HALL, John C. HALL, Lindsey C. HALL ... contest on my part in relation to the validity of the will of Charles C. HALL, deceased. They also hold a note on Betsey or Elizabeth SHROPSHIRE, to which I am security. If I pay notes when they come due, this deed to be void.
16 Jan. 1827   JOHN G. NEELY
Test: I. M. MARTIN, Thos. L. DOUGLASS, Jos. W. HORTON
[p411]

POLLY McCAIN & others of ISAAC JOHNSON
16 Nov. 1827   Deed of Gift
I, Isaac Johnson, have in time past given my son-in-law John McCain and my Daughter, Betsey McCain, one hundred and twenty acres of land, one mare, saddle & bridle, one Bed & furniture and other valuable property and John McCain, having disposed of the same and his family likely to want and I, for the love and respect I have for ten of my Grandchildren, herein named, give the following property for their maintainance & support: 1st I give to my granddaughter Polly McCain one feather bed and furniture and ten barrels of corn. 2nd I give to my grandson, John McCain, the first colt Roberts sorrel mare brings, one mans saddle and ten barrels of corn. 3rd I give to my grandson, Charles McCain, one cow & calf, ten head of hogs & ten barrels of corn and the first colt that a certain Gray mare brings (which Gray mare I intend to give to my Grandson, Isaac McCain). 4th I give to my Granddaughter, Matilda McCain, one cow & calf, and ten barrels of corn. 5th I give to my grandson William McCain, one cow & calf, one Bay colt and ten head of hogs and ten barrels of corn. 6th I give to my grandson, Robert McCain, one cow & one yoke of oxen, one sorrel mare, ten head of hogs and ten barrels of corn. 7th I give to my granddaughter, Selah Emeline McCain, one Bed & furniture, one cupboard & furniture, four chairs, one skillet and ten barrels of corn. 8th I give to my granddaughter, Almira McCain, one bed & furniture, one side saddle, four chairs, one dutch oven, one loom and gear and

ten barrels of corn. 9th I give to my grandson, Isaac McCain, one Gray mare, one cow & calf, ten head of hogs, ten barrels of corn. 10th I give to my Granddaughter, Marget McCain, one Bed & furniture, one fall leaf table, one trunk, one looking glass, two chairs, one pot & hooks and ten barrels of corn. All of the above was sold as said John McCains property, for which I have bought, and have given for the maintaining and schooling of said ten children, under the care of their uncles, Robert McCain & Thomas JOHNSON as guardians. 22 Oct. 1827   ISAAC (X) JOHNSON
Test: Saml EWING, B. GRAY   [pp412/413]

JOEL PARISH of ANDREW HAYS
22 Nov. 1827   Deed
Whereas on 27 Dec. 1825 Andrew Hays executed a Deed of Trust to Joel Parrish of certain slaves for the purpose of securing James C. Hays, George W. GIBBS, & Thomas CLAIBORNE on a certain note and since that time they authorized Joel Parrish to transfer said deed of Trust to Wm DICKINSON ...this instrument is to be made a part of said Deed of Trust. 12 Oct. 1827   ANDREW HAYS
Test: Thomas H. CRUTCHER, Benjamin M. HINCHMAN, N. B. PRYOR Jno. NICHOL   [pp413/414]

REUBIN P. GRAHAM of JOSEPH S. LOVING
22 Nov. 1827   Deed of Trust
I, Joseph S. Loving, am indebted to Reubin P. Graham and to secure the said debt have confirmed unto Graham a negro boy slave by the name of Thomas, aged about eighteen years. The possession of said boy is to remain in said Graham, and I have delivered the said boy to him. 18 Oct. 1827 Jos. S. LOVING [p414]

JOSEPH PIERCE of ELIZABETH PIERCE
22 Nov. 1827   Bill of Sale
I, Elizabeth Pierce, have sold and delivered the following negroes to Joseph Pierce: Nanny, Jack, Moses, Jim, Lewis, Alley, Rilly, Laris, Milly, Matilda, Artimecy, David, Marina, Ned, Jefferson, Jim, Moses, Westley, Jack, Evaline & Malvina.
29 July 1826   ELIZABETH (X) PIERCE
Test: William R. WARREN, Micajah RACKBY   [p415]

DICKINSON & SHREWSBERRY of A. & J. B. HAYS
23 Nov. 1827   Deed of Trust
This Indenture between Andrew Hays, of Davidson County, John B. Hays, of Maury County, of the one part and William Dickinson & Joel

Shrewsberry, trading under the firm of *Dickinson & Shrewsberry* of the other part. A Deed of Trust was executed on 2 April 1825 by Andrew Hays and John B. Hays together with James C. Hays, who is now dead, and whose only heirs and distributees are the said Andrew Hays and John B. Hays, which deed of trust was executed to Francis B. FOGG & Ephraim H. FOSTER, for the benefit of Dickinson & Shrewsberry in consideration of delivery of a certain quantity of salt. 12 Oct. 1827   ANDREW HAYS   JOHN B. HAYS, by his attorney in fact, Thos. WASHINGTON
Test: Thomas H. CRUTCHER, Benjm M. HINCHMAN, N. B. PRYOR, Jno. NICHOL   [pp415/416]

BENAJAH GRAY of THOMAS BOAZ
7 Dec. 1827   Deed of Trust
I, Thomas Boaz, in consideration of one dollar and for the further consideration of the natural love and affection I have for my wife, Frances Boaz, give to Benajah Gray, the following negro slaves, which slaves I received by my present wife: Violet, Gilbert, Sinah, Dafney, Elvey & Benjamin. In trust - for the use and benefit of Frances Boaz and myself during our joint lives ... I am, during my natural live, to retain possession of said slaves. The increase of said slaves during our joint life to be the absolute property of me and my heirs.
5 Nov.1827   THOMAS BOAZ   [pp416/417]

THOMAS BRANDON, Admr of JAMES LANG
7 Dec. 1827   Deed of Mortgage
James Lang conveys to Thomas Brandon, adm. of the estate of James COCKRAN, dec'd, of Huntsville, Ala. the following property: three featherbeds, pair of blankets, pair of sheets, one sideboard, three Bedsteads, three tables, all the chinaware, one candlestand, one washstand, twelve chairs,   spoons of silver, one Looking glass, one rag carpet, sundry miscellaaneous books to secure judgments obtained in the County Court of Madison County, Ala, July Term 1822 by John McKINLEY. 21 Nov. 1827   JAMES LONG   [pp417/418]

LEVEN BROWNING of CALDWELL & SMITH
30 Dec. 1827   Bill of Sale
I have this day sold to L. Browning a negro slave named Maria, about eighteen years old. 2 Jan. 1827   P[HEBE] CALDWELL
Test: Hugh ELLIOT, Wm ARNOT, Saml A. HOLMES
- I do also relinquishs to Levin Browning all my right to above mentioned slave, Maria. 2 Jan. 1827 Jno. H. SMITH
Test: Wm ARROTT, Sam'l A. HOLMES   [p419]

JAMES DAVIDSON of JOHN H. MARTIN
31 Dec. 1827   Bill of Sale
I have sold to James Davidson a negro woman slave named Amey,
about forty years old. 13 Dec. 1827 J. H. MARTIN   [p419]

JOHN C. McLEMORE of JAMES P. PETERS
16 Jan. 1828   Bill of Sale
Whereas in 1825 James P. Peters purchased in North Carolina and
Tennessee the following described negro slaves: Rose and her child,
Job, Dorcas, Milley, Merrick, Jessee, Phoebe, Burwell, Ned, Aron,
Brittain, Peter, Fagan, Abram, Sarah and her three girl children,
Charlotte and her children, five or six boys & girls, Tempey, Tilda,
Tom, Gloster & Lucy. The above, with their increase, are rightfully
the property of James P. Peters and John C. McLemore equally ... said
Peters having made the purchase of said negroes for and on account of
McLemore & Peters, but the Bills of sale were taken in the name of
Peters ... I transfer and vest in McLemore one equal half of all the
before named negroes and their increase .. all now in the possession of
McLemore and Peters at their Pidgeon Roost plantation in Carroll
County, TN except Abram, Gloster, Temper & her child, now in
possession of Peters at his plantation in Maury county.
28 July 1827 JAMES P. PETERS
Test: Tho. B. EASTLAND, Jos. SHAW   [p420]

GEORGE HAIL of ROBERT S. HEATON
16 Jan. 1828   Bill of Sale
I, Robert S. Heaton, have swapt to George Hale one negro woman
and child named Priss & Ellick, aged about eighteen years for a negro
woman named Mourning plus eighty five dollars.
12 July 1827 ROBERT S. HEATON
Test: Jas. LOVELL   [pp420/421]

JAMES TILFORD of ELIZABETH McCAUN
16 Jan. 1828   Power of Attorney
I, Elizabeth MacCAUN, hath this day appointed James Tilford my
lawful attorney in fact, to lease lots in the Town of Nashville and to
purchase timber, materials, etc, employ workmen, build houses. I
further authorise him to settle with Lawrence McGUIRE and receive
from him sundry negroes sold me in the state of KY...authorize him to
receive the balance due me in the state of Kentucky on account of my
Interest in my late fathers estate in KY.
21 June 1827 ELIZABETH (X) MACCAUN

Test: Alex. GRAY, Thomas PATTISON   [p421]

CHARLES COOPER of GEORGE W. GIBBS
30 Jan. 1828   Bill of Sale
I hereby sell to Charles Cooper a mulatto boy named Ned, sixteen
years of age. 12 March 1825   G. W.GIBBS   [p422]

PHILIP LINDSLEY of PETER P. SCALES
15 Feb. 1828   Bill of Sale
I have sold to Philip Lindsley a negro man named Dick, about forty
five years of age, of dark complexion.
28 Nov. 1827   PETER P. SCALES
Test: Andrew HAYS, Nathan EWING   [p422]

FELIX GRUNDY of RAMSAY S. MAYSON
15 Feb. 1828   Bill of Sale
I, Ramsay S. Mayson, of Sumner County, TN, in consideration of
notes held by Felix Grundy on me, have delivered up the following
negroes: a negro woman, Eliza, which I received from Grundy, about
twenty four years old, also her three children named Henry, Margaret
and Cynthia, also my interest in the unsold part of South Gallatin.
15 Jan. 1828 RAMSAY S. MAYSON
Test: Nathan EWING, Henry EWING   [p423]

JOSEPH L. EWING of WILLIAM W. RICE
15 Feb. 1828   Bill of Sale
I, William W. Rice, of the county of Muhlenberg, KY, have this day
sold to Joseph L. Ewing a negro boy slave, Charley, thirteen years of
age. 13 Oct. 1827 WM W. RICE
Test: James McGAVOCK, Lysander McGAVOCK [pp423/424]

JOHN WATERS of EDWARD C. WATSON
15 Feb. 1828   Bill of Sale
I, Edward C. Watson, have sold to John Waters a negro boy named
Arthur, between 11 & 12 years old. 31 Dec. 1827
              EDWARD C. WATSON
Test: John MARSHALL, Jacob WILLIAMS [p424]

JOHN J. HINTON of HENRY STRANGE
15 Feb. 1828   Bill of Sale

I have sold to John J. Hinton a negro woman and her two children. Milley is about twenty two years, Austin about three years old and Mary about 18 months old.
22 Jan. 1828   HENRY STRANGE   [pp424/425]

SAMUEL FORSYTHE of P. W. CAMPBELL
15 Feb. 1828   Bill of Sale
I have sold to Samuel Forsythe a negro woman named Tracy, about twenty five years of age. 25 Jan. 1828   P. W. CAMPBELL
Test: W. H. McLAUGHLIN   [p425]

JOHN HOBSON of JOHN RICE
15 Feb. 1828   Bill of Sale
I have sold to John Hobson a negro boy named Frank, about twelve years old. 7 June 1827   JOHN RICE
Test: Dyes PEARL, Francis CAMPBELL   [p425]

JAMES STEPHENSON of GRANVILLE S. PEARCE
15 Feb. 1828   Bill of Sale
I have sold James Stephenson a negro boy named Solomon, aged eleven years. 25 Jan. 1828   GRANVILLE S. PEARCE
Test: R. H. BARRY, Seymour PLUMMER   [p426]

RICHARD H. BARRY of JOHN E. FENN
15 Feb. 1828   Bill of Sale
I have sold to Richard H. Barry a negro woman named Lucinda, twenty two years old. 1 Nov. 1827   J. E. FENN
Test: Seymour PLUMMER, Collin S. HOBBS   [p426]

JAMES COOPER of JOHN BILLINGS
16 Feb. 1828   Bill of Sale
I, John Billings of the state of KY, have sold James Cooper one negro man named Isaac. 30 July 1827   JOHN BILLINGS
Test: Galvin MALONE, William BUMPASS [p427]

ELISHA CRUTCHFIELD of BENJAMIN BUGG & wife
15 Feb. 1828   Bill of Sale
I, Benjamin Bugg and Nancy Bugg, my wife, have sold Elisha Crutchfield a negro woman named Chaney about twenty four years old. 17 Jan. 1828 BENJAMIN BUGG NANCY BUGG
Test: Thos. BUCHANON, Charles H. WALDEN   [p427]

BENJAMIN COX of WILLIAM TAYLOR
15 Feb. 1828   Bill of Sale
I, William Taylor, have sold Benjamin Cox one negro woman named
Mariah, thirty years old; Kirsey age twenty five; Reuben, seven years
old; Simon, age five years; Albeon, three years; Peter, one year old.
25 Aug. 1827   WM TAYLOR
Test: Thomas COX, Joel R. TAYLOR, Eldridge COX, John B.
CARRINGTON   [p428]

BENJAMIN COX of WILLIAM TAYLOR
15 Feb. 1828   Bill of Sale
I have sold Benjamin Cox one Sorrel horse, one Bay mare, one Sorrel
mare, one Bay colt, four cows & calves, eight yearlings, fifty head of
hogs, two ploughs and swingletrees & haims & stretcher, one
cupboard & furniture, one sugar chest, one desk, one crib, two chests,
one candlestand, three beds & furniture, seven chairs, two smoothing
irons, five water vessels, kitchen furniture, eighty barrels of corn and
four stacks of fodder, two thousand weight of seed cotton, thirty head
of geese, two saddles (mans & womans) & bridles, one loom, three
sleighs & harness, four weeding hoes, Tongues & shovel.
24 Nov. 1827   WM TAYLOR
Wit: William COX, Eldridge COX, John B. CARRINGTON
[pp428/429]

JAMES P. CLARK of THOMAS JAMES' Exrs
15 Feb. 1828   Bill of Sale
We, Elizabeth James, Extx, & Thomas G. James, Exr., of the Last Will
of Thomas James, dec'd, have sold to James P. Clark a negro man
named Harry, about thirty years old, to pay debt recovered by Mary
HYDE, adm'st in the Circuit Court of Davidson County. 21 Jan. 1828
ELIZABETH JAMES THO. G. JAMES   [p429]

MARTHA NORVELL of LIPSCOMB NORVELL
15 Feb. 1828   Bill of Sale
I, Lipscomb Norvell, in consideration of the natural love I have for my
daughter, Martha Norvell, assign to her a negro woman, named Fanny,
about 26 years old and her three children; Bob, about eleven years old,
Wilson, about 6 years old & Mary Jane, between three & four. 20 Dec.
1827 LIPSCOMB NORVELL
Wit: Nathan EWING, Edwin H. EWING   [p430]

JOHN SHELBY of ISAAC EARTHMAN, Constable
15 Feb. 1828   Bill of Sale

William PORTER recovered a judgment against Jolly PARRISH before William LYTLE, Esq. on 19 July 1827; Jno. R. DABBS recovered a judgment against said Jolly on 11 Dec. 1827 before Samuel McMANUS, Esq.; Jesse PARRISH recovered a judgment against Jolly before McManus on 13 Dec. 1827... Executions were issued and levied upon a negro woman named Jsaas? as the property of Jolly Parrish by Isaac Earthman, constable and purchased at public sale by John Shelby by his attorney in fact, Washington BARROW.
29 Dec. 1827   I. EARTHMAN, constable
Wit: David BARROW, Lewis EARTHMAN [pp430/431]

JOHN WATERS of JOHN R. DABBS, Constable
15 Feb. 1828   Bill of Sale
Alexander PORTER recovered a judgment against Charles M. HALL and was executed by John R. Dabbs, constable, and levied on a negro man named Flanders, of black colour, about forty years of age, as the property of Hall, and Dr. John Waters was last and best bidder at public sale. 12 Oct. 1826   J. W. HORTON, shff, by JNO. R. DABBS [pp431/432]

BURNELL, SHELTON & KEEBLE of THOMAS BURNELL
15 Feb. 1828   Deed of Trust
Jeremiah Burnell, Godfred Shelton & Walter Keeble have become security for Thomas Burnell for debt to Joseph DERECHSON. I convey the following property to them to be sold if debt is not paid: three feather beds & furniture, one bureau, two tables, one loom, one sugar chest, sugar canister, one looking glass, one set cupboard furniture, two smoothing irons, one trunk, two pairs of ploughing gear, three ploughs, three axes, one grubbing hoe, three weeding hoes, one mans saddle, one bay filly, one sorrel horse, two cows & calves, two head of hogs, six hundred lbs bacon, one hand saw, one draw knife, two augers, ten geese. 9 Jan. 1828   THOS. BURNELL
Test: E. ENSLEY   [pp432/433]

THOMAS SMITH of THOMAS VAUGHN
15 Feb. 1828   Deed of Trust
Thomas Vaughn is indebted to David ABERNATHY and to secure the loan assignes the following property to Thomas Smith: a negro boy slave named Lewis, about fifteen years old; a black horse, a sorrel horse, twelve head of cattle. If debt is paid this deed to be void.
3 Jan. 1828   THOMAS VAUGHN
Test: Freeman ABENATHY, Logan DRAKE [pp433/434]

CHRISTOPHER BROOKS of WILLIAN T. BROOKS
15 Feb. 1828   Mortgage Deed
I sell to Christopher Brooks the following property: one copper still &
heater, twenty tubs, one mare & colt, 10 head of cattle, forty head of
hogs, three beds, bedsteads & furniture, one cupboard & furniture, one
clock, one looking glass, two tables, 1/2 dozen windsor chairs, one
common chair, all other furniture & kitchen furniture, three ploughs,
two weeding hoes, one mattock, four axes, 25 geese, five barrels of
brandy, one barrel of whiskey, one stack fodder, 40 barrels of corn
two bee hives, two fishing gigs & canoe, one mans & one womans
saddle, bridles, etc., one apple mill, the hire of one negro man, George,
for one year. In trust to secure debts, note to *Crutcher, Wood & Co.*,
& bond as Constable.4 Jan. 1828   WM T. BROOKS
Test: Nathan EWING, Henry EWING [pp434/435]

TRABUE and LA FRENCY CHANOIN
21 March 1828   Deed of Trust
Joseph WOODS & Robert WOODS convey the following property to
Joseph La Frency CHAUVIN, of St. Louis County, Missouri, and
Charles C. TRABUE, of Ralls County, Missouri: 5 bed quilts, 8 table
cloths, 8 sheets, 6 blankets, 8 pillow cases, 4 pillows, 2 matrasses, 2
bolsters, 12 towels, 2 Bedsteads, 1 Bureau, 2 tables, 1 candlestand, 12
chairs, 2 carpets, 2 Tea Boards, 2 waters, 1 Bread Casket, 1 pr silver
plated candlesticks, pr Brass candlesticks, 2 pr Snuffers, 1 large
Looking glass, 1 small looking glass, 2 dozen plates, 6 dishes, 1/2
dozen cups & saucers, 1/2 dozen cupplates, 5 bowls, 1/2 dozen knives
& forks, 6 pitchers, 2 Teapots, 6 earthenwar Jars, 2 Glass jars, 1/2
dozen tumblers, 1 dozen wine glasses, 2 decanters, 1 pr Brass
andirons, 1 pr Cast Iron andirons, 2 sugar bowls, 1 pr salt sellars, 1/2
dozen tablespoons, 1/2 dozen teaspoons, 1 large soup spoon, 1 castor
stand, 5 tin pans, 3 tin buckets, 2 tin coffee pots, 1 large pot, 1 small
pot, 1 oven & lid, 2 skillets, 1 tea kettle, 1 pr waffle irons, 1 pr sad
irons, one wash tub, 2 pails, 2 falling axes, 1 spade, 3 trunks, 1 box
candles, 1 box soap, 1 Bag coffee, 1 Barrel sugar and any cattle that
we may purchase in the state of Missouri. To hold in Trust for the use
of Andrew WOODS and his family, and ultimately the benefit of the
children of Andrew, at present of Nashville, TN, but about to remove
to Missouri. 18 March 1828   JOS. WOODS   ROBERT WOODS
Test: Nathan EWING, Henry EWING [pp436/437]

ROBERT ELLIS of WILLIAM S. BURT
22 March 1828   Power of Attorney

I, William S. Burt, of Halifax County, N.C., appoint Robert Ellis, of Northampton, N.C., my Attorney, to sell such negroes as I have have in the state of Tennessee. 24 Jan. 1828   W. S. BURT
State of North Carolina - Halifax County - 24 Jan. 1828
...appeared before Elisha B. SMITH & James HOLLIDAY, acting Justices of the Peace.   Mark H. PETTEWAY, Clerk of the Court of Pleas & Quarter Pleas by S. M. JOHNSON [pp437/438]

JOHN STEWART of GEORGE R. ROYSTER
24 March 1828   Deed of Mortgage
I, George R. Royster, of Sumner County, TN, for notes to Reese & Franklin, Daniel SAFFARAN, James HOUSE, Thomas W. ROYSTER & The Bank of State of Tennessee, that John Steward is bound to pay for me convey to him the following property: one negro waman named Jane about twenty five or six years old; her son, Jerry, about five or six years old; her son Richard, about three or four years old; her youngest son, Patrick, about one year old. Also all my household & kitchen furniture. 30 June 1826   GEORGE R. ROYSTER
Test: F[ranklin] B. WILSON, J[ames] WOOD   Test: A. H. DOUGLAS, Clerk Sumner County, TN   [pp438/439]

WILLIAM TAYLOR of NATHAN SMITH
8 April 1828   Bill of Sale
I, Nathan Smith, of Limestone County, Ala., have sold William Taylor a negro man named Sam, black complexion, thirty years old.
19 July 1826   NATHAN SMITH
Test: Sala N. SHARP, Thos. L. ROBINSON
Test: Tho. HARDIMAN, clerk of Williamson County, TN   [p439]

JAMES PORTER of NATHANIEL A. McNAIRY
19 April 1828   Bill of Sale
Willie BARROW, in his lifetime, did on 27 Jan. 1821 convey to me in trust certain negroes and as trustee I did sell to James Porter one negro man named Peter, about thirty seven years of age, one negro boy, Egbert, about seventeen years of age, and one negro boy, Aaron, about twelve years of age. 15 March 1828 N. A. McNAIRY
Circuit Court of the U.S. for District of West Tennessee
Jno. CARRON, Dep. Clerk [pp439/440]

THOMAS L. WILLIAMS of JOSEPH WILLIAMS
14 May 1828   Deed of Trust

Joseph Williams, Sr., of Surry Co., N.C., conveys to Thomas L. Williams, of Knox County, TN, the following property: one negro woman named Claret, one boy named Thomas, one girl named Maria, one boy, Squire, & one girl, Rose; one piano Forte and all the goods & chattels now in the use & possession of John P. ERWIN, which were conveyed by the executor of Robert SEARCY, dec'd, to the said Joseph, by deed dated 6 Oct. 1821, together with all the goods and chattels now in the possession of John P. Erwin, which were conveyed by Robert PURDY, Marshall for West Tennessee, by deed dated 28 Nov. 1821, for the use and benefit of the joint heirs & children of John P. Erwin & his present wife, Frances L. Erwin. Joseph Williams, Sr. also transfers the following: note on Dr. TAIT, of Alabama; note of William M. BENNJHILL?, note of James CARTER, Wm BROFORD.
8 Nov. 1822   JO WILLIÁMS   [pp440/442]
Test: Alex. WILLIAMS, H. P. POINDEXTER, Nicholas L. WILLIAMS
Court of Pleas & Quarter Sessions - Surry Co., N.C. Nov. 1822
Deed of Trust proven -
Test: Jo Williams, C. C. by Jo Williams, Jun., Dep. C.
J. MATTHEW, M. HUGHES, Public Register
29 March 1828 - Surry Co., N.C. - I, Alvin S. DUVALL, a presiding magistrate ... certify Joseph Williams is the sworn & acting Clerk of the County Court of Surry, and that Joseph Williams, Jun., is the lawful & acting deputy.
31 May 1823 - I, Matthew BARROW, register for Davidson County, TN certify the foregoing Deed of Trust is registered in Deed Book P, pp128-131.   [pp442/443]

THOMAS F. HARDGRAVE & FRANCIS HARDGRAVE
23 May 1828   Bill of Sale
I, Francis Hardgrave give & convey to my grandson, Thomas Francis Hardgrave, one negro boy named Henry, about six years old.
1 May 1828   FRÁNCIS HARDGRÁVE
Test: Jno. DAVIS, Lewis JOSLIN, Wm RAMSEY, Jr.   [p444]

GEORGE W. CHARLTON of HENRY BURNELL'S Exrs
23 May 1828   Bill of Sale
I, Elizabeth SEAT, Executrix of Henry Burnell, dec'd, (will recorded 18 Nov. 1817) have this day sold a negro boy, Frank, 15 years old, to George W. Charlton, Esqr.
Test: Henry BURNELL, Pleasant M. MARKHAM, Joseph Burnell, Sr.28 May 1827   [p444]

HENRY HALL of WILLIAM HOWLETT
23 May 1828   Bill of Sale
I have transfered to Henry Hall the following property: one black
mare, one grey mare, one mule, one cart, one feather bed & furniture,
a parcel of Hogs, one cow, 4 ploughs, 6 chairs, 1 cupboard, a parcel of
kitchen furniture, hoes, axes, etc. that I bought at the sale of John
Halls property by virtue of executions in my favour. He has paid me
the amount of his debt. 31 Oct. 1827   WM HOWLETT
Test:Thomas HOPPER, Hance H. HOPPER [pp444/445]

JOHN HARMON of MICHAEL BROWN
23 May 1828   Bill of Sale
I have sold to John Harmon a negro man named Jack. 13 March 1828
MICHAEL (X) BROWN
Test: J. NORMAN, Wm. Y. RANDOLPH   [p445]

WILKINS TANNEHILL of JACOB V. D. STOUT
23 May 1828   Deed of Trust
I convey to W. Tannehill the following named negroes, Lots & notes: 1
lot on Cedar St. sold by Stephen CANTRELL, Exr. of Robert
SEARCY, dec'd to William A. COOK; two negroes named Fanny and
Bill, two notes drawn by S. V. D. Stout in favour of Jacob V. D.
Stout, note payable in the U. S. Bank of Discount & Deposit, passed
to John WILLIAMS. 28 March 1828   J. V. D. STOUT
Wit: Thos. CARRAWAY, A. L. DONOVAN   [pp445/447]

JOHN THOMPSON of OPIE DUNNEWAY
23 May 1828   Mortgage
I convey to John Thompson the following negro slaves: one negro
man named Armstead, about forty five years old; one negro man
named Leroy, about twenty seven years; a negro woman, Penny, about
twenty years; a boy named Thomas, about ten; a boy named Daniel
about eight; also all the stock of horses, cattle, hogs & sheep now in
the possession of Opie Dunneway and all his household & kitchen
furniture. Opie Dunneway is indepted , with John Thompson his
security, to the following: David McGAVOCK, Robert C. FOSTER,
Samuel WEAKLEY for the use of the heirs of William WHARTON,
dec'd. 3 May 1828   OPIE DUNNEWAY   [pp447/448]

MATTHEW BARROW of NICHOLAS PERKINS
23 May 1828   Deed of Trust
I convey to Nicholas Perkins the following property: one waggon, four
horses & gear. I purchased all the property from Thomas J. STUMP

with Henry PERKINS my security. If debt is paid, this deed to be void. 29 Dec.   NICHOLAS PERKINS
Test: E. P. MITCHELL, ANDERSON (X) TUCKER   [pp448/449]

JOHN SHUTE of FRANCIS OGDEN
23 May 1828   Deed of Trust
I, Francis Ogden, for debts to John Shute, Lew Shute, John A. Shute, I convey the following property to John Shute: 5 head horses, one waggon & 4 pair of gear, 2 ploughts, two oxen, one rifle gun, two cows, four beds, bedsteads & furniture, one Yankee clock, all now in my possession, and one hogshead of tobacco in Sumner County at Richart S. LESTERS, also all my household and kitchen furniture.
22 March 1828   FRANCIS OGDEN
Test: Philip SHUTE, Robt. JOHNSON   [pp449/450]

THOMAS SMITH of THOMAS VAUGHN
26 May 1828   Deed of Trust
Thomas Vaughn is indebted to David ABERNATHY & to secure debt does convey the following property to Thomas Smith In Trust - a negro boy, Lewis, about fifteen years old; a Black horse, a sorrel horse, twelve head of cattle, property previously conveyed to Thomas Smith in Trust, also one yoke of Oxen & Oxcart, three beds & furniture, 45 head of hogs, 7 head of sheep, fifty barrels of corn.
20 Feb. 1828   THOMAS VAUGHN
Test: Henry EWING, Nathan EWING [pp450/451]

SOLOMON CLARK of GEORGE WHITSON
26 May 1828   Deed of Trust
George Whitson has conveyed to Solomon Clark the following property upon consideration that Whitson is indebted to John SHUTE, Stephen CANTRELL, Lee SHUTE: two sorrel horses, two mens saddles, one womans saddle, two ploughs & gear, four feather beds, their furniture & bedsteads, two tables, twelve chairs, one clock, one rifle gun, two stone jugs, one Looking glass, seven head of cattle, twelve plates, one set cups & saucers, six Tumblers, two dishes, twelve knives & forks, and the corn & Oats on thirty acres of ground, a crop of potatoes and the hire of negro Charles, a boy hired for the present year from Lee Shute.
13 May 1828   GEO WHITSON   SOLOMON CLARK
Test: A. CUNNINGHAM, I. EARTHMAN, Jr. [pp451/453]

DAVID B. LOVE of JESSE R. FAULKNER
26 May 1828   Deed of Trust

I convey to David B. Love the following personal property: five negro slaves, Keziah and her three children, Richard, James, and a male infant at present unnamed, a mulattress called Tarrersa, together with every article of household and kitchen furniture now in the possession of Jesse R., also two cows and one sorrel horse. Jesse is indebted to his brother, William Faulkner, Esqr., and William also being security on note payable to Nelson PATTERSON. If debts are paid, this deed to be void. 29 April 1828   JESSE R. FAULKNER
D. B. LOVE   WM FAULKNER   [pp453/454]

SAMUEL V. D. STOUT of OLIVER HART
26 May 1828   Deed of Trust
Oliver Hart does convey to Samuel V. D. Stout the following personal property: five feather beds & bedding, one moss mattress, four low post bedsteads and bedsteads, one set of dining tables, one Jackson press, one clothes press, twelve windsor chairs, one Bureau, four small tables, eight split bottom chairs, two rag carpets, one copper Dyers kettle & sixteen feet of stove pipe, three kettles (two brass), eight pots and ovens, one Gridiron and one griddle, one churn, three tubs, four pails of cedar, two dozen plates, knives & forks, eleven silver teaspoons, three silver tablespoons, and one silver soup ladle, one and half dozen tea cups & saucers, two pitchers, three bowls and one tureen, two coffee pots and two teapots, one pair of brass & iron andirons, shovel & tongs, one pair of large hatters iron and three sad irons & one machine for dressing an winding ribbons, all in the possession of Oliver Hart.   Hart is indebted to Joseph WARD of Alabama. 26 April 1828   OLIVER HART
Test: John MORRIS, Thos. CARRAWAY   [pp454/455]

JOHN WALKER of THOMAS McCASLIN
26 May 1828   Deed of Trust
Thomas McCaslin does sell & deliver to John WALKER of Morgan County, Georgia the following negro slaves: Amy, a woman about thirty five years old; Silvey, a girl about nine years old; England, a boy about seven; Minty, a girl about three, John, a boy about nine months; Isaac, a mulatto boy about twenty seven. Upon Trust - Thomas McCaslan is desirous [out of her own property] to provide a safe, secure & comfortable support for Mrs. Ann GOWDY, wife of Thomas GOWDY, and daughter of said Thomas. John Walker is to hold the slaves and their future increase for the benefit of Ann Gowdey and is to permit her to have the possession, labour and services of the above named slaves but at her death John Walker is to convey the slaves and

their increase unto the heirs of the body of Ann Gowdey.1 Feb. 1828
THOS. McCARTAN
Nathan EWING, Clerk of Court of Pleas & Quarter Sessions
Will WILLIAMS, Presiding Magistrate of the Court of Pleas &
Quarter Sessions   [pp456/457]

THOMAS T. SHAW of PILMORE CROSSWY
27 May 1828   Bill of Sale
I have sold and delivered to Thomas T. Shaw a negro man named
John. 8 Feb. 1828   PILMORE CROSSWY
Test: Timothy DEMONBREUN   [p457]

SAMUEL EDMONDSON of WILLIAM P. WALLACE
27 May 1828   Bill of Sale
I, William P. Wallace, have sold to Samuel Edmondson a negro
woman named Loucy, about thirty or thirty five years old.
28 Feb. 1828 WILLIAM P. WALLACE
Test: Eroslus COXE, Sterling DAVIS   [p458]

SAMUEL EDMONDSON of WILLIAM P. WALLACE
27 May 1828   Deed of Trust
I, William P. Wallace, in consideration of the natural love and affection
I have for my infant son, William Houston Wallace, grant to him my
two negro girl slaves, Kissy, about five years old, and Maria, about
nineteen months. I shall permit Samuel Edmondson the use and benefit
until the said W. H. Wallace shall arrive at the age of twenty one years.
12 April 1828   WILLIAM P. WALLACE
Test: B. W. SMART, Jas. CONDON [pp458/459]

SILVESTER PEARL of WILLIAM L. WARD
3 June 1828   Bill of Sale
I, William L. Ward, have sold to Silvester Pearl a negro boy named
Chapman, about seven or eight years old.
18 June 1827   W. L. WARD
Test: Dyer PEARL   [p459]

DYER & SILVESTER PEARL of JAMES RUCKS
3 June 1828   Bill of Sale
I, James Rucks, have sold to Dyer & Sylvester Pearl a negro boy,
Willis, about 16 years old.12 Feb. 1828 J. RUCKS [pp459/460]

MICHAEL & BERNARD McANULTY of B. RICHMOND

7 June 1828   Bill of Sale
I have sold to Michael McAnulty and Bernard McAnulty a mulatto
boy slave named Jack, about thirteen years old.
19 May 1828 B. RICHMOND   [p460]

CHALONER & HENRY of ANTHONY LATAPIE

7 June 1828   Deed of Mortgage
To secure his note to *Chaloner and Henry* of Philadelphia, Anthony
Latapie does sell the following negro slaves; one negro man named
Stephen, about 30 years of age; one negro man named Baden, about
20 years of age; one negro girl named Mary, about 18 years old. If the
note is paid, this deed becomes void. 27 Nov. 1827   A. LATAPIE
Test: Henry BEEKMAN, G. M. FOGG   [p461]

JOSEPH COOK of FRANKLIN SAUNDERS

5 July 1828   Bill of Sale
I, Franklin Saunders, have sold to Joseph Cook all the interest I am
entitled to as a devisee of my father, William Saunders, dec'd, estate or
all the interest I am entitled to after the death of my mother, who has a
life estate in said estate. 11 August 1827 FRANKLIN SAUNDERS
Test: Tho. H. FLETCHER, Will A. COOK   [p462]

JAMES P. CLARK of LEWIS JOSLIN

13 Aug. 1828   Bill of Sale
I have sold to James P. Clark a negro woman, named Farra, about
twenty three years old. 16 Feb. 1828   LEWIS JOSLIN
Test: I. J. ANTHONY, Geo. S. YERGER   [p462]

JAMES C. CROSSWY of JOHN H. CROSSWY

13 Aug. 1828   Bill of Sale
I have sold to James C. Crosswy one negro girl, Caty, about thirteen
years old. 21 July 1828 JOHN H. CROSSNY
Test: Thos. P. YEATES, Jesse GLASGOW [p463]

JOHN A. CHEATHAM of SHADRACH F. ELLIN

13 Aug. 1828   Bill of Sale
I, Shadrach F. Ellin, of Carroll County, TN, have sold to J. A.
Cheatham a negro woman named Clarissa.
22 July 1828   S. F. ELLIN   [p463]

JOHN NICHOL of EDWARD S. BARKER
13 Aug. 1828   Bill of Sale
I, Edward S. Barker, of Clarksville, Montgomery County, TN, have
sold to John Nichol a negro girl slave named Patsey, about twenty
years of age. 6 March 1828 EDWARD S. BARKER
Test: Thos. WASHINGTON   [p464]

JOHN NICHOL of LEONARD DUNNWANT
13 Aug. 1828   Bill of Sale
I, Leonard DUNAVENT, of Williamson County, TN, have sold to
John Nichol a negro boy named Andy, dark complexion, about
fourteen years old. 23 July 1828 LEONARD DUNAVENT
Test: Saml. EWING   [p464]

SALLY WALLER of JOEL WALLER
13 Aug. 1828   Bill of Sale
In consideration of the love and affection I bear to my daughter, Sally
Waller, I convey to her a negro girl slave named Leah, about eight or
nine years old.21 July 1828   JOEL WALLER   [p465]

ROBERT WEAKLEY of WILKINS TANNEHILL
13 Aug. 1828   Bill of Sale
By virtue of a Deed of Trust executed by Jacob V.D. Stout on 28
March 1828, to secure debts, [Book P, pp445/446] I, Wilkins
Tannehill have this day offered at public sale a mulatto boy named Bill
and Robert Weakley became the purchaser.15 July 1828
W. TANNEHILL, Trustee
Wit: Edmond LANEAR, Matthew PORTER   [p465]

REUBEN PAYNE of THOMAS GLEAVES
13 Aug. 1828   Bill of Sale
I, Thomas Gleaves, have sold to Reuben Payne a negro boy by the
name of Austin, about five or six years old. 15 Jan. 1828   THOS.
GLEAVES
Test: James CAIN, Wm PAYNE   [p466]

REUBEN PAYNE of THOMAS GLEAVES
13 Aug. 1828   Bill of Sale
I have sold to Reuben Payne a negro man slave by the name of Alex,
about 24 years old. 1827   THOS. GLEAVES, Jr.
Test: M. B. FRAZER, A. R. CARWRIGHT [p466]

REUBEN PAYNE of THOMAS GLEAVES
13 Aug. 1828   Bill of Sale
I have sold to Reuben Payne the following described negroes: Fanny,
about twenty eight years of age; Eliza, about six; John, about four;
Parker, about two and a half years and Hagar, about one year old. I
warrant all to be sound, healthy and sensible except Hagar who
appears puny and not healthy.
18 July 1828   THOMAS GLEAVES, JR.
Test: Wm P. BRYN, Jno. B. HALL   [p467]

JOSEPH S. LOVING of REUBEN P. GRAHAM
13 Aug. 1828   Release of Mortgage
I have this day relinquised to Joseph S. Loving all right to a negro boy,
Thomas, who has been mortgaged to me.
13 July 1828   REUBEN P. GRAHAM
Test: S. B. MARSHALL   [p467]

HENRY R. CARTMILL of JOHN M. ROBERTSON
13 Aug. 1828   Deed of Trust
John McNairy Robertson is justly indebted to William WATKINS and
to secure the debt does transfer to Henry R. Cartmill the following
negro slaves: Abram, a man about twenty eight years; Henderson, a
boy about eighteen years; Moses, about seventeen years; Julia, a girl
about fourteen; Caty, a girl about twelve years and Bill, a boy about
eleven years.   1 July 1828   JOHN M. ROBERTSON
Test: Edmond LANEAR, Leven BROWNING [pp468/469]

WILKINS TANNEHILL of JAMES EDMONDSON
13 Aug. 1828   Deed of Trust
James Edmondson has executed notes payable to Boyd McNAIRY of
the Bank of the United States at Nashville and to secure the notes does
convey to Wilkins Tannehill- IN Trust - the following negro slaves: a
woman named Caty and her two children, Paulina & Prince; a woman
named Rose and her child, Patsey; a negro woman named Milley and a
negro woman named Sukey.16 June 1828   JS EDMONDSON
Test: Duncan ROBERTSON, L. H. TANNEHILL   [pp469/470]

WILLIAM WILKINSON of DANIEL DUNNEVANT
13 Aug. 1828   Deed of Trust
I hereby transfer to William Wilkinson a negro man named Anthony,
about twenty three years old.   I am justly indebted to Jesse J.
EVERETT by note payable 1 Jan. 1829. If debt is paid this deed to be
void. 5 Jan. 1828   DANIEL DUNAVENT

Test: J. EARTHMAN, Jr., Daniel BRIM [pp470-472]

JABEZ OWEN of SAMUEL SHORT
20 Aug. 1828   Mortgage Deed
I have sold to Jabez Owen the following; one small bay mare and colt, one grey colt, one red cow and calf, one white cow and spotted calf, one Brindle cow & calf. If debt is paid this deed is void.
7 June 1828   SAMUEL SHORT
Test: Ira H. OWEN   [p472]

JOHN C. McLEMORE of JAMES MOORE
20 Aug. 1828   Bill of Sale
I, James Moore of Tipton County, TN, have sold to John C. McLemore three negro slaves; a mulatto woman named Dafney, about twenty two years and her two boy children, Franklin, a mulatto boy about four years of age and Sam, about two years of age and dark complexion. 17 July 1828   JAMES MOORE
Test: John MITCHEL   [p473]

JAMES WHITSETT of LEVI CARICO
20 Aug. 1828   Bill of Sale
I, Levi Carico of Spencer County, KY, have sold a negro girl named Frances, aged seventeen or eighteen, to James Whitsett.
24 Dec. 1827   LEVI CARICO
Test: William BROOKS, James M. WHITSETT   [p473]

BRAXTON LEE of M. V. GRANT
20 Aug. 1828   Bill of Sale
Received of Braxton Lee full payment for a negro boy named Moses, now in his fourteenth year. 5 Aug. 1827 M. V. GRANT
Test: R. WEAKLEY, W. A. WATTHALL   [p474]

HENRY EWING of ELIZABETH CROSTHWAIT
20 Aug. 1828   Bill of Sale
I, Elizabeth Crosthwair of Rutherford County, TN, have sold to Henry Ewing a negro woman named Sookey, dark complexion, aged about twenty three years and her children, William, a boy about seven years; Fanny, a girl about eighteen months and May Birneum, a boy about seven weeks. 21 June 1828 ELIZABETH CROSTHWAIT
Test: E. P. SHALL, Geo SHALL   [p474]

JAMES GRIZZARD of NICHOLAS GORDON
20 Aug. 1828   Deed of Trust

131

I have sold to James Grizzard the following property: one hundred and twenty four thousand sigars, fourteen Doz. Snuff in bottles, two hundred pounds Wose snuff, one Tobacco press and crow bar, one ten plate stove & pipe, one high post bedstead & bedding, two low post bedsteads & furniture, one tea table, one side board, one dozen red Windsor chairs, Also the hired time of two negro men, Albert & Reuben for the present year. In Trust - for judgment in favor of Solomon PAYNE, judgment in favor of *Robertson & Elliot*, judgment in favor of E. HUGHS, judgment in favor of T. DONLEY, judgment in favour of James MULHERRINS.
2 May 1828   N. GORDON   [p475]

BASS & SPENCE of CALEB GOODRICH
20 Aug. 1828   Mortgage Deed
Caleb Goodrich conveys the following property to Brent Spence and Peter Bass: one waggon and team of five horses, one yolk of oxen, two cows, two yearlings, three bedsteads, bedding & furniture, one cupboard, two tables, seven chairs and kitchen utensils, fifteen barrels of corn, fifteen hundred lbs of pork, twenty head of stock hogs. If debt and interest are paid, this deed to be void.
18 Dec. 1827   C. GOODRICH
Test: Simon O'REILLY, William M. YOUNG   [pp476/477]

THOMAS WALLACE of WALLACES & TURBEVILLE
10 Sept. 1828   Bill of Sale
We, Hartwell H. Wallace, Effy Wallace & Benjamin Turbeville have sold to Thomas Wallace a negro girl named Nancy, which I, H. Wallace & Effy, got as part of our legacy of Jesse Wallace, dec'd estate for and in consideration of Sarah, another negro girl which Thomas Wallace got as part of his legacy of said estate. 27 July 1826
HARTWELL H. WALLACE   EFFY WALLACE   BENJAMIN TURBEVILLE
Test: Humphrey GWYNN, Hugh LYNCH   [p477]

JOHN HAYWOOD of GEORGE HAYWOOD
11 Sept. 1828   Bill of Sale
I, George Haywood of Limestone County, Alabama, sell to John Haywood the land due to me by McLEMORE and assigned to me on 8 Jan. 1823 by John Haywood, also negroes, Jacob & Austin.
9 April 1825   G. H. HAYWOOD
Test: Chas CASSEDY, Thos HAYWOOD E. HAYWOOD JAMES (X) TAYLOR   [p478]

DAVID SAFFARANS of B. S. WELLER
6 Oct. 1828   Bill of Sale
I sell to David Saffarans the following for two notes due 24 Dec.
1827: one Jackson Press, one Bureau, two folding leaf tables, one
small table, one high post bedstead, one dozen windsor chairs, one
rocking chair, one large table, one trunk, one bed and clothing, one
cupboard, two dozen china plates, two dozen cups & saucers, one
stand of Castors, two small pitchers, one tea pot and sugar boll, two
large pitchers, one dozen tumblers, one half dozen large silver spoons,
one half dozen small silver spoons, two celery stands, two watches,
one pair of dog irons, one tea kettle, one large oven, one skillet, one
Gridiiron, two smoothing irons, two cut decanters, one half dozen
knives & forks, one cream jug. 28 Apr. 1828   B. S. WELLER
Test: Stephen HAIL, Thos. C. KING [pp478/479]

CHARLES PUGSLEY of ELIZABETH McCOWN
7 Oct. 1828   Bill of Sale
I, Elizabeth McCoun sell to Charles Pugsley a negro woman, aged
twenty three or twenty four and her son David, between five and six
years old. 5 July 1827   ELIZABETH (X) McCOUN
Test: Corry McCONNELL, A. G. GOODLET [p479]

ALEXANDER RAY of JAMES BIGGS
15 Nov. 1828   Bill of Sale
I have sold to Alexander Ray one spinning machine. 5 June 1828
JAMES BIGGS
Test: Robert LANEAR, Thos. McAFEE   [p480]

SARAH E. FAULKNER of EDWARD WOODWARD
15 Nov. 1828   Deed of Gift
Edward Woodward for and in consideration of the natural affection he
bears to Sarah Elizabeth Faulkner, daughter of James and Rebecca
Faulkner, gives and conveys to Sarah E. a negro female slave named
Zaday, aged nine or ten years.
27 Oct. 1828   EDWARD WOODWARD
Test: Benjamin W. BEDFORD, M. GLEAVES [pp480/481]

JOHN AUSTIN of GARNETT & MURRELL
15 Nov. 1828   Bill of Sale
I have sold to John Austin a negro girl, Sally, healthy and sound and
between the ages of 14 & 16.
23 Oct. 1828 M. GARNETT Wm MURREL   [p481]

PETER KNIGHT of ALLEN KNIGHT
15 Nov. 1828   Bill of Sale
I, Allen Knight, have sold Peter Knight two negro slaves: Molice, a
girl about sixteen years old; Albert, a boy about fifteen years old. 21
Oct. 1828 ALLEN KNIGHT [p481]

JOHN NICHOL of ARRINGTON & DAVIS
15 Nov. 1828   Bill of Sale
We, James H. Arrington and Benjamin Davis, both of Henry County,
TN, have sold to John Nichol a negro boy named Albert, about
nineteen years old. 11 Aug. 1828
        JAS. H. ARRINGTON   BENJ. DAVIS
Test: Saml EWING   [p482]

JOHN NICHOL of PHILIP SHUTE
15 Nov. 1828   Bill of Sale
I have sold John Nichol a negro girl of a dark complexion, about
eleven years old, named Rosetta. 11 Oct. 1828 PHILIP SHUTE
Test: A MAXWELL   [p482]

GREEN B. GREER of HENRY JEFFERSON
17 Nov. 1828   Mortgage Deed
I have conveyed to Green B. Greer certain property: two bay mares,
one bay colt, one sorrell, fifteen head of cattle and fifty head of hogs,
two beds and steads, a bureau cupboard, table and candlestand, chairs
and other household and kitchen furniture, 5 ploughs, 3 pair of gears -
to secure debt. If debt is paid, this deed to be void.
1 Apr. 1828   HENRY JEFFERSON
Test: James EZELL, Thomas JEFFERSON [p483]

MICHAEL&BERNARD McANULTY of DURHAM HAIL
17 Nov. 1828   Bill of Sale
I, Durham Hail of Simpson County, KY, have sold to Michael
McAnulty and Bernard McAnulty a negro boy slave named Cornelius,
about seventeen years old. 21 Aug. 1827 D. HAIL
Test: Henry EWING, Nathan EWING [pp483/484]

RICHARD H. BARRY of EGBERT HAYWOOD
17 Nov. 1828   Bill of Sale
I have sold R. H. Barry a negro woman named Mary, about twenty
four years old. 27 Oct. 1828   E. HAYWOOD
Test: Edw'd HALL, Leman HAIL   [p484]

WILLIAM H. MOORE of JESSE WHARTON
17 Nov. 1828   Bill of Sale
I have sold to William H. Moore a negro man slave named Abram,
about thirty three years of age. 17 June 1828   J. WHARTON
[pp484/485]

WILLIAM FAULKNER of WILLIAM R. WRIGHT
17 Nov. 1828   Bill of Sale
Sumner County, TN - I have sold to William Faulkner a negro girl by
the name of Rachel, about six years old.
10 May 1828   WM R. WRIGHT
Test: Jno. L. BUGG, James NICHOL, Peterfield JEFFERSON,
Edward SANDERSON   [p485]

SAMUEL MOLLOY of HENRY C. DICKINSON
17 Nov. 1828   Bill of Sale
I, Henry C. Dickinson, have sold to Samuel Mulloy, a free man of
colour, a negro woman slave named Kitty, about thirty three years of
age. 17 Nov. 1828   C. H. DICKINSON
Test: Henry EWING, Nathan EWING   [pp485/486]

DAVID & ROBERT JOHNSON of JOSIAH RICHARDS
17 Nov. 1828   Deed of Trust
I have sold to David and Robert Johnson of Williamson County, TN
all my household furniture, stock, farming tools etc: Three beds &
furniture, seven chairs, one table, one chest, two trunks, one bay mare
and her colt, one Roan mare, one bay horse, one dun horse, three red
cows, three white cows, four white young cattle, one red and one
black yearling, forty head of hogs, two ploughs, three hoes, three axes,
one mattock, one cane hoe, one hand axe ... to have possession of the
property from this date until Richards shall repay the debt with
interest.3 Nov. 1828 JOSIAH RICHARDS   [pp486/487]

ROBERT WEAKLEY of JOHN BARFIELD
17 Nov. 1828   Bill of Sale
I, John Barfield of Williamson County, TN, have sold Robert Weakley
the following negroes: a negro woman, Judy, thirty five years old; her
daughter, Winney, eight years old, last December; her son, Jack, six
years old the 12th of Oct. last. 31 Jan. 1828   JOHN BARFIELD
Test: James RIDLY, Edmond CHARLTON, S. GLENN   [p487]

ROBERT WEAKLEY of MASSINGILL and PORTER
17 Nov. 1828   Bill of Sale

We, William Massingill of Washington County, TN, and Alexander Porter, of the town of Nashville, TN, have sold to Robert Weakley three negroes: Rose, a girl fourteen years old; George, a boy twelve years old, 8 July next; Carey, a boy eight years old. 30 June 1828
WM MASSENGILL   ALEXR PORTER
Test: W. CAMPBELL, James J. GILL   [p488]

SHIVERS and SHAW of JAMES CUNNINGHAM
17 Nov. 1828   Mortgage Deed
I have sold to Jonas Shivers and William W. Shaw four head of horses, ten head of cattle, forty head of hogs, one cupboard, one Bureau, one Table, one chest, eight chairs, four feather beds and furniture, three ploughs, three hoes, three axes, one oven, two kettles, six water vessels. If debt is paid, this deed to be void. 12 June 1828
JAMES CUNNINGHAM
Test: Henry EWING, Nathan EWING   [pp488/489]

DAVID C. WATERS and JOHN C. HICKS Agreement
18 Nov. 1828   Mortgage Deed
John C. Hicks being indebted to David C. Waters and having no security agrees to assign to him all debts now due and owing to him for his professional services as a physician.
25 April 1828 JNO. C. HICKS   D. C. WATERS
Test: Orville EWING, Henry EWING, Nathan EWING [pp490/491]

JOHN C. HICKS of DAVID C. WATERS
18 Nov. 1828   Power of Attorney
I, David C. Waters, now moving, do appoint my friend Doct. John C. Hicks, my true and lawful attorney to receive all sums of money, accounts or debts that may become due by virtue of an article of agreement between John C. Hicks and myself bearing date the 25th April 1828.   D. C. WATERS
Test: Nathan EWING, Henry EWING [pp491/492]

GEORGE BURTON of WILLIAM C. ZACHERY
18 Nov. 1828   Deed of Trust
William C. Zachery is indebted to Greenberry GREER and to secure debt does sell unto Greer the following described property: all the interest in a negro woman named Polly, about 24 years old; Patience, her daughter, about 9 years old; Hannah, about 7 years; Jenny, about 5 years of age; and infant son of Polly; also one sorrel horse. William C. Zachery shall remain in possession of said property.
27 Aug. 1828   WILLIAM C. ZACHERY

Test: W. H. GREER, Will LYTLE   [pp493/494]

LEWIS EARTHMAN'S Admrs of ISAAC EARTHMAN, constable
18 Nov. 1828   Bill of Sale
The following writs were placed in the hands of Lewis Earthman,
constable for Davidson County, for collection:
Lewis Earthman against John L. YOUNG; Truman ABERNATHY
agst John L. Young; Daniel BRIM agst John L. Young; all issued by
James MARSHALL, Esquire, justice of the peace for Davidson
County. Execution of ANDERSON & KNOSE against John L.
Young; execution of Robert T. & James WALKER against John L.
Young; execution of David RALSTON against John L. Young;
execution of Samuel & John MARSHALL against Young; execution
of Iredale REDDING against Young; last six executions issued by
Buchanon LANEAR, Esq., a justice of the peace for Davidson
County. Execution of Henry HOLT against Young, by William
LYTLE, Esq., a justice of the peace for Davidson county. Execution
of Jesse J. EVERETT against Young, issued by Jonathan DRAKE,
Esq., justice of the peace for Davidson County. Execution of Nelson
JACKSON against Young & Lewis Earthman, issued by John
STUMP, Esq., justice of the peace for Davidson County. In execution
of the above writs Isaac Earthman levied on and took in execution the
following negro slaves: Sealey, a woman about twenty years of age,
her child, Jacob, about three or four years old; Armistead, a boy aged
fifteen. After being legally advertised Isaac Earthman offered the
above at public auction and Lewis Earthman, being best bidder for the
same on 29 Aug. 1825. Since the day of sale Lewis Earthman has
departed this life intestate and letters of administration have been
granted to John S. COX and Judah EARTHMAN and Isaac Earthman,
constable, conveys the same above named slaves to the administrators
for the use of said estate. 1 Nov. 1828 I. EARTHMAN, constable
Test: Nathan EWING   [pp493/495]

JOHN FITZGERALD of ANDREW HAMILTON
19 Nov. 1828   Deed of Trust
I, Andrew Hamilton, of Dickson County, TN, convey to John
Fitzgerald a mulatto woman named Amelia, about 25 years old, and
her infant son, James, about nine months. In Trust - Andrew is
indebted to John Fitzgerald and if debt is paid within twelve months
John is to reconvey the named slaves. John is to keep possession and
have the services until payment is made.
22 Oct. 1828   A. HAMILTON

Test: Jno OVERTON   [p496]

HENRY CRABB of SAMUEL K. BLYTHE
19 Nov. 1828   Bill of Sale
Blythe, living in Sumner County, has sold to Henry Crabb a negro man
slave named Solomon, aged twenty four years, he having worked two
years at the blacksmith business and being a good coarse blacksmith.
29 Aug. 1825   S. K. BLYTHE
Test: Wm COMPTON, John MITCHELL   [p497]

HENRY CRABB of WILLIAM B. CARTER
19 Nov. 1828   Bill of Sale
I, William B. Carter, of Carter County, TN, have sold to Henry Crabb
a negro boy about sixteen years old, named Martin, dark yellow
colour. 4 Oct. 1827   W. B. CARTER
Test: Jno BELL, Stephen CANTRELL   [p497]

HENRY CRABB of MATTHEW BARROW
19 Nov. 1828   Bill of Sale
I, Matthew Barrow, sell to Henry Crabb a negro woman named
Rachel, black colour, about 19 years of age, which James GORDON
delivered to Crabbs plantation in Louisiana last spring.
22 Oct. 1827   M. BARROW   [p498]

HENRY CRABB of HENRY EWING
19 Nov. 1828   Bill of Sale
I, Henry Ewing, have delivered to Henry Crabb a negro man named
Nelson, about twenty years of age, of black colour.
27 June 1827   HENRY EWING
Test: Nathan Ewing   [p498]

ELIZABETH BEASLEY of ANN BURTON
21 Nov. 1828   Deed of Gift
I, Ann Burton of Wilson County, TN, in consideration of the natural
love and affection I have to my daughter Elizabeth Beasley and her
offspring and also divers good reasons, Ann Burton hereunto moving,
grant and confirm unto the children of daughter, Elizabeth, as well as
those who may hereafter be born of her body, one negro woman
named Cloe and her increase.
6 Oct. 1828 at Nashville   ANN (X) BURTON
Test: Was. L. HANNUM, Rich'd HANKS, Joseph RUFF   [p499]

JOHN OVERTON of EGBERT HAYWOOD
21 Nov. 1828   Bill of Sale
I have this day sold to John Overton a negro man by the name of
Adam, aged twenty eight years.10 Nov. 1828   E. HAYWOOD
Test: R. H. BARRY, Lmn HAIL   [pp499/500]

SIMON BRADFORD of HUGH ROLAND
26 Nov. 1828   Mortgage Deed
Hugh Roland for the sum of ten thousand dollars does convey to
Simon Bradford a Steam Sawmill erected on a lot of ground leased by
Bradford & Roland of Nathaniel A. McNAIRY running two saws and
a Shingle machine attached to each. If debt is paid before 1 Jan. 1829
this conveyance to be void.16 June 1828   H. ROLAND
Test: Nathan EWING, Henry EWING   [pp500/501]

FRANCIS B. FOGG of GEORGE W. GIBBS
26 Nov. 1828   Bill of Sale
I have sold to Francis B. Fogg a negro woman, Minta, aged about
twenty five. 8 April 1828   G. W. GIBBS
Test: Jacob McGAVOCH   [p501]

JAMES FAULKNER of JESSE R. FAULKNER
27 Nov. 1828   Bill of Sale
I have sold to James Faulkner a female slave named Tarracy, aged
thirteen or fourteen years.
17 Nov. 1828 JESSE R. FAULKNER   [p501]

SIMON BRADFORD of KENDAL WEBB
27 Jan. 1829   Mortgage
I convey to Simon Bradford the following property: twenty new pair
of boots, thirty pairs of shoes, eight dozen calf skins, one set of lasts &
one set of trees and all other article now on hand or may purchase for
the purpose of the shoe and boot making business. Kendal Webb is
indebted to Bradford for money loaned to enable him to purchase
materials. If debt is paid this deed to be void.
26 Jan. 1829   KENDALL WEBB
Test: Henry EWING   [p502]

PHILIP HOOVER of WALTER WILLIS
12 Feb. 1829   Bill of Sale
Whereas I, Walter Willis, am entitled to one half of a negro girl slave
named Milley, aged about twenty two, in right of my wife, Catherine

L. Willis, upon the decease of her mother, Ann E. WILSON, have sold the interest I now have to Philip Hoover.
8 Jan. 1829   WALTER WILLIS
Test: H. A. WISE, Th. A. DUNCAN [p503]

JAMES EDMONDSON to WILKINS TANNEHILL
12 Feb. 1829   Deed of Trust
James Edmondson has rented a house from the Nashville Bank known by the name of the *City Hotel* and executed a note payable to Alexander PORTER and to secure said note sell to Wilkins Tannehill the following negroes: A negro woman named Caty and her children, Paulina & Prince; a negro woman named Rose and her child, Patsey; a negro woman naamed Milley; a negro woman named Sukey.
21 Jan. 1829   JAMES EDMONDSON
Test: John AUSTIN, Geo. BACKUS [pp503/504/505]

JAMES STEVENSON of ROLAND & GRIZZARD
12 Feb. 1829   Bill of Sale
I, Hugh Roland, have sold to James Stephenson a negro man named Sterling. 5 Jan. 1829   HUGH ROLAND
Test: Henry EWING, Nathan EWING
- I hereby release all claim to negro man Sterling by virtue of executions against Hugh Roland   J. W. HORTON, shff by his Deputy JAS GRIZZARD 12 Jan. 1829   [p505]

CORNELIUS WAGGONER of LEONARD P. CHEATHAM
12 Feb. 1829   Bill of Sale
I have this day sold to Cornelius Waggoner my two negro boys Charles & Sandy. 29 Jan. 1829   L. P. CHEATHAN
Wit: I. EARTHMAN, Jr.   [pp505/506]

JOHN L. BROWN of FRANCIS B. FOGG
12 Feb. 1829   Bill of Sale
I, Francis B. Fogg have sold a negro boy slave named John, which I purchased of Pleasant M. MILLER, to John Lucien Brown.
24 Jan. 1829   FRANCIS B. FOGG [p506]

JOHN SHELBY of PATRICK H. OVERTON
12 Feb. 1829   Bill of Sale
I have sold to John Shelby a negro man slave named Ireland, about thirty eight years old. 20 Jan. 1829   PATRICK H. OVERTON
Test: J. OVERTON, C. J. F. WHARTON   [pp506/507]

LABAN ABENATHY Senr and DAVID ABENATHY
12 Feb. 1829   Agreement & Loan
I, David Abenathy, in consideration of the filial regard and respect I
have for my father, Laban Abenathy, Senr., and to promote his ease,
confort and maintainance have loaned and delivered to him a negro
boy slave named Jupiter, to be used during his natural life and at his
death the said negro slave is to revert back to me. 21 Jan. 1829
DAVID ABENATHY
Test: Freeman ABENATHY, W. W. GARRETT   [p507]

ELLEN KIRKMAN of JOHN B. CARTER
12 Feb. 1829   Bill of Sale
I have this day sold to Mrs. Ellen Kirkman a negro man slave named
Richmond, about 25 years old. 24th   1829   JOHN B. CARTER
Test: R. P. SMITH   [p508]

SAMUEL V. D. STOUT of CARLES J. F. WHARTON
12 Feb. 1829   Bill of Sale
I, C. J. F. Wharton have sold to Samuel V. D. Stout one negro girl by
the name of Mayan. 20 Jan. 1829   C. J. F. WHARTON
Test: Saml M. PARRY   [p508]

JOSEPH T. ELLISTON of DAVID R. COLE
12 Feb. 1829   Deed of Trust
I, David R. Cole, being indebted to Joseph T. Elliston as Guardian for
John B. MULLIN convey to him all my household and kitchen
furniture together with my stock of hogs, about thirteen head; six head
of horses, nine head of cattle and all my farming utensils. Property
shall remain in my possession until due date.
1 Jan. 1829   DAVID R. COLE   [p509]

JAMES OVERTON of PATRICK H. OVERTON
12 Feb. 1829   Bill of Sale
I have this day sold to James Overton a negro woman named Dolly
and her two children, Nancy and Mary.
26 Jan. 1829   PATRICK H. OVERTON
Test: John SHELBY, C. J. F. WHARTON [pp509/510]

JOHN HALL of SHADRACH NYE
12 Feb. 1829   Bill of Sale
I, Shadrach Nye, have sold to John H. Hall one negro girl by the name
of Hester, about twenty three years old.
24 Jan. 1829   SHADRACH NYE   [p510]

ALLEN M. PERRY of GEORGE PERRY
13 Feb. 1829   Bill of Sale
I, George Perry, have given unto Allen M. Perry, a negro man by the
name of David and a negro man by the name of Peter and a negro girl
by the name of Melinda.
20 Jan. 1829 GEORGE PERRY   [p510]

JOHN NICHOL of WILLIAM MASSENGILL
13 Feb. 1829   Bill of Sale
I, William Massengill of Washington County, TN, have sold to John
Nichol a negro girl named Dicey, of yellow complexion, about twenty
years old. 6 Nov. 1828   Wm MASSENGILL
Test: Samuel EWING   [p511]

JAMES YARBOROUGH of GEORGE E. SANDERSON
13 Feb. 1829   Bill of Sale
I have sold to James Yarborough a negro girl named Vicey, agen ten
of twelve years. 27 Feb. 1827 GEO. E. SANDERSON
Test: S. SHANNON, W. WILKINSON, Jr. [p511]

WILLIAM RICHARDSON of RICHARD DABBS, dec'd Admrs.
13 Feb. 1829   Bill of Sale
We, Elizabeth Dabbs and John R. Dabbs, have sold to William
Richardson a negro man named Robin and his wife Aney and three
children named Mariah, Richard and Washington.
31 Dec. 1828   ELIZABETH DABBS   JOHN R. DABBS, Admrs
of Richard Dadds
Test: John WILLIS, T. E. HARRISON, I. K. BUCHANON [p512]

DANIEL B. JACKSON of GARDNER MAYS
13 Feb. 1829   Deed of Trust
I have conveyed to Daniel B. Jackson a negro woman Mariah and her
two children, Judah and Milley - also three feather beds, bedsteads and
furniture. In Trust - Mays is indebted to Jackson and if note is paid
with interest this conveyance to be void. 29 Jan. 1829
GARDNER MAYES   [pp512/513]

CATO, ALLEY & YEATS of ABEL ALLEY
13 Feb. 1829   Mortgage
Whereas Rolin Cato, Peter Alley, Abner ALLEN & William Yeats
have become my security for my appearance at the next Circuit Court

for Davidson County they are to have my title in the Lease as well as the crop now growing.23 Aug. 1828   ABEL ALLEY
Test: William CATO   [p513]

ALBERT G. EWING of ALEXANDER FOOTE
13 Feb. 1829   Bill of Sale
I, Alexander Foote of Prince William County, VA, sell to Albert G. Ewing a mulatto negro boy named Albert, about six years old.
29 Oct. 1828   ALEXR FOOTE
Test: Edmond RIEVES   [pp513/514]

ALBERT G. EWING of ELIAS S. BOWMAN
13 Feb. 1829   Bill of Sale
I, Elias S. Bowman, have sold Albert G. Ewing a negro man slave named Ellich or Alexander, aged twenty five years, of yellow complexion, stout made. 27 Nov. 1828   ELIAS S. BOWMAN
Test: Th. CLAIBORNE, Nathan EWING, Henry EWING   [p514]

ALBERT G. EWING of MASSINGILL & PORTER
13 Feb. 1829   Bill of Sale
We, William Massingell & Alexander Porter have sold Albert G. Ewing the following negroes: a boy named Simon, aged twelve years; a boy named Orphey, aged twelve years; a girl named Mary, aged thirteen years. 5 Nov. 1828   WM MASSINGILL ALXR PORTER, Surety
Test: Henry EWING, Nathan EWING   [p515]

ALBERT G. EWING of JOSEPH W. HORTON, Shff
13 Feb. 1829   Bill of Sale
July Session 1828 of the Court of Pleas & Quarter Sessions Alvah GUION recovered a judgment against M. WINBOURN & John PIRTLE. A Writ was issued and served by David B. LOVE, a deputy under Joseph W. HORTON, shff, executed on two negro slaves, property of the Defendants; Jack, a man about thirty years and Patsey, his wife, aged about thirty five years and they were exposed to sale on 17 Jan. 1829 with Albert G. Ewing being best bidder.
29 Jan. 1829 JOSEPH W. HORTON, Shff [pp515/516]

INDEX

---

* free black

144

BARROW
  Alexander, 5
  David, 44, 120
  M., 51, 64
  Matthew, 47, 50,
    51, 80, 89,
    106, 123, 124,
    138
  S., 91
  W., 15, 98
  Washington, 120
  Willie, 11, 15,
    122
BARRY
  R. H., 66, 72,
    110, 118, 139
  Richard H., 43,
    72, 118, 134
BASS
  Mr., 44
  Peter, 132
BASS & SPENCE,
  31, 58
BATES
  Robert, 90
BAXTER
  Robert, 73
BAYLOR
  Robert T., 48
  Robt. T., 48
BEARLEY
  John, 7
BEASLEY
  Elizabeth, 138
BEAZLEY
  John, 7
BEDFORD
  Benjamin W., 31,
    48, 53, 59, 74,
    79, 93, 133
  Edwin W., 43, 67
  W. H., 31, 53, 59,
    67, 93
BEEKMAN
  Henry, 128
BELL
  Alex, 98
  Alexander, 98

Hugh F., 65
Hugh T., 65
James, 13
Jno., 25, 111, 138
John, 46, 75
L., 54
Montgomery, 39
Samuel, 52, 53
Bell Tavern, 15
BENNETT
  Nathan, 8, 84, 87
BENNJHILL
  William M., 123
BENOIT
  Ernest, 21
BENSON
  J. C., 77
BERRYHILL
  W. W., 40
  William M., 34
  Wm. M., 73
BIBB
  Benjamin, 53
BIDWELL
  C., 102
  Charles, 16
BIGGS
  James, 133
BILLINGS
  John, 118
BINKLEY
  Frederick, 55
  William, 16
BIRDWELL
  Andrew, 56
  Isaac, 56, 83, 87
  Jane, 56
  Samuel, 56
BLACK
  Alexr., 52
  Samuel P., 97
BLACKBURN
  J. N., 66
BLACKFAN/BLAC
  KSPAN
  J., 5, 14
BLACKMAN

Hays, 13, 20, 23,
  27, 56
John, 53
BLACKSPAN
  Jesse, 4
BLAIR
  John, 24
  Samuel, 101
BLAND
  A., 42
  Arthur, 42
  Elizabeth J G W,
    42
  Elizabeth J. G.
    W., 42
  Len-d Mary Ann
    W, 42
  Mary O., 42
  Polly O., 42
BLUE
  Alexander, 64
BLYTHE
  S. H., 102
  Samuel K., 138
BOAZ
  Frances, 115
  Thomas, 115
BODWELL
  John A., 2
BOON
  Bryant, 36
BOOTH
  Samuel, 70
BOOTHE
  George C., 70
BORDEN
  Elisha, 43
BOSLEY
  Beal, 13, 77, 109
  Charles, 82, 85
  John, 57, 77, 82,
    85
BOWMAN
  Elias S., 108, 143
BOYD
  Arch., 18
  Archibald, 18
  Jno., 91

John, 67
Richard, 13
BRACKEN
John, 6
BRADFORD
Simon, 104, 139
T. G, 15
Thomas G., 15,
20, 38
BRADLEY
Thomas, 62
BRADSHAW
J. F., 97
Polly, 97
Tabitha W., 97
BRADY
R., 74
BRANDON
Thomas, 115
BRAUGHTON
John, 76
BRAY
William, 36
*Breedlow, Bradford
& Robinson*, 78
BRIDGES
Joseph J., 105
BRIM
Daniel, 48, 131,
137
BROFORD
Sm., 123
W., 34
BROOKS
Chas. M., 71
Christopher, 96,
121
Moses F., 100
William, 55, 89,
131
William T., 121
Wm, 37
Wm., 37
Wm. T., 121
BROWN
John, 109
John L., 140
Michael, 124

Robert L., 12
Thomas L., 83,
86
Thos., 102
BROWNING
Leven, 115, 130
BRUTON
James, 102
BRYAN
Hardy S., 36, 48,
102, 103, 109
Stephen, 39
BRYANT
Hardy S., 16
William, 58
Wm., 58
BRYN
Wm. P., 130
BUCHANON
Alexander, 54
I. K., 142
J. S., 66
James B., 100
John, 72, 100
Major John, 72
Thomas, 42
Thos., 80, 118
BUCKNER
Homer, 110
Mary, 48
Prettyman M.,
110
BUGG
Benjamin, 118
Jno. L., 111, 135
Nancy, 118
BUIE
Daniel, 36, 48
BUMPASS
William, 118
BURGES
John, 38
BURKE
Jno. R., 74
John R., 105
BURNELL
Henry, 123
Jeremiah, 120

Joseph, Sr., 123
Thomas, 120
BURNETT
Joseph, Jr., 42
Joseph, Sr., 42
Samuel, 78
BURT
William S., 121
BURTON
Ann, 138
Elizabeth P., 76
George, 136
George W., 76
BUTLER
John D., 107
BUTTERWORTH
John, 106
BYRN
Wm P., 96

C

CABELL
William S., 101,
108
Wm. S., 108
CAIN
James, 129
CALDWELL
Phebe, 115
William, 30
CAMERON
D., 75
Daniel, 55, 105,
107, 110
CAMPBELL
Cynthia, 91
Cynthia A., 91
Cyrus, 72
Francis, 66, 118
J. W., 109
John W., 91
Michael, 27
P. W., 118
Patrick W., 47
R. C., 92
Robert C., 91
W., 136

COLLINS
  A., 109
  Patk., 67
  Thomas, 46
  William F., 77
COLLINSWORTH
  Alice, 109
  Jas., 44
COMBS
  James W., 32
COMPTON
  W. S., 44
  William, 75, 97
  William S., 47
  Wm., 74, 102,
    138
  Wm. L., 60, 69
CON
  Jno. S., 74
CONDON
  James, 102
  Jas., 2, 127
CONNELL
  E. P., 69, 96
  Enoch P., 68, 83,
    86, 90, 92
  Oliver S., 39
  W. P., 90
CONNETT
  E. P., 43
Constitutional
  Advocate, 38
COOK
  Dempsey, 67
  Joseph, 128
  Mr., 12
  Will A., 128
  William A., 124
COOPER
  C., 25, 36, 77,
    79, 91, 106
  Charles, 23, 117
  Edm'd, 5
  Edmund, 5
  James, 53, 118
  John C., 38
  W., 23
  Will, 4

William, 41
COOTS
  Letitia, 52
COTTON
  Allen, 103
COUNCELL
  J., 3
COWEN
  V. D., 31
COX, 40
  Benjamin, 119
  Christopher G.,
    75
  Eldridge, 119
  Jno. S., 8
  John S., 137
  Thomas, 119
  William, 119
COXE
  Eroslus, 127
CRABB
  Henry, 5, 18, 44,
    56, 73, 74, 75,
    81, 97, 98,
    111, 138
CRADDOCK
  Henry, 36
  P., 20
CRAIGHEAD
  David, 60
CRAIN
  John, 90
CRAWFORD
  James, 11
CREEL
  Wm., 100
CRIDDLE
  Col. John, 62
  Jn., 7
  Jno, 50
  Jno., 7, 18, 22, 44
  John, 7, 13, 22,
    50, 62, 64
  L. G., 54, 105
  Smith, 69, 83, 87,
    88, 105
CRIGHTON
  Joseph, 95

Robert, 95
CRITCHLOW
  Henry, 53
CRITZ
  Jacob, 62
CROCKETT
  David, 51
  George, 94
CROSS
  James B., 30
  Maclin, 95
  Nancy M, 30
  Nancy M., 30
  Poettan B., 30
  Richard C., 5
  William E. R., 30
CROSSWY
  James C., 128
  John H., 128
  Pilmore, 127
CROSTHWAIT
  Elizabeth, 131
CRUTCHER
  Tho., 83
  Tho. H., 2
  Thomas, 9, 13,
    15, 27, 32, 56
  Thomas H., 114,
    115
  Thos., 87
  Crutcher, Wood &
    Co., 121
CRUTCHFIELD
  Elisha, 118
CUMMINS
  David, 54
CUNNINGHAM
  A., 125
  James, 136
  John, 52, 53
CURD
  Spencer, 48
CUREN, 32
CURREY
  Isaiah, 7, 21
CURRIN
  John, 66

CURRY
B. F., 55
Isaiah, 16
Jane, 89
Robert B., 89
CURTIS
Frances, 20
Wm., 30
CUTLER
Jervis, 104

D

DABBS
Elizabeth, 80,
142
Jno. R., 120
John R., 80, 120,
142
Richard, 80, 142
DANCE
Wm. S., 37
DANDRIDGE
B., 41
DANIEL
Edward, 40, 74,
75, 77, 79, 90
DANSFORTH
James B., 62
DARBY
Patrick H., 14, 38
DAVENPORT
Samuel, 54
DAVIDSON
James, 116
S., 94
DAVIS
Benjamin, 134
E., 108
Elisha, 108
Estate of, 9
Isaac, 55
James, 43
Jno., 36, 123
Sterling, 127
William F. J.,
109

William Franklin
Jones, 109
DEADRICK
George M., 5
DEAN
Francis M., 51
DECKER
John, 14, 95
DEGRAFFENRIED
A. M., 46
DEMONBREUN
Timothy, 21, 127
Timothy, Jr., 21
DERECHSON
Joseph, 120
DIBRELL
Martha, 101
DICK & Co.
N. & J, 19
DICKERSON
William, 5
DICKINSON
Andrew J., 11
Arraminta, 11
Henry C., 135
Jacob, 11
Julia Ann, 11
Minerva, 11
Mrs., 11
Sophia, 11
Thomas J., 11
William, 69, 114
Wm., 114
Dickinson &
Shrewsberry, 69
DILL
Thomas, 106
DILLAHUNTY
James, 54
William, 54
Wm., 54, 72
DISMUKES
F., 78
DIXON
Wallace, 78
DOCKERTY
William, 82, 86

DODSON
Elias, 51
DONELSON
Andrew J., 95
John, Jr., 95
DONLEY
T., 132
DONNELLY
William O., 63
DONOLY
Henry O., 84, 88
DONOVAN
A. L., 112, 124
DOOLIN
Harris, 48
DORRIS
W. D., 35
Wm. D., 75
DOSSELL
Nancy, 95
DOUGLAS
A. H., 122
Peter, 20, 21, 67,
68, 77
DOUGLASS
H. L., 62
Harry L., 62
Peter, 40
Thos. L., 113
DRAKE
Benjamin, 40
Britain, 27
John, 54, 70
Jonathan, 54, 137
Logan, 120
Richard, 55
Sevier, 70
William B., 46,
52
Wm. B., 52
DREWEY
Richardson C.,
100
DREWRY
Jno., 31
John, 14, 31
R. C., 100
Ric'd, 31

Richard, 30, 31,
36, 48, 72
Richardson C., 30
DUFF
Robert L., 57
DUNCAN
A., 93
Charles, 112
Th. A., 107, 140
Th. S., 73
Thomas A., 98
DUNCAN & KEYS,
42
DUNHAM
D. A., 89
Daniel A., 18
DUNNAVANT
Abraham, 83, 87
Umphrey B., 83,
87
DUNNEVANT
Daniel, 130
DUNNEWAY
Opie, 124
DUNNWANT
Leonard, 129
DUVALL
Alvin S., 34, 123

E

EARHART
Abraham, 95
John, 46
Lucinda, 53
Rodney, 37
EARLE
Wm. H., 111
EARTHMAN
I., 85
I., Jr., 125, 140
Isaac, 81, 85,
102, 103, 107,
119, 137
Isaac F., 103
Isaac, Jr., 16, 44,
103, 107
J., Jr., 64, 90, 131

John, 62, 81, 84,
85
John H., 103
Judah, 137
L., 62
Lewis, 16, 37, 64,
81, 85, 102,
103, 113, 120,
137
Polly, 81, 85
EAST
Addison, 3, 19
E. H., 42, 80
EASTLAND
Tho. B., 116
ECHOLS
Rich'd A., 6
Echols & Drake, 46
ECKOLS
Joel, 27
Richard A, 27
Richard A., 27
EDMISTON
John, 36
Th., 52
William, 36, 53
Wm., 102
EDMONDSON
James, 130, 140
Samuel, 127
William Houston,
127
EDNEY
Edmond, 54
Samuel, 54
ELAM
John, 13
Robert, 100
Sam, 15
Samuel, 13, 15
Watters, 112
ELLIN
Shadrach F., 128
ELLIOT
H., 49
Hugh, 97, 115
ELLIS
Robert, 121

ELLISTON
James M., 73
Jno., 3
John, 22, 35
Joseph T., 2, 107,
141
Emerald, 58, 78
EMMETT
William C., 86
Wm. C., 83
EMMITT
Wm. C., 98
ENSLEY
E., 120
Joseph, Jr., 53
ERWIN
Frances, 34
John P., 34
ERWIN
Andrew, 15
F. L., 31
Frances L., 34,
93, 123
G. W., 88
J. P., 17, 26, 31,
42, 56
James, 32
John, 2
John P., 4, 10,
19, 34, 93, 123
Jos., 2
Joseph, 2
EVANS
Robert, 3
EVERETT
Amariah B., 63
Jesse, 43
Jesse J., 84, 87,
130, 137
Nicey, 108
Simon, 108
EWING
Nathan, 136
EWING
A. G., 72, 99
Albert G., 143
Alex., 20

John, 9, 10
GARDNER
  Dempsey, 81
  Henry, 81, 85,
    111
  Joshua, 81, 85,
    110, 111
GARLAND
  Elisha, 94
GARNER
  W., 35
GARNETT
  M., 133
GARRETT
  W. W., 141
GERMAN
  Zacheus, 53
GIBBS
  G. W., 25, 91
  George W., 25,
    57, 114, 117,
    139
GILBERT
  Thomas, 58, 78
GILL
  I. J., 101
  James J., 136
  Wm., 38
GILSON
  R., 13
  Wm., 13
GINGRY
  Andrew, 108
  J., 101
  Joseph, 110
GLASGOW
  Jesse, 128
GLEAVES
  M., 34, 68, 82,
    86, 102, 133
  Michael, 7, 39,
    64, 77, 88, 103
  Mich'l, 7
  Thomas, 55, 129,
    130
  William B., 55
GLENN
  S., 135

Simon, 65
GOODE
  Martha, 84, 88
  William, 84, 88
GOODLEf
  A. G., 133
GOODRICH
  Caleb, 132
  William, 108
GOODWIN
  W. W., 72
GORDAN
  N., 132
GORDON
  J., 81
  James, 36, 38,
    47, 138
  Nicholas, 131
GOULD
  James, 44, 45
GOWDY
  Ann, 126
  Thomas, 126
GRAHAM
  John, 110
  Reuben P., 130
  Reubin P., 114
GRANT
  John, 35
  M. V., 131
GRAVES
  Henry, 60
GRAY
  Alex., 117
  B., 105, 114
  Benajah, 115
GREEN
  J. H., 6
  S., 105
  Sam'l L. F., 17
  Samuel F., 17
  W. F., 21
GREENE
  R. W., 20
  Robert W., 35
  Robt W., 22
  Robt. W., 6, 22
  Samuel F., 112

GREER
  D. B., 5
  Green B., 134
  Green Berry, 76
  Greenberry, 136
  J. W., 76
  Joseph, 40
  W. H., 137
GRERRARD
  James, 15
GRIFFARD
  James, 13
GRIFFIN
  Edwin, 81, 85
GRIZAN
  Joseph B., 50
GRIZZARD
  James, 66, 104,
    131
  Jas., 44, 79, 140
GRUBBS
  William, 13, 64,
    103
GRUNDY
  Felix, 68, 117
GUELL
  J. C., 4
GUILD
  J. C., 23
GUION
  Alvah, 143
GULLIDGE
  John, 62
GUNNING
  John, 15, 67, 82,
    86
GWINN
  Thos. W., 83, 86
GWYNN
  Humphrey, 132

H

HACKNEY
  Daniel, 43
  Hackney, 43
  Jemima, 68, 92
  Jemina, 68, 90

Jemmina, 43
Jesse, 90
William, 68, 69
Wm, 68
HAIL
Durham, 134
George, 116
Leman, 134
Lmn, 139
Lurnan, 79
Stephen, 133
HALE
George, 116
HALL
Allen S., 79
Charles C., 113
Charles M., 76,
95, 96, 113,
120
E. S., 44, 47, 67,
74
Edw'd, 134
Elihu F., 39
Elihu S., 11
Henry, 124
Jno. B., 130
John, 141
John B., 76, 95
John C., 113
Lindsey C., 113
Linsey C., 76
N. C., 38
Nancy B., 96
Nicholas, 39
William, 95
HAMILTON
A., 137
Andrew, 137
John, 50, 90, 91
Joseph S., 40
Joseph, Jr., 74
Robert, 74
William, 34
Wm., 50
HAMLET
Elizabeth, 80
HANDY
George, 54

HANKS
Richard, 16
Rich'd, 138
Sarah, 15
HANNUM
Was. L., 57, 67,
68, 72, 79, 138
HARBISON
John, 51
HARDEN
Joab, 63, 70
HARDGRAVE
Francis, 123
Thomas F., 123
HARDIMAN
Tho., 122
HARDING
Jno. B., 3
John, 37
John B., 3
Tho., 3
HARDINGS
John, 19
HARMAN
John, 21
HARMON
Hardeman, 47
John, 22, 51, 100,
124
HARRIS
William, 106
Wm., 58
HARRISON
Isaac, 92, 93
Rolla, 93
T. E., 142
HART
Oliver, 126
R. W., 2
HAYES
John T., 51
O. B., 24
Roswell P., 76
S. D., 14
HAYNES
William, 41
Wm., 41

HAYNIE
John, 11
John N., 11
HAYS
Andrew, 69
James C., 69
John B., 69
HAYS
Andrew, 15, 41,
44, 57, 59, 69,
114, 115, 117
Campbell, 55
Charles, 56
David, 68
James, 105
James C., 57, 58,
59, 69, 78,
114, 115
James Campbell,
74
Jane, 105
JAS. C., 69
JOHN B, 69
John B., 59, 69,
114, 115
John C., 55
Polly, 100
Sarah, 105
HAYWOOD
E., 43, 80, 132
Egbert, 134, 139
George, 132
John, 42, 43, 132
Thomas, 42, 43,
80
Thos., 132
HAZARD
H. F., 21
HEATON
Robert S., 116
William, 8
HELAND
Geo. W., 53
HENDERSON
James, 6
HENING
A., 90

MANIFEE
Jonas, Jr., 18
MANNIFEE
John B., 7
Mansion House, 97
MARKHAM
Pleasant M., 123
MARLIN
Samuel C., 35
MARR
George W. L.,
103
MARSHALL
Elihu, 39, 54, 55
James, 16, 137
John, 72, 98, 117,
137
S. B., 31, 46, 130
Sam'l B., 38
Samuel, 72, 137
MARTIN
Geo. W., 54
George W., 54
I. M., 113
J. H., 73, 93, 116
J. M., 105
John H., 113, 116
William, 8
William D., 70
MASSENGILL
William, 142
MASSINGILL
William, 135,
143
MASTERSON
William, 101,
102
MATHIS
A., 112
MATTHEW
J., 123
MATTHEWS
Edward, 100
MATTHIAS
Stephen, 72
Thomas, 72
MATTHIS
Allan, 96

MAURY
A. P., 83, 87
James H., 51
MAXWELL
A., 134
MAYFIELD
Isaac, 84, 87
John, 5
MAYS
Drewry, 64
Drury, 64
Gardner, 142
MAYSON
Ramsay S., 117
McAFEE
Thos., 133
McALONES
W., 61
McANULTY
Bernard, 128,
134
Michael, 128,
134
McBRIDE
J., 48
McCAIN
Almira, 113
Betsey, 113
Charles, 113
Isaac, 113, 114
John, 17, 113,
114
Marget, 114
Matilda, 113
Polly, 113
Robert, 113, 114
Selah Emeline,
113
William, 113
McCARTAN
Thos., 127
McCASLAND
Isaac, 112
John, 43
McCASLIN/McCA
RTAN
Thomas, 126

McCAULEY
B. E., 110
McCAUN
Elizabeth, 116
McCLELLAN
John, 13
William B., 22
McCOMBS
J. W., 6
James W., 64, 93
McCONNELL
Corry, 133
McCOWN
Elizabeth, 133
McCUTCHEN
James, 9
John, 93, 102
Jos., 53
McDANIEL
John, 91
S. C., 46
McDONALD &
RIDGELEY, 39
McEWIN
J. H., 18
Jos. H., 18
Joseph H., 67
McFADDEN
Guy, 3
McGAVOCH
Jacob, 139
McGAVOCK
David, 124
H. W., 76, 78
Jac., 39, 77
Jacob, 24, 27
James, 117
John, 61
Lysander, 117
McGEHEE
George W., 91
McGUIRE
Lawrence, 116
McINTOSH
Alex., 97
McKAY
Francis, 74, 76

158

PRYOR
N. B., 23, 69,
100, 114, 115
Nicholas B., 23,
27, 36, 44
PUGSLEY
Charles, 133
Chas., 81, 84
Doctor Charles,
81, 85
PUGSLY
Chas., 90
PULLIAM
Washington, 100
PURDY
Rob., 10
Robert, 9, 10, 34,
123
PURKINSON
Jackman, 71
Martha, 71

Q

QUESTENBURY
Henry, 108
QUINN
M. H., 2, 51
Matthew H., 44,
48
*Quinn, Elliston &
Co.*, 44

R

RACKBY
Micajah, 114
RAINEY
G. Duncan, 97
RAINS
Wilford H., 13
RALSTON
David, 137
William, 71
Wm, 71
Wm., 71
RAMSEY
Wm, 90

Wm., Jr., 123
RANDAL
Amandey Green,
8
Cordeley, 8
Greenberry, 8
RANDALL
Aquilla, 8, 92, 93
Elizabeth, 8
RANDOLPH
Wm. Y., 124
RAWLINGS
John A., 32
RAY
Alexander, 133
REACE
John, 7
READ
Alex., 20
Cornelia, 28, 29
Jane, 58
John A., 28
Jones, 28, 29, 33,
58
Mary Jane, 28,
29, 33
Polly, 29
Tho. J., 58
Thomas, 29
Thomas J., 28,
29, 58
READY
Aaron, 44
REDDING
Iredale, 137
REED
Alexander, 20
REEDER
John, 106
REESE
John, 16
Rega, 67
RICE
John, 118
William W., 117
RICHARDS
Josiah, 135

RICHARDSON
Alex, 19
Alex., 18
Alexander, 18, 50
Booker F., 24, 28
William, 142
RICHMOND, 35
Barton, 99, 128
Harriet, 99
RIDLEY
James, 91
RIDLY
James, 135
Riego, 62, 63
RIEVES
Edmond, 143
RIGHT
Hollis, 55
RINKLE
John, 44
ROANE
J., 33
ROANEY
M. C., 13
Robertson, 132
ROBERTSON
Betsey, 17
C., 99
Charles, 24, 28
Christopher, 99
Duncan, 7, 15,
47, 48, 52, 55,
75, 83, 87, 97,
130
Duncan G., 16
E. B., 38, 71
Eldridge B., 24,
25, 33, 38, 47,
71, 95
Elijah, 24, 28
F. D., 108
Felix, 12
Felix W., 69
John McNairy,
130
N. H., 37, 90,
104
Peyton, 108

SHREWSBERRY
  Joel, 69, 114
SHROPSHIRE
  B., 95
  B. S., 95
  Betsey, 113
  Elizabeth, 113
SHULTZ
  James C., 51
SHUMATE
  Willis L., 22
Shute
  Philip, 33
SHUTE
  John, 14, 46, 61,
    63, 67, 86, 125
  John A., 125
  Lee, 32, 125
  Lev, 110
  Lew, 125
  Philip, 18, 43, 44,
    50, 64, 65, 72,
    75, 76, 97,
    125, 134
  William, 67
SHUTE &
  CRIDDLE, 48
SIMS
  Walter, 88
SITLER
  Isaac, 25, 48, 49,
    55
  J. W., 5, 34
  James W., 4
SMART
  B. W., 127
SMILEY
  Arraminta, 11
  David, 8
  Robert, 11
SMITH, 39
  Charles, 20
  Edwin, 32, 76
  Elisha B., 122
  I. H., 89
  J. M., 10, 11
  Jacob C., 32, 56,
    78

Jno. F., 61
Jno. H., 53, 115
John H., 73
Mark W., 62
Martin, 65
Martin, 32, 56,
  61, 62, 65, 78
Nathan, 122
R. P., 141
Thomas, 61, 62,
  120, 125
Thomas C., 56
W. M., 60
SNEED
  Absalom D., 64
  H. D., 64
  William, 11
SNOW
  David C., 3
SOMMERVILLE
  Alen H., 73
  Jno., 102
  Jno. H., 66
  John, 24, 35
SOUGHTY
  h., 19
SPENCE
  Brent, 31, 132
SPIECE
  Thomas L., 77
  Thos. L., 77
STAMPS
  John, 50
STANCILL
  Jesse, 105
STANFIELD
  Ashley, 41
STEELE
  John, 41
  Samuel, 96
STEPHEN
  Robert, 57
STEPHENSON
  James, 118, 140
STEVENS
  Moses, 2
STEVENSON
  James, 140

STEWART
  Agness, 12
  James, 19, 51, 78
  John, 111, 122
  Rebecca, 12
  Thomas, 12
STILLWELL
  John, 62
STOBAUGH
  Jno., 9
STOCKTON
  A., 59
  Aaron, 59, 67
  Aron, 66
STOTHART
  R., 47
  Robt., 82, 86
STOUT
  Jacob V. D., 124
  Jacob V. D., 129
  S. V. D., 6, 15
  Samuel V. D., 99,
    112, 126, 141
STRANGE
  Henry, 117
STROTHER
  John, 14
STUDEVANT
  J. M., 46
STULL
  Geo., 67
  George, 61
  Nancy, 61
  Sam'l, 17
  Zachariah, 8
Stump
  Frederick, 33
  Philip S., 33
  Tennessee M. A.,
    33
  Thos. J., 33
STUMP, 40
  Catherine, 52
  Christopher, 43
  Frederick, 18, 33,
    43, 50, 64, 76,
    77, 78
  Jno., 16

166

WRIGHT
    James, 60
    James W., 60
    Thomas, 71
    William R., 135
    Wm. R., 135
WYATT
    Martha M., 97
    Spencer R., 97
WYNN
    Devereux, 6
WYNNE
    Deverin, 27

Y

YARBOROUGH
    James, 142
YEATES
    Thos. P., 128
YEATMAN
    Th., 93

Thomas, 10, 19,
    93, 94
Yeatman & Woods,
    78
YEATS
    Thos. P., 7
    William, 142
YERGER
    Geo. S., 33, 75,
        93, 128
    Geof., 66
YOUNG
    Amanda Malvina,
        96
    Amanda Malvina
        F., 95
    Amelia Elizabeth
        Ann, 95, 96
    Daniel, 16, 95, 96
    Estate of, 9
    Ferdinand Jones,
        95, 96

J. L., 16, 96
John B., 95, 96
John L., 29, 95,
    103, 137
Mark, 61, 91
Napoleon B., 95,
    96
Samuel, 84, 87
William, 100
William F. L. B.,
    96
William M., 132

Z

ZACHERY
    William C., 136
ZACK
    Dr., 34

SLAVE INDEX

Aaron, 40, 109,
121
Abbady, 42
Abby, 66
Abraham, 10, 31,
55, 64, 76, 77
Abram, 82, 86,
115, 129, 134
Absalom, 40, 46
Acry, 98
Adam, 138
Addison, 55
Aggy, 51, 111
Agnes, 8
Agness, 30
Ailcey, 95
Albeon, 118
Albert, 64, 68,
83, 87, 88,
131, 133
Alen, 59
Alex, 128
Alexander, 22,
36, 51, 142
Alfred, 12, 56,
81, 85
Alice, 55, 98
Alick, 77, 83, 87
Allen, 17, 63
Alley, 67, 89, 113
Ally, 67, 91
Alsey, 88
Ama, 13
Amanda, 26, 111
Amelia, 136
Amey, 24, 48,
115
Amos, 42, 46
Amy, 14, 46, 54,
56, 59, 100,
107, 125
Anaca, 88
Anarchy, 99

Andrew Jackson,
1
Andy, 128
Aney, 141
Angelina, 10, 32,
57
Anjea, 12
Ann, 98
Ann Jane, 99
Anna, 40, 107
Anne, 73, 78, 90
Annis, 54
Anny, 46
Anthony, 52, 81,
84, 90, 129
Armistead, 15,
46, 136
Armon, 50
Armstead, 50,
123
Aron, 115
Arthur, 82, 86,
97, 116
Artimeca, 67
Artimecy, 113
Artimesa, 91
Artimicey, 67
Astimecy, 89
Atkins, 14
Austin, 117, 128,
131
Baden, 127
Barbary, 11
Beck, 1, 53
Bella, 33
Ben, 1, 13, 24,
65, 68, 76, 87,
104
Benjamin, 66, 79,
114
Benn, 80
Bentley, 64, 77
Bently, 31

Bes, 62
Betsey, 24, 58,
78, 95, 97, 105
Betsy, 53
Betty, 24, 26, 37
Bill, 48, 81, 85,
123, 128, 129
Billey, 1
Billy, 14, 59, 65,
78, 111
Binkley, 55
Bird, 99, 104
Bob, 1, 17, 57,
109, 118
Bobb, 40
Bonaparte, 17
Braddock, 99
Brittain, 115
Bryant, 24
Burwell, 115
Carey, 135
Carlos, 82, 97
Carloz, 86
Caroline, 46, 74,
103
Carter, 24, 78
Cary, 5
Caster, 66
Caswell, 72
Catherine, 14,
109
Caty, 127, 129,
139
Ceila, 105
Cela, 41
Celey, 108
Celion, 88
Chaney, 112, 117
Chans, 63
Chany, 75, 78
Chapman, 126
Charity, 27, 58

---

* free black

Heritage Books by Mary Sue Smith:

Davidson County, Tennessee Deed Book H: 1809–1821

*Davidson County, Tennessee Deed Book P:
Personal Property Deeds, 15 Nov. 1821–13 Feb. 1829*

Davidson County, Tennessee Deed Book T and W: 1829–1835

*Davidson County, Tennessee Deed Book Z:
Personal Property Deeds, September 5, 1835–January 2, 1838*

*Superior Court of Law and Equity, Mero District of Tennessee,
1803–1805, Middle Tennessee*

*Superior Court of Law and Equity, Mero District of Tennessee,
1806–1809, Middle Tennessee*

*Superior Court of Law and Equity, Mero District of Tennessee,
1810–1813, Middle Tennessee*